Arsenal

POCKET ANNUAL
1994-95

D0796500

Edited by
John Jackson

Arsenal Pocket Annual 1994-95

Copyright © John Jackson – Author 1994

ISBN: 1-898351-09-0

Typeset by Bruce Smith Books Ltd

Cover photograph: Paul Merson

All photographs supplied by Empics Ltd

Statistics supplied by Football Information Services.

The right of John Jackson to be identified as the Author of the Work has been asserted by him in accordance with the *Copyright, Designs and Patents Act 1988.*

First published in 1994 by
Words on Sport

Words on Sport Ltd
PO Box 382
St. Albans
Herts, AL2 3JD

Registration Number: 2917013

Registered Office:
Worplesdon Chase, Worplesdon, Guildford, Surrey, GU3 3LA

Printed and Bound in Great Britain by Ashford Colour Press Ltd, Gosport.

CONTENTS

Acknowledgements

Many thanks to all those people who, in one way or another, have contributed something to this first *Arsenal Pocket Annual*. In particular, I would like to thank Ray Spiller and Brian Mellowship at the Association of Football Statisticians, Paul Rainbow, Daniel Unwin and Mark Jeffrey.

And finally thanks to Sharon, Duncan, Nicola and Ben.

Disclaimer

Introduction

This first edition of the independent Arsenal Pocket Annual chronicles the 1993/94 season's success, match by match, blow by blow, goal by goal. But it contains much else besides: all the records, facts and statistics associated with this great football institution.

Arsenal Football Club hold a unique and revered place in the history of English football. It was in the 1930s that they became established as one of the most famous clubs in the world. This was due not only to their success on the field, but also their determination off it and both assured that the club would always stand amongst the elite in all aspects of the game.

Sixty years on, this philosophy still stands and the name Arsenal still remains one of the most charismatic in the world of football. Ten League Championships, FA Cup winners six times, League Cup winners twice and winners of two European trophies – the Gunners can certainly lay claim to be considered as one of football's true greats.

Welcome, therefore, to the first edition of the Arsenal Pocket Annual. The annual has been designed to be the fan's guide to the club and all manner of facts and statistics about the Gunners, past and present, have been included. Alongside the major historical records, there is a complete run-down and report of all Arsenal's games in the 1993/94 season. For those travelling away there is a visitor's guide to all the Premiership grounds.

Arsenal fans everywhere can look forward to another year of high expectancy and success. Undoubtedly this Pocket Annual will help contribute to your enjoyment of the 1994/95 Premiership season – have a great spectating year.

The Season Reviewed

The winning of the FA Cup and the Coca-Cola Cup in 1993 had left the Arsenal fans quietly confident of further success in the 1993/94 season. But their dreams were quickly shattered by another horrendous opening day home defeat. After Norwich City the previous year, it was the turn of Coventry City to inflict an early, painful blow to the Gunners' Premiership title aspirations with a 3-0 victory, Mick Quinn scoring a hat-trick.

Arsenal, however, soon turned around this set-back and strung together a run of good results climbing up into second place in the league. They were to remain undefeated until the top-of-the-table clash with Manchester United in mid-September. During this six match run, Arsenal came to rely heavily on the goalscoring exploits of Ian Wright – as they continued to do all season. Kevin Campbell finally redressed the balance somewhat with a hat-trick in the 4-0 demolition of Ipswich Town.

Defeat at Old Trafford brought a halt to Arsenal's initial Premiership title charge and, following a narrow win over Southampton a week later, the Gunners failed to win another league game until the 20th November. Incredibly, they only suffered one loss in this spell – a 2-1 home defeat by Aston Villa – but their goalscoring problems were highlighted by the fact that they failed to score a single league goal in October. This alarming statistic was balanced by not conceding any either, but those four goalless draws put paid to any hopes Arsenal had of mounting a serious title challenge to Manchester United.

In the meantime the cup competitions had got under way and, by contrast, Arsenal were having no problems in finding the net in these games. In the Coca-Cola Cup, Huddersfield Town were comfortably despatched by a 6-1 aggregate victory, with Ian Wright scoring a hat-trick in the 5-0 first-leg win in Yorkshire. In the third round, the holders struggled to overcome Norwich City at Highbury, but two Ian Wright goals helped the Gunners to an impressive 3-0 success in the replay at Carrow Road.

In the European Cup-Winners' Cup, Arsenal got their challenge under way against Odense Boldklub of Denmark. Despite the lowliness of their opposition Arsenal struggled to a 3-2 aggregate victory. However, it was enough to earn them a second round tie against Belgian Cup winners Standard Liege.

The first leg at Highbury was comfortably won by the Gunners 3-0, but in the second leg, with Ian Wright rested, Arsenal turned in the finest performance of the season as they thrashed the Belgians 7-0. It was a result.to send a shudder around the rest of Europe.

Back in the Premiership, Arsenal were still struggling to find any sort of consistent form although they had at last found their goalscoring touch. Newly promoted Newcastle United were defeated in an entertaining 2-1 home game at the end of November but, at the other end of the scale, the Gunners travelled to Coventry City one week later and produced probably their worst league performance of the season, going down 1-0 at Highfield Road. Sheffield Wednesday were beaten 1-0 at Highbury before the Gunners travelled to Elland Road just before Christmas and went down to a 2-1 defeat. That was to be the turning point of the season – Arsenal were to remain undefeated in the Premiership until the 30th of April, a run of 19 games.

In the Coca-Cola Cup, the Gunners finally relinquished their hold on the trophy when they crashed 1-0 at home to Aston Villa in the fourth round. It was Arsenal's first defeat in the domestic cup competitions for 26 games.

Three impressive wins over Swindon, Sheffield United and Wimbledon over the Christmas and New Year period took them up into fourth place in the league. It also saw talk of a possible title challenge to Manchester United. However, five successive draws during January and February put an end to any lingering hopes the Gunners had of Premiership honours for the season.

The FA Cup competition got under way at the start of January and the Gunners overcame the stiff hurdle of First Division Millwall in the third round – a last-minute Tony Adams goal giving them a hard-earned victory over the promotion-challenging Lions. But, in the fourth round, they became the latest victims of giant-killers Bolton Wanderers, who shocked the Highbury fans with a fully deserved 3-1 replay victory.

March saw Arsenal break their draw deadlock and impressive victories followed over Premiership title challengers Blackburn Rovers, Ipswich Town and Southampton – Ian Wright helping himself to hat-tricks in the games against the two Premiership strugglers. Champions-elect, Manchester United, were held to a 2-2 draw at Highbury while Liverpool were beaten by a single goal which took Arsenal into third position in the table.

The European Cup-Winners' Cup competition got under way again at the beginning of March and Arsenal overcame a difficult tie against Torino, 1-0 on aggregate. After holding the Italians to a goalless draw in Turin, a Tony Adams goal in the second leg at Highbury was enough to earn the Gunners a semi-final tie against top French side, Paris St. Germain.

Again, Arsenal were drawn away in the first leg and came back to Highbury with an excellent 1-1 draw under their belts after Ian Wright had given them a first half lead. In the second leg a fifth minute goal from Kevin Campbell put the Gunners into the Final to meet the holders and favourites for the cup – Italian side Parma.

With their minds probably more on their European adventures, Arsenal continued their inconsistent form in the Premiership. Draws over relegation strugglers Swindon Town and Sheffield United were followed by good wins over Chelsea and Aston Villa. They still remained undefeated however, a record that was finally broken by West Ham United on the penultimate Saturday of the season just a few days before their European Cup-Winners' Cup Final game. Two late goals from Trevor Morley and Martin Allen brought a disappointing end to the Gunners' Highbury programme for the 1993/94 season.

That defeat was soon forgotten four days later however, as Arsenal travelled to Copenhagen and produced one of their finest ever displays. They beat Parma in the European Cup-Winners' Cup Final thanks to a single Alan Smith goal. Weakened by injuries and suspension the 1-0 victory was a glowing testament to Arsenal's commitment, professionalism and tactical awareness.

The Gunners flew back to finish their league programme with a 2-0 defeat at Newcastle United and a final placing of fourth in the Premiership. Despite their European success, Arsenal had again been too inconsistent in the league and, during the summer months, no doubt manager George Graham will have been looking for additional flair in his midfield and maybe a goalscorer who can ease the burden on Ian Wright.

Gunners' Diary 1993/94

August

The 1993/94 season gets underway with Highbury welcoming just one arrival during the summer – Republic of Ireland international Eddie McGoldrick, a £1 million signing from relegated Crystal Palace. Arsenal draw with Manchester United in the FA Charity Shield but lose the penalty shoot-out 5-4, with goalkeeper David Seaman missing the vital final kick. The new North Bank Stand welcomes Coventry City for the opening match of the league programme but the visitors ruin the Gunners' day with a comprehensive 3-0 victory, with City striker Mick Quinn grabbing a hat-trick. Arsenal soon get back on the tracks however and successive wins over Tottenham Hotspur, Sheffield Wednesday, Leeds United and Everton take them into second place in the Premiership by the end of the month. Ian Wright seemingly sets out on a personal goalscoring crusade with five of Arsenal's first seven goals of the season.

September

The unbeaten run in the Premiership continues with a battling draw at Blackburn Rovers and an impressive 4-0 demolition of Ipswich Town at Highbury, with Kevin Campbell scoring a hat-trick. Halfway through the month, the top of the table clash with leaders Manchester United sees the current champions come out on top, in front of an Old Trafford crowd of 44,000, thanks to a spectacular Eric Cantona strike. The Gunners maintain their challenge though with a 1-0 victory over Southampton a week later. The cup competitions get underway and goals from Paul Merson and Ian Wright give Arsenal a 2-1 away win over Danish side Odense Boldklub in the first leg of their European Cup-Winners' Cup First Round match. In the second leg two weeks later, the Danes manage to earn themselves a creditable 1-1 draw, but the first leg victory was enough to take Arsenal through to the second round. The defence of the Coca-Cola Cup begins with a 5-0 hammering of Huddersfield Town in a Second Round First Leg match at Leeds Road – Ian Wright scores a hat-trick. Tony Adams, Ian Wright and David Seaman all play for England in their World Cup Qualifying match win over Poland.

October

Arsenal's challenge for the Premiership begins to falter as they fail to score a single goal in the league during the month – they still remain undefeated though as all four league games finish 0-0. In the second leg of their second round Coca-Cola match against Huddersfield Town, the Gunners are held to a disappointing 1-1 draw at Highbury, but go through 6-1 on aggregate. In the third round they are drawn at home to Norwich City and are grateful to Ian Wright for a valuable equaliser ten minutes from time in a 1-1 draw. Wright is on target again in the European Cup-Winners' Cup Second Round, scoring twice in a comfortable 3-0 first leg victory over Standard Liege at Highbury – Paul Merson scores the other goal which should ensure a comparatively easy passage to the quarter-finals of the competition in the second leg. David Seaman, Tony Adams, Paul Merson and Ian Wright all play for England in their 2-0 World Cup defeat in Holland – a loss which just about put paid to any hopes they had of qualifying for the finals in the United States in 1994.

November

After their goalscoring problems in October, Arsenal begin the month in spectacular fashion against Standard Liege in their Second Leg European Cup-Winners' Cup match, returning from Belgium with a 7-0 victory under their belts and earning an easy passage to the quarter-final stages of the competition in March. The win gives the Gunners their biggest individual and aggregate victory in European football – more amazingly, Ian Wright was not playing. In the Premiership Aston Villa inflict Arsenal's second home defeat of the season as goals from Whittingham and Townsend give them a 2-1 victory. Arsenal finally achieve their first league victory since the end of September with a 2-0 win at struggling Chelsea on the 20th November. The Newcastle game at the end of the month sees Highbury fully operational as an all-seater stadium for the first time with a capacity of 39,000. Goalkeeper David Seaman is sent off for the first time in his career in the goalless draw at West Ham United. Ian Wright scores four goals for England in their 7-1 win over San Marino, but it is all to no avail as Holland win 3-1 in Poland to secure second spot and a place in the finals in America. In the same match David Seaman suffers the indignity of conceding a goal after just nine seconds to the part-timers. Eddie McGoldrick does make it to the World Cup Finals, as he plays in the Republic of Ireland's 1-0 win over Northern Ireland, which clinches their place. Despite an impressive 3-0 win at Norwich City in their third round replay, it's goodbye to the Coca-Cola Cup in the fourth round as Aston Villa dump the holders out of the competition, courtesy of a Dalian Atkinson goal after just four minutes – it is their first cup defeat in 26 cup-ties.

December

The Gunners continue to struggle to find any sort of consistency in the Premiership. Probably their worst performance of the season sees them crash 1-0 at Coventry City, with Mick Quinn again on the scoresheet – it was the first goal the defence had conceded away from home in eight outings. Ian Wright earns Arsenal a point in the local derby against Tottenham Hotspur and is again on the scoresheet with a dramatic 90th minute winner in the 1-0 home win over Sheffield Wednesday. Defeat follows at Leeds United before the Gunners finally find their shooting boots and get back to winning ways over the Christmas period. Strugglers Swindon Town and Sheffield United are both comfortably beaten, 4-0 and 3-0 respectively, Kevin Campbell hitting his second hat-trick of the season in the game against the Wiltshire side.

January

The first game of the New Year sees Arsenal continue their impressive form with a 3-0 win at Wimbledon, before Queens Park Rangers bring a halt to the winning run in a predictably goalless draw at Highbury – the fourth successive such scoreline between the clubs. The 0-0 scoreline is the start of a run of five successive draws in the Premiership which puts a huge dent into the Gunners' title aspirations. The defence of the FA Cup begins with a hard-earned 1-0 victory at Millwall, with captain Tony Adams scoring the last-minute winner. In the fourth round Arsenal are drawn away at First Division giantkillers, Bolton Wanderers, and bring the Lancashire side back to Highbury for a replay after a 2-2 draw.

February

Disaster strikes in the first game in February as Bolton Wanderers deservedly win 3-1 in the FA Cup fourth round replay at Highbury. It is the club's first FA Cup defeat since Janaury 1992 when they lost to Wrexham. To cap a disappointing evening, Martin Keown is sent off in the last minute of the game and Ian Wright picks up an injury that will put him out for the rest of the month. In the Premiership Norwich City and Everton both hold Arsenal to 1-1 draws, before the Gunners get back to winning ways with a 1-0 victory over title challengers Blackburn Rovers at the end of the month.

March

In the Premiership, Ian Wright returns from injury and shows the Arsenal fans just what they have been missing with two stunning hat-tricks. The first comes in a 5-1 win at struggling Ipswich Town and the second comes two weeks later in a 4-0 victory at Southampton. Leaders Manchester United attract the biggest crowd of the season to Highbury and maintain their lead at the top in a 2-2 draw. Eric Cantona is controversially sent off for the second time in four days. Four days later a Paul Merson goal is enough to defeat Liverpool. The transfer deadline passes with no new arrivals at Highbury, but leaving are Anders Limpar who joins Everton for £1.6 million and Neil Heaney who signs for Southampton for a fee of £300,000. The first leg of the quarter-finals of the European Cup-Winners' Cup sees Arsenal gain a creditable goalless draw in Italy against highly-fancied Torino. Two weeks later at Highbury, a Tony Adams goal in a 1-0 victory is enough to give the Gunners a semi-final tie against French league leaders, Paris St-Germain. In the first leg Ian Wright scores a vital away goal in the 35th minute to give his side a 1-1 draw and leave them just ninety minutes from a place in the final.

April

A wonderful night at Highbury on the 12th of April as Arsenal beat Paris St-Germain to reach the final of the European Cup-Winners' Cup, where they will meet holders Parma on May 4th in Copenhagen. Kevin Campbell scores the vital goal after just five minutes. The evening is tinged with disappointment however, when a booking for Ian Wright means he will miss the final because of suspension.

The Gunners' unbeaten record in the Premiership stretches to 19 games by the time they draw 1-1 at Queens Park Rangers on the 27th of April. During the month Chelsea and Aston Villa are beaten and matches are drawn against Swindon Town, Sheffield United, Wimbledon and Rangers. The unbeaten run finally comes to an end at the end of April when the Gunners lose their final home fixture 2-0 to West Ham United. Just four days before their European final Arsenal are hit by an injury crisis with Martin Keown and John Jensen definitely out of the game and goalkeeper David Seaman doubtful with a rib injury.

It's a glory night for the Gunners in Copenhagen as Arsenal beat Parma 1-0 in the final of the European Cup-Winners' Cup. Although weakened by injuries and suspension, Arsenal produce a superb team performance with Alan Smith scoring the winning goal with a shot from 15 yards after 20 minutes. Returning from Copenhagen, Arsenal play their last league match of the season at Newcastle United and go down 2-0, to finish fourth in the Premiership. Steve Bould receives a surprise call up – at the age of 31 – to the England squad by Terry Venables and wins his first England caps in the games against Greece and Denmark. Eddie McGoldrick is picked for the Republic of Ireland World Cup squad. The month ends with George Graham finally entering the transfer market when he signs the Swedish international midfielder Stefan Schwarz from Benfica for a reported fee of £1.75 million.

Arsenal FC – Cup-Winners' Cup winners 1993-94

The Season
Match by Match

The Pre-season Friendlies 1993/94

Tuesday 20th July 1993
Away *v.* Leyton Orient   Drew   3-3
Scorers: A. Limpar, P. Merson, I. Wright

Tuesday 3rd August 1993
Away *v.* Charlton Athletic   Lost   1-2
Scorer: I. Wright

SOUTH AFRICAN TOUR

Sunday 25th July 1993
Manchester United   Won   2-0
Scorer: I. Wright (2 pens)

Wednesday 28th July 1993
Olando Pirates   Won   1-0
Scorer: A. Smith

Saturday 31st July 1993
Iwisa Kaiser Chiefs   Won   1-0
Scorer: K. Campbell

ARSENAL RESULTS SUMMARY 1993/94

Date	Type	Opponents	Scores	Scorers	Att
07/08/93	FACS	Manchester Utd	1-1	Wright	66,519
14/08/93	FACP	Coventry City	0-3		26,397
16/08/93	FACP	Tottenham H	1-0	Wright	28,355
21/08/93	FACP	Sheffield Wed	1-0	Wright	26,023
24/08/93	FACP	Leeds United	2-1	Merson (og)	29,042
28/08/93	FACP	Everton	2-0	Wright(2)	29,063
01/09/93	FACP	Blackburn R	1-1	Campbell	14,051
11/09/93	FACP	Ipswich Town	4-0	Campbell(3), Wright	28,563
15/09/93	ECWC1/1	Odense	2-1	Wright, Merson	9,580
19/09/93	FACP	Manchester Utd	0-1		44,009
21/09/93	CCC2/1	Huddersfield T	5-0	Wright(3), Merson, Campbell	14,275
25/09/93	FACP	Southampton	1-0	Merson	26,902
29/09/93	ECWC1/2	Odense	1-1	Campbell	25,689
02/10/93	FACP	Liverpool	0-0		42,750
05/10/93	CCC2/2	Huddersfield T	1-1	Smith	18,789
16/10/93	FACP	Manchester C	0-0		29,567
20/10/93	ECWC2/1	Standard Liege	3-0	Wright(2), Merson	25,258
23/10/93	FACP	Oldham Ath	0-0		12,105
26/10/93	CCC3	Norwich City	1-1	Wright	24,539
30/10/93	FACP	Norwich City	0-0		30,516
03/11/93	ECWC2/2	Standard Liege	7-0	Adams, McGoldrick, Selley, Smith, Merson, Campbell(2)	15,000
06/11/93	FACP	Aston Villa	1-2	Wright	31,773
10/11/93	CCC3R	Norwich City	3-0	Wright(2), Merson	24,539
20/11/93	FACP	Chelsea	2-0	Wright, Smith	26,839
24/11/93	FACP	West Ham Utd	0-0		20,279
27/11/93	FACP	Newcastle Utd	2-1	Wright, Smith	36,091
30/11/93	CCC4	Aston Villa	0-1		26,453
04/12/93	FACP	Coventry City	0-1		12,722
06/12/93	FACP	Tottenham H	1-1	Wright	35,669
12/12/93	FACP	Sheffield Wed	1-0	Wright	22,026
18/12/93	FACP	Leeds United	1-2	Campbell	37,515
27/12/93	FACP	Swindon Town	4-0	Campbell(3), Wright	17,651
29/12/93	FACP	Sheffield Utd	3-0	Campbell(2), Wright	27,035
01/01/94	FACP	Wimbledon	3-0	Parlour, Wright, Campbell	16,584
03/01/94	FACP	QPR	0-0		34,935

Date	Type	Opponents	Scores	Scorers	Att
10/01/94	FAC3	Millwall	1-0	Adams	20,093
15/01/94	FACP	Manchester C	0-0		25,642
22/01/94	FACP	Oldham Ath	1-1	Wright	26,524
31/01/94	FAC4	Bolton Wdrs	2-2	Adams, Wright	18,891
09/02/94	FAC4R	Bolton Wdrs	1-3	Smith	33,863
13/02/94	FACP	Norwich City	1-1	Campbell	17,667
19/02/94	FACP	Everton	1-1	Merson	19,891
26/02/94	FACP	Blackburn R	1-0	Merson	35,030
02/03/94	ECWCQF1	Torino	0-0		32,480
05/03/94	FACP	Ipswich Town	5-1	Wright(3), Parlour, (og)	18,656
15/03/94	ECWCQF2	Torino	1-0	Adams	34,678
19/03/94	FACP	Southampton	4-0	Wright(3), Campbell	16,790
22/03/94	FACP	Manchester Utd	2-2	Merson. (og)	36,203
26/03/94	FACP	Liverpool	1-0	Merson	35,556
29/03/94	ECWCSF1	Paris St-Germain	1-1	Wright	46,000
02/04/94	FACP	Swindon Town	1-1	Smith	31,634
04/04/94	FACP	Sheffield Utd	1-1	Campbell	20,019
12/04/94	ECWCSF2	Paris St-Germain	1-0	Campbell	34,212
16/04/94	FACP	Chelsea	1-0	Wright	34,314
19/04/94	FACP	Wimbledon	1-1	Bould	21,192
23/04/94	FACP	Aston Villa	2-1	Wright(2)	31,580
27/04/94	FACP	QPR	1-1	Merson	11,442
30/04/94	FACP	West Ham Utd	0-2		33,701
04/05/94	ECWC F	Parma	1-0	Smith	33,765
07/05/94	FACP	Newcastle Utd	0-2		32,216

Key: FACP = FA Carling Premiership
       FAC = FA Cup
       CCC = Coca-Cola Cup
       FACS = FA Charity Shield
       ECWC = European Cup-Winners' Cup

Arsenal
Manchester United

(1) 1
(1) 1

Saturday 7th August 1993, Wembley Stadium   Att.: 66,519

ARSENAL			MANCHESTER UNITED		
1	David	SEAMAN	1	Peter	SCHMEICHEL
2	*Lee*	*DIXON (†45)*	2	Paul	PARKER
3	Nigel	WINTERBURN	3	Denis	IRWIN
4	Paul	DAVIS	4	Steve	BRUCE
5	Andy	LINIGHAN	14	Andrei	KANCHELSKIS
6	Tony	ADAMS	6	Gary	PALLISTER
7	Kevin	CAMPBELL	16	Roy	KEANE
8	Ian	WRIGHT	8	Paul	INCE
10	Paul	MERSON	7	Eric	CANTONA
15	*Anders*	*LIMPAR (+74)*	10	Mark	HUGHES
17	John	JENSEN	11	*Ryan*	*GIGGS (†68)*

Subs

14	*Martin*	*KEOWN (†45)*	12	*Bryan*	*ROBSON (†68)*
11	*Eddie*	*McGOLDRICK (+74)*		Brian	McCLAIR
	Ian	SELLEY		Lee	SHARPE
	Neil	HEANEY		Darren	FERGUSON

Match Facts

- This was the 72nd Charity Shield match.

- Apart from sharing the trophy with Tottenham in 1991, Arsenal have not won the Charity Shield since 1953.

- From 1930 to 1938 Arsenal appeared in the Charity Shield on seven occasions, winning it five times.

- Manchester United were the first winners of the Charity Shield in 1908 when they beat Queens Park Rangers 4-0 after a replay.

- Goalkeeper David Seaman missed the penalty which gave United victory.

Score Sheet

M. HUGHES 8 min – 0-1

I. WRIGHT 44 min – 1-1

*Manchester United win
5-4 on penalties*

Referee:
Mr. G. Ashby (Worcester)

FA Charity Shield

Charity Share Out

Football's traditional curtain raiser to the season saw England's finest – champions against double cup-holders – produce a rather stale draw with the trophy finally ending up at Old Trafford after a penalty shoot-out.

It took referee Gerald Ashby just 14 seconds to blow for the first foul of the game and what followed manifested exactly the kind of football that would probably be produced over the next nine months of the season although the two goals executed by Mark Hughes and Ian Wright were both superb strikes.

It was Hughes who put United in front in the seventh minute when an immaculate touch by Eric Cantona gave the Welshman the time and space to drive the ball past David Seaman. It was United who continued to control most of the first half with Andrei Kanchelskis causing the Gunners most problems on the right hand side and he was unlucky with a 30 yard free kick which whisked just past Arsenal's left post.

Gradually the Gunners fought their way back into the game and equalised a minute before half time when Ian Wright superbly volleyed home a Paul Davis nod-on from the edge of the penalty area.

The second half was very much an even affair with both goalkeepers dealing comfortably with all that was thrown at them and it seemed almost inevitable that the game would have to be decided by a penalty shoot-out. United's Denis Irwin and Arsenal's Ian Wright both missed their kicks and after Keane converted his kick it was left to keeper David Seaman to keep the Gunners in the frame but his rather lazy shot was easily saved by Schmeichel to earn his side a 5-4 victory.

Charity Shield Record

	P	W	D	L	F	A
All-time Charity Shield Record	13	7	2	4	22	14

Arsenal
Coventry City

(0) 0
(1) 3

Match Two

Saturday 14th August 1993, Highbury   Att.: 26,397

ARSENAL

1	David	SEAMAN
2	Lee	DIXON
3	Nigel	WINTERBURN
4	Paul	DAVIS
5	Andy	LINIGHAN
6	Tony	ADAMS
17	John	JENSEN (†67)
8	Ian	WRIGHT
7	Kevin	CAMPBELL
10	Paul	MERSON (+73)
15	Anders	LIMPAR

Subs

11	Eddie	McGOLDRICK (†67)
14	Martin	KEOWN (+73)
13	Alan	MILLER (gk)

COVENTRY CITY

23	Jonathan	GOULD
19	Tony	SHERIDAN
6	David	RENNIE
4	Peter	ATHERTON
20	Phil	BABB – *Booked*
11	*Stewart*	*ROBSON* (†10)
17	Roy	WEGERLE
12	Peter	NDLOVU
7	John	WILLIAMS
10	Mick	QUINN – *Booked*
18	Sean	FLYNN

3	*Steve*	*MORGAN* (†10)
9	Mick	HARFORD
27	Tim	DALTON (gk)

Match Facts

- A 3-0 win at Wimbledon on the 25th August 1990 was the last time Arsenal won on the opening day of the season
- Mick Quinn's three goals gave him the first hat-trick of the 1993/94 season.

Score Sheet

M. QUINN 34 min Pen – 0-1
M. QUINN 63 min – 0-2
M. QUINN 66 min – 0-3

Referee:

A. Wilkie (Chester-le-Street)

Result of this Season's Fixture

Arsenal
Coventry City

The Mighty Quinn

For the second season running Arsenal suffered a heavy opening day defeat at Highbury. Last year it was unfancied Norwich City who returned home with a 4-2 victory under their belts – this time a 3-0 defeat saw the equally unfancied Coventry City deal a heavy blow to the Gunners' Premiership hopes for the coming season.

It was the combination of Mick Quinn and the much-travelled Roy Wegerle which caused Arsenal problems all afternoon. Wegerle played just behind the front two which gave him the opportunity to run at opponents rather than play with his back to the goal. He had a direct hand in two of Quinn's three goals.

Arsenal had opened brightly and looked well capable of celebrating the opening of the new all-seated North Bank Stand with a comfortable victory. But, once Anders Limpar's bright opening burst had been curtailed, Coventry took control with Wegerle's passing and intuition continually unlocking the Arsenal defence.

The game had not started so well for Mick Quinn. He was booked after eight minutes for throwing the ball away when a decision went against him – but he ended up taking the ball home with him. His first goal came after 34 minutes from the penalty spot after Lee Dixon had blocked Peter Ndlovu's run – Quinn's powerful spot-kick leaving David Seaman with no chance. Ndlovu himself should have had the visitors three up by the break but he failed to convert two chances with just Seaman to beat.

The second half was dominated by the Sky Blues with Wegerle the provider for the goal-hungry Quinn on two occasions. In the 63rd minute Wegerle sold Andy Linighan a dummy, backheeling the ball on the run into Quinn's path who finished with a fierce shot from the edge of the area. Three minutes later he ran on to another pass from Wegerle, cut in and blasted the ball inside the far post for his – and his side's – third.

Another disappointing opening day home defeat for the Gunners and no doubt they'll be hoping that the start of the 1994/95 season will see them begin their fixtures with an away match.

League Record

	P	W	D	L	F	A	Pts	Pos
93-94 Premiership Record	1	0	0	1	0	3	0	
All-time Premiership Record	43	15	11	17	40	41	56	
All-time League Record	3567	1552	881	1134	2884	4768		

	Home	Away	Total
League Attendances	26,397	–	26,397

Tottenham Hotspur (0) 0
Arsenal (0) 1

Monday 16th August 1993, White Hart Lane   Att.: 28,335

TOTTENHAM HOTSPUR

1	Erik	THORSTVEDT
2	Dean	AUSTIN – *Booked*
23	Sol	CAMPBELL
4	Vinny	SAMWAYS – *Booked*
5	Colin	CALDERWOOD
6	Gary	MABBUTT – *Booked*
14	Steve	SEDGELEY
8	Gordon	DURIE
15	*David*	*HOWELLS* (†66)
10	Teddy	SHERINGHAM
12	Jason	DOZZELL

Subs

20	*Darren*	*CASKEY* (†66)
13	Ian	WALKER (gk)
25	John	HENDRY

ARSENAL

1	David	SEAMAN
14	Martin	KEOWN – *Booked*
3	Nigel	WINTERBURN
4	Paul	DAVIS
5	Andy	LINIGHAN
6	Tony	ADAMS
17	John	JENSEN
8	Ian	WRIGHT – *Booked*
7	Kevin	CAMPBELL
11	Eddie	McGOLDRICK
23	Ray	PARLOUR – *Booked*

22	Ian	SELLEY
9	Alan	SMITH
13	Alan	MILLER (gk)

Match Facts

- Ian Wright collected Arsenal's first booking of the season following his third minute caution.
- Tottenham's first league defeat of the season and Arsenal's first victory.
- This was the 113th league meeting between the two clubs, this being Arsenal's 47th victory, whilst Tottenham have won 42.

Score Sheet

I. WRIGHT 86 min – 0-1

Referee:
Mr. D. Elleray (Middlesex)

Result of this Season's Fixture
Tottenham H

Arsenal

Wright Away

Ian Wright, whose last visit to Tottenham ended with a misconduct charge and a three-game suspension, made it the happiest of returns to White Hart Lane by heading the 87th minute winner of a rousing local derby. Despite being booked after only three minutes, for not allowing Vinny Samways to take a free kick, Wright had the last word in the most positive of ways.

It was a game that saw the Gunners gain a deserved first win of the season. The late goal helped take the emphasis away from an incident in the 36th minute when they had what looked like a perfectly good goal disallowed. From McGoldrick's corner, the ball fell to Tony Adams whose shot was clearly over the line when Spurs defender Colin Calderwood cleared.

It was Arsenal's first League triumph over Tottenham in five matches. David Seaman was a virtual spectator in the first half and Spurs had only two noteworthy goalscoring opportunities. After 33 minutes Seaman failed to collect a high ball and it fell to Sheringham. The Spurs striker could not find the space to shoot and Seaman recovered. Then with nine minutes remaining, Seaman made a superb diving save from a Jason Dozzell header.

With the recalled Ray Parlour nullifying the threat of Vinny Samways, and the Arsenal midfield cutting off the supply to Sheringham and Gordon Durie, the Gunners took control in the second half. The deserved winner came just three minutes from time after Andy Linighan headed on Eddie McGoldrick's left-wing corner. As the Tottenham defence stood still Wright, unmarked, flicked the ball past keeper Erik Thorstvedt to earn his side their first three Premiership points and erase the painful memories of the 3-0 home defeat by Coventry City just two days earlier.

League Record

	P	W	D	L	F	A	Pts	Pos
93-94 Premiership Record	2	1	0	1	1	3	3	
All-time Premiership Record	44	16	11	17	40	41	59	
All-time League Record	3568	1552	881	1134	5885	4768		

	Home	Away	Total
League Attendances	26,397	28,335	54,752

Sheffield Wednesday (0) 0
Arsenal (1) 1

Saturday 21st August 1993, Hillsborough   Att.: 26,023

SHEFFIELD WEDNESDAY

1	Chris	WOODS
3	Nigel	WORTHINGTON
18	*Phil*	*KING (†67)*
17	Des	WALKER
12	Andy	PEARCE
11	*John*	*SHERIDAN (†67)*
4	Carlton	PALMER
16	Graham	HYDE
15	Andy	SINTON
9	David	HIRST
7	Paul	WARHURST

Subs

14	*Chris*	*BART-WILLIAMS (†67)*
13	Kevin	PRESSMAN (gk)
10	*Mark*	*BRIGHT (†67)*

ARSENAL

1	David	SEAMAN
14	Martin	KEOWN
3	Nigel	WINTERBURN
4	Paul	DAVIS
5	Andy	LINIGHAN
6	Tony	ADAMS
17	John	JENSEN
8	Ian	WRIGHT
7	Kevin	CAMPBELL
11	Eddie	McGOLDRICK
23	Ray	PARLOUR

10	Paul	MERSON
22	Ian	SELLEY
13	Alan	MILLER (gk)

Match Facts

• Arsenal's second consecutive 1-0 away victory of the season.

• Sheffield Wednesday's third Premiership league match without a win.

• This was the fifth meeting between the two clubs since April.

Score Sheet

I. WRIGHT 8 min – 0-1

Referee:
Mr. R. Hart (Darlington)

FA Carling Premiership

		P	W	D	L	F	A	Pts
7	Blackburn Rovers	3	2	0	1	5	4	7
8	Tottenham Hotspur	3	2	0	1	2	1	6
9	**Arsenal**	**3**	**2**	**0**	**1**	**2**	**3**	**6**
10	Aston Villa	3	1	2	0	6	3	5
11	Wimbledon	3	1	2	0	5	3	5

Result of this Season's Fixture

Sheffield Wed
Arsenal

Same Old Story

Arsenal, the bane of Sheffield Wednesday's 1992/93 season, plunged the Owls into more gloom with this 1-0 success at Hillsborough. Another Ian Wright strike in the first half was enough to give the Gunners a second successive away win and left Wednesday with just one point from their opening three Premiership matches.

Arsenal took the lead after just eight minutes when a weak back-pass by Wednesday's Graham Hyde allowed Kevin Campbell to draw the whole of the home defence to the near post and his pass was gratefully tapped home by Ian Wright. It was Kevin Campbell who impressed all afternoon and his magnificent all-round performance should have been capped off with at least one goal from the three chances he had.

First of all, having rounded Andy Pearce with consummate ease Campbell ran the ball into Chris Woods' hands. Then, after exchanging passes with Wright and being put clear by Ray Parlour, the Arsenal striker was twice denied by sprawling saves from Woods.

Manager George Graham was entitled to be delighted with the composure, patience and passing skill his team showed all afternoon and for all their frantic attacking early and late in the game Wednesday looked like scoring only twice. Warhurst ought to have done better than head Carlton Palmer's centre over the bar and Palmer himself was thwarted at the last second, when he broke through and was magnificently tackled by Tony Adams as he was in the act of shooting.

After their disappointing defeat by Coventry City on the first day of the season, two successive away wins have seen the Gunners quickly back on the rails – more concern was clearly being shown in the Sheffield Wednesday camp. Despite a £6 million transfer outlay during the summer – including beating Arsenal to the signature of £2.7 million Andy Sinton – the end of the game left the Owls with just one point and no goals from their first three games

League Record

	P	W	D	L	F	A	Pts	Pos
93-94 Premiership Record	3	2	0	1	2	3	6	9th
All-time Premiership Record	45	17	11	17	41	41	62	
All-time League Record	3569	1554	881	1134	5886	4768		

	Home	Away	Total
League Attendances	26,397	54,378	80,775

Arsenal
Leeds United

(1) 2
(0) 1

Tuesday 24th August 1993, Highbury   Att.: 29,042

ARSENAL

1	David	SEAMAN
14	Martin	KEOWN
3	Nigel	WINTERBURN
4	Paul	DAVIS (†45)
5	Andy	LINIGHAN
22	Ian	SELLEY
10	Paul	MERSON
8	Ian	WRIGHT – Booked
7	Kevin	CAMPBELL
11	Eddie	McGOLDRICK
23	Ray	PARLOUR

Subs

15	Anders	LIMPAR
18	David	HILLIER (†45)
13	Alan	MILLER (gk)

LEEDS UNITED

1	John	LUKIC
22	Gary	KELLY
3	Tony	DORIGO
5	Chris	FAIRCLOUGH
16	Jon	NEWSOME
7	Gordon	STRACHAN
10	Gary	McALLISTER – B'ked
4	David	BATTY
11	Gary	SPEED
9	Brian	DEANE
25	Noel	WHELAN (†45)

8	Rod	WALLACE (†45)
18	David	WETHERALL
13	Mark	BEENEY (gk)

Match Facts

• Paul Merson became the first player apart from Ian Wright to score for the first team in the 1993/94 season. • This was only Arsenal's third home win in the league since November 1992. • Leeds last away win was their 3-2 victory at Sheffield United which clinched the Football League Championship at the end of the 1991/92 season

Score Sheet

J. NEWSOME 2 min o.g. – 1-0

P. MERSON 57 min – 2-0

G. STRACHAN 70 min – 2-1

Referee:
Mr. K. Hackett (Sheffield)

FA Carling Premiership

		P	W	D	L	F	A	Pts
4	Ipswich Town	3	3	0	0	5	0	9
5	Blackburn Rovers	4	3	0	1	7	4	9
6	**Arsenal**	**4**	**3**	**0**	**1**	**4**	**4**	**9**
7	Coventry City	4	2	2	0	9	5	8
8	Norwich City	3	2	0	1	7	4	6

Result of this Season's Fixture

Arsenal
Leeds United

Newsome's Gift Brings the Points

Arsenal won their third successive Premiership game in less than convincing fashion as Leeds recovered strongly after conceding an own goal inside the first minute. The visitors can consider themselves unlucky to have left Highbury without a point.

Ex-Arsenal favourite, David O'Leary, was forced to miss the game because of injury and it was his replacement, Jon Newsome, who put the Gunners ahead with an own goal after just 56 seconds. Ian Selley started the move with a good pass to Paul Merson on the right. His centre was missed by Kevin Campbell on the near post but the ball hit Newsome on the knee and went over the line to spare the blushes of the Arsenal striker who should have done much better.

Leeds rallied well and had the better of an ordinary first half where much of the football was played in a congested midfield. David Batty did a man-marking job on Paul Merson to prevent his strong runs from behind the two strikers.

The second half saw Arsenal add a further goal in the 57th minute when Wright's pass left Gary Kelly with both Merson and Campbell to mark. Merson brushed off the young full-back and beat John Lukic from 15 yards – the first Arsenal player apart from Ian Wright to score for the Gunners in the season so far.

Gordon Strachan gave Leeds a glimmer of hope with a 69th minute strike. Brian Deane chested the ball down and Strachan slid the ball from his right foot to his left and gave David Seaman no chance with a low shot from just inside the penalty area. Deane himself should have equalised with seven minutes remaining. Gary Speed's left-wing centre was deflected and the ball fell perfectly for Deane, but his header went straight into the arms of the Arsenal keeper.

Arsenal were grateful for the three points at the end of the ninety minutes but Leeds' dreadful away run continued. Their last away victory was more than a season before when they beat Sheffield United at Bramall Lane at the end of their championship season 1991/92.

League Record

	P	W	D	L	F	A	Pts	Pos
93-94 Premiership Record	4	3	0	1	4	4	9	6th
All-time Premiership Record	46	18	11	17	43	42	65	
All-time League Record	3570	1555	881	1134	5888	4769		

	Home	Away	Total
League Attendances	55,439	54,378	109,817

Arsenal
Everton

(0) 2
(0) 0

Saturday 28th August 1993, Highbury

Att.: 29,063

ARSENAL

1	David	SEAMAN
14	Martin	KEOWN
3	Nigel	WINTERBURN
18	*David*	*HILLIER (†45)*
5	Andy	LINIGHAN
6	Tony	ADAMS
17	John	JENSEN
8	•Ian	WRIGHT
7	Kevin	CAMPBELL
11	Eddie	McGOLDRICK
23	Ray	PARLOUR

EVERTON

1	Neville	SOUTHALL
12	Paul	HOLMES
3	Andy	HINCHCLIFFE
2	Matthew	JACKSON
6	Gary	ABLETT
8	*Graham*	*STUART (†58)*
10	Barry	HORNE
14	John	EBBRELL
7	Mark	WARD
15	Paul	RIDEOUT
9	*Tony*	*COTTEE (+72)*

Subs

10	*Paul*	*MERSON (†45)*
22	Ian	SELLEY
13	Alan	MILLER (gk)

16	*Pedrag*	*RADOSAVLJEVIC (†58)*
19	*Stuart*	*BARLOW (+72)*
13	Jason	KEARTON (gk)

Match Facts

• Arsenal's fourth consecutive league win. After winning their opening three games this was Everton's second consecutive defeat.

• Ian Wright's two goals brought his total in the league to four and his first goal was his 60th for Arsenal.

Score Sheet

I. WRIGHT 48 min – 1-0

I. WRIGHT 78 min – 2-0

Referee:
Mr. K. Burge (Tonypandy)

FA Carling Premiership

		P	W	D	L	F	A	Pts
1	Manchester United	5	4	1	0	11	3	13
2	Liverpool	5	4	0	1	13	3	12
3	**Arsenal**	**5**	**4**	**0**	**1**	**6**	**4**	**12**
4	Norwich City	5	3	1	1	8	4	10
5	Ipswich Town	5	3	1	1	6	2	10

Result of this Season's Fixture

Arsenal

Everton

So Wright for the Gunners

Ian Wright was once again the man Arsenal had to thank as they recorded their fourth successive Premiership win with a 2-0 victory over a rather ordinary Everton side who, after winning their first three games, left Highbury having lost their last two.

Although Ian Wright took the accolades for his two goals it was the introduction of Paul Merson for David Hillier at half-time that turned the game after an inept first half display from both teams. Merson – playing behind Campbell and Wright – announced his presence just two minutes after the interval when he crashed the ball into the side-netting; he also beat Southall and clipped the top of the crossbar but it was the prompting he gave Arsenal's strikers that brought such a turnaround in the fortunes of the team.

Both Wright's goals were special although the striker himself dismissed them rather airily. His first came three minutes into the second half. Kevin Campbell flicked on David Seaman's goal kick and Wright controlled the ball with one touch before shooting low past Neville Southall from just outside the right corner of the six-yard box.

His second, in the 78th minute, was greeted by a spontaneous standing ovation from the Highbury crowd. Again Seaman kicked, again Campbell flicked on to Wright who went round Matthew Jackson once and then brought the ball back to do it all over again. This time he went the other way, flicking the ball over the defender, before hoisting it above a transfixed Southall and into the roof of the net. A euphoric crowd rightly celebrated the genius of Wright's goal-scoring.

Everton, who badly missed their injured captain Dave Watson in the middle of their defence, desperately hoped for some Merson or Wright-like inspiration when they brought on Preki for Graham Stuart in the 58th minute and introduced the pace of Stuart Barlow for an out-of-sorts Tony Cottee 14 minutes later. But they still continued to look second best. They would have been very hard pushed to find any striker in the country capable of measuring up to the quality of Ian Wright's finishing this particular Saturday afternoon.

League Record

	P	W	D	L	F	A	Pts	Pos
93-94 Premiership Record	5	4	0	1	6	4	12	3rd
All-time Premiership Record	47	19	11	17	46	42	68	
All-time League Record	3571	1556	881	5890	4769			

	Home	Away	Total
League Attendances	84,502	54,378	138,880

Blackburn Rovers **(1) 1**
Arsenal **(0) 1**

Wednesday 1st September 1993, Ewood Park   Att.: 14,051

BLACKBURN ROVERS

1	Bobby	MIMMS
20	Henning	BERG
6	Graeme	Le SAUX
2	David	MAY
21	Kevin	MORAN (+76)
4	Tim	SHERWOOD
12	Nicky	MARKER
11	Jason	WILCOX
8	Kevin	GALLACHER (†53)
10	Mike	NEWELL
7	Stuart	RIPLEY

Subs

9	Alan	SHEARER (†53)
22	Mark	ATKINS (+76)
13	Frank	TALIA (gk)

ARSENAL

1	David	SEAMAN
14	Martin	KEOWN
3	Nigel	WINTERBURN
17	John	JENSEN
5	Andy	LINIGHAN
6	Tony	ADAMS – *Booked*
10	Paul	MERSON
8	Ian	WRIGHT
7	Kevin	CAMPBELL
11	Eddie	McGOLDRICK
23	Ray	PARLOUR

22	Ian	SELLEY
20	Pål	LYDERSEN
13	Alan	MILLER (gk)

Match Facts

- Arsenal's unbeaten run was extended to five matches.
- Kevin Campbell's first goal of the season.
- Arsenal gained their first point off Blackburn since Rovers' promotion to the Premier League.

Score Sheet

K. GALLACHER 36 min – 1-0
K. CAMPBELL 75 min – 1-1

Referee:
Mr. D. Allison (Lancaster)

FA Carling Premiership

		P	W	D	L	F	A	Pts
1	Manchester United	6	5	1	0	14	3	16
2	**Arsenal**	6	4	1	1	7	5	13
3	Liverpool	6	4	0	2	13	4	12
4	Coventry City	6	3	3	0	11	6	12
5	Norwich City	6	3	2	1	11	7	11

Result of this Season's Fixture

Blackburn Rvrs
Arsenal

31

Campbell Clincher

The Gunners extended their unbeaten run to five matches with a typically spirited comeback to gain a valuable point at Blackburn's Ewood Park. However, Rovers only had themselves to blame for not putting the outcome beyond even Arsenal's well-known powers of recovery after wasting some good chances before the interval.

Arsenal were forced to defend in depth as Blackburn pushed forward but Nicky Marker, Kevin Gallacher and Jason Wilcox were all guilty of missing good chances when they should have at least forced saves from David Seaman.

Rovers finally took the lead in the 36th minute when David May put Mike Newell clear down the right and he forced his way past Tony Adams before centring. Gallacher beat Andy Linighan to the ball and although Seaman got a hand to the Scot's 15 yard shot he was unable to prevent it entering the net.

Not for the first time under George Graham Arsenal showed a different attitude after the manager's half-time team talk. Within five minutes of the re-start Arsenal almost equalised when Tony Adams' header from Eddie McGoldrick's corner was cleared off the line by Jason Wilcox.

The introduction of Alan Shearer as substitute once again galvanised Rovers back into action but the Arsenal defence, who were a much tighter unit in the second half, continued to hold firm and frustrate the home side.

The equaliser the Gunners had threatened came in the 75th minute when Martin Keown's long pass eluded Kevin Moran and found Kevin Campbell. May should have cleared the danger but Campbell took advantage of this lapse to score his first goal of the season with a rising shot from 15 yards. Campbell had previously struck the underside of the crossbar after beating two defenders and was grateful to see his luck at last change with this goal. With their unbeaten away record still intact no doubt manager George Graham was equally delighted to see the equaliser coming from a player other than Ian Wright.

League Record

	P	W	D	L	F	A	Pts	Pos
93-94 Premiership Record	6	4	1	1	7	5	13	2nd
All-time Premiership Record	48	19	12	17	46	43	69	
All-time League Record	3572	1556	882	1134	5891	4770		

	Home	Away	Total
League Attendances	84,502	68,429	152,931

Arsenal
Ipswich Town

(2) 4
(0) 0

Match Eight

Saturday 11th September 1993, Highbury   Att.: 28,563

ARSENAL

1	David	SEAMAN
14	Martin	KEOWN
3	Nigel	WINTERBURN
4	Paul	DAVIS
5	Andy	LINIGHAN
6	Tony	ADAMS
17	*John*	*JENSEN (†68)*
8	Ian	WRIGHT
7	Kevin	CAMPBELL
10	*Paul*	*MERSON (+80)*
11	Eddie	McGOLDRICK

Subs

18	*David*	*HILLIER (†68)*
15	*Anders*	*LIMPAR (+80)*
13	Alan	MILLER (gk)

IPSWICH TOWN

1	Craig	FORREST
2	Mick	STOCKWELL
3	Neil	THOMPSON
6	David	LINIGHAN
15	Phil	WHELAN
18	Steve	PALMER
7	Geraint	WILLIAMS
5	John	WARK
14	Steve	WHITTON
11	Chris	KIWOMYA
12	Paul	GODDARD

9	Bontcho	GUENTCHEV
19	Frank	YALLOP
13	Clive	BAKER (gk)

Match Facts

- Kevin Campbell hit Arsenal's first hat-trick of the season.
- Ian Wright scored his 62nd goal in just 87 matches for the Gunners.
- Arsenal's fourth Premiership away match without defeat.

Score Sheet

I. WRIGHT 30 min – 1-0
K. CAMPBELL 38 min – 2-0
K. CAMPBELL 55 min – 3-0
K. CAMPBELL 64 min – 4-0

Referee:
Mr. J. Worrall (Warrington)

FA Carling Premiership

		P	W	D	L	F	A	Pts
1	Manchester United	7	5	1	1	14	4	16
2	**Arsenal**	**7**	**5**	**1**	**1**	**11**	**5**	**16**
3	Coventry City	7	3	4	0	11	6	13
4	Liverpool	6	4	0	2	13	4	12
5	Aston Villa	7	3	3	1	9	5	12

Result of this Season's Fixture

Arsenal
Ipswich Town

Campbell's Kingdom

A comprehensive 4-0 victory over a poor Ipswich side saw Arsenal draw level on points with Manchester United in the Premiership. England's Tony Adams and Ian Wright once again impressed but both were upstaged by a hat-trick from the eager and combative Kevin Campbell. From the start he gave his marker Phil Whelan an uncomfortable afternoon though the defender did well to block his first real chance after 18 minutes.

That chance sparked the sort of pressure that inevitably brings goals and Arsenal obliged by scoring two before half-time. In the 30th minute a Campbell header put Wright free on the left. He beat full-back Stockwell easily before slotting the ball accurately just inside the far post from a narrow angle.

Eight minutes later Wright did even better when he dummied two defenders before curling his shot against the bar. His disappointment was very short-lived however; Kevin Campbell latched on to the rebound and volleyed it joyously into the net. It was all Arsenal from then on with Ipswich goalkeeper Forrest performing heroics to tip over a shot from Wright, although he was lucky to escape having a penalty awarded against him when he brought down Campbell in full flight.

The second half saw Arsenal continue their dominance and they were obviously in no mood to sit on their lead. Campbell and Merson both had good chances stopped after a Winterburn cross in the 55th minute before Campbell celebrated his return to goal-scoring form with a neat header that brought him a second goal.

His hat-trick was completed in the 65th minute after a brilliant burst of possession. The ball went from Adams in deep defence to McGoldrick on the right, inside to Wright, who curled such a beautiful pass to Campbell that it made scoring a formality.

In between Ipswich flattered to deceive with John Wark hitting wide in front of an open goal and Seaman had to intercept expertly to deny Kiwomya but their manager Mick McGiven knew they had been given a footballing lesson and was quick to praise the five-star performance from the Gunners.

League Record

	P	W	D	L	F	A	Pts	Pos
93-94 Premiership Record	7	5	1	1	11	5	16	2nd
All-time Premiership Record	49	20	12	17	50	43	72	
All-time League Record	3573	1557	882	1134	5895	4770		

	Home	Away	Total
League Attendances	113,065	68,429	181,494

Odense Boldklub
Arsenal

(1) 1
(1) 2

Match Nine

Wednesday 15th September 1993, Odense Stadion   Att.: 9,580

ODENSE BOLDKLUB

1	Lars	HOGH
2	Thomas	HELVEG
3	Michael	HEMMINGSEN – B'ked
4	Torben	SANGLID (†80) – B'ked
5	Steen	NEDERGAARD
6	Allan	NIELSEN
7	Brian	STEEN NIELSEN
8	Brian	SKARRUP
9	Jess	THORUP
10	Carsten	DETHLESSEN
11	Alphonse	TCHAMI

Subs

12	Per	HJORTH (†80)
13	John	DAMSTED
14	Lars	BROGGER
15	Steen	PETTERSEN
16	Tom	STEROBO (gk)

ARSENAL

1	David	SEAMAN
2	Ian	SELLEY
3	Nigel	WINTERBURN
4	Paul	DAVIS
5	Andy	LINIGHAN
6	Martin	KEOWN
7	John	JENSEN – Booked
8	Ian	WRIGHT (†86)
9	Kevin	CAMPBELL – Booked
10	Paul	MERSON
11	Eddie	McGOLDRICK – B'ked

12	Alan	SMITH (†86)
13	Alan	MILLER (gk)
14	Steve	BOULD
15	David	HILLIER
16	Ray	PARLOUR

Match Facts

- Ian Wright's 36th minute goal was Arsenal's 100th in Europe.
- The 2-1 victory meant that Arsenal maintained their record of never actually losing a game in the European Cup-Winners' Cup.
- In their other season in the competition (1979/80) the Gunners lost in the final to Valencia only after a penalty shoot-out.

Score Sheet

M. KEOWN 18 min o.g. – 1-0
I. WRIGHT 36 min – 1-1
P. MERSON 69 min – 1-2

Referee:
Mr. M. Kakar (Turkey)

European Cup Winners' Cup – First Round, First Leg

Over the First Hurdle

Arsenal, who might have conceded two goals in the opening four minutes of this European Cup-Winners' Cup tie, staged another of their famous recovery acts to emerge as firm favourites to advance to the second round of the competition.

In the opening stages they were overwhelmed by the Danish league leaders who had only themselves to blame for not taking an early grip on the match as Arsenal struggled to find any sort of rhythm or pattern.

Only two minutes had elapsed when Andy Linighan tackled Jess Thorup and while the Arsenal defender got the ball, the Dane fell over and the Turkish referee pointed to the spot. There was an early escape for Arsenal though as Thorup's penalty struck Seaman's right-hand post and rebounded for a goal kick. Two minutes later Linighan's weak back pass left Allan Nielsen with only Seaman to beat but he shot wide.

It was no surprise when Odense Boldklub took the lead in the 18th minute. Brian Skaarup played a short corner, took the return pass and drilled a low centre into the Arsenal goalmouth where the ball struck Martin Keown's knee and flew past a startled Seaman.

Arsenal slowly put their game together and equalised in the 36th minute. A well-worked free kick routine ended with Nigel Winterburn shooting from 25 yards. Lars Hogh only half-saved, the ball rebounded to Merson whose effort was blocked but Wright was on hand to score.

Merson's 69th minute winner was a superb individual effort. Receiving Kevin Campbell's pass Merson beat two defenders and despite almost losing possession regained the ball, before beating Hogh from 15 yards.

An evening in the birthplace of Hans Christian Andersen which had started so grimly for the visitors ended with a much relieved Gunners side taking a valuable goal advantage into the second leg at Highbury – OB certainly paying the price for letting Arsenal off the hook in the early stages of the game. That price was almost certain elimination from the tournament.

ECWC Record

	P	W	D	L	F	A
ECWC Record 93-94	1	1	0	0	2	1
All-time ECWC Record	10	5	4	1	15	6

	Home	Away	Total
ECWC Attendances	–	9,580	9,580

Manchester United (1) 1
Arsenal (0) 0

Sunday 19th September 1993, Old Trafford   Att.: 44,009

MANCHESTER UNITED

1	Peter	SCHMEICHEL
2	Paul	PARKER
3	Denis	IRWIN
4	Steve	BRUCE
5	Lee	SHARPE
6	Gary	PALLISTER
7	Eric	CANTONA
8	Paul	INCE
16	Roy	KEANE – *Booked*
10	*Mark*	*HUGHES (†89) – B'ked*
11	Ryan	GIGGS

Subs

9	*Brian*	*McCLAIR (†89)*
14	Andrei	KANCHELSKIS
13	Les	SEALEY (gk)

ARSENAL

1	David	SEAMAN
14	Martin	KEOWN – *Booked*
3	Nigel	WINTERBURN
18	*David*	*HILLIER (†79)*
5	Andy	LINIGHAN
6	Tony	ADAMS
17	John	JENSEN
8	Ian	WRIGHT
7	Kevin	CAMPBELL
10	*Paul*	*MERSON (+79)*
11	Eddie	McGOLDRICK

4	*Paul*	*DAVIS (†79)*
9	*Alan*	*SMITH (+79)*
13	Alan	MILLER (gk)

Match Facts

- Arsenal's first away defeat of the season.
- The 1-0 defeat meant that Arsenal had failed to score against Manchester United in their last three league meetings.
- The crowd of 44,009 was the biggest gate to watch Arsenal in the Premiership so far this season.

Score Sheet

E. CANTONA 38 min – 1-0

Referee:
Mr. V. Callow (Solihull)

FA Carling Premiership

		P	W	D	L	F	A	Pts
1	Manchester United	8	6	1	1	15	4	19
2	**Arsenal**	**8**	**5**	**1**	**2**	**11**	**6**	**16**
3	Aston Villa	8	4	3	1	11	6	15
4	Everton	8	5	0	3	10	6	15
5	Tottenham H	8	4	2	2	12	6	14

Result of this Season's Fixture

Manchester Utd

Arsenal

37

Manchester Misery

The clash of the top two teams in the Premiership produced a fast, furious and exciting match. the pace of which left Old Trafford breathless. An Eric Cantona 25-yard free kick was enough to take Manchester United three points clear at the top of the Premiership.

Arsenal set out to frustrate United from the start, employing Eddie McGoldrick as a sweeper which left the home side somewhat bemused for the opening period. However, they soon found their feet with Lee Sharpe and Ryan Giggs on the flanks leading Martin Keown and Nigel Winterburn some merry dances.

It was all United in the first half – Cantona saw a shot deflected wide, Hughes had a header well saved and Giggs also went close. Then, after 37 minutes, David Hillier obstructed Giggs and United had a free-kick some 25 yards out. Ince touched the ball to Cantona, whose right foot arrowed a spectacular strike high into David Seaman's right corner.

Ince and Sharpe could have added to United's lead minutes into the second half after two more incisive moves, but both finished weakly enabling Seaman to collect. Sensing their chance of getting back in the game, Arsenal now began to assert themselves in a way they had failed to in the first half when they had not managed one shot on target.

Kevin Campbell headed McGoldrick's corner straight at Schmeichel to serve notice of intent. Merson then slipped Campbell through but Denis Irwin was in smartly to intercept, whilst Schmeichel had to react swiftly to thwart Wright and Campbell.

United though, led by the magnificent Bruce and Pallister, came through this period of Arsenal pressure with their goal still intact and Roy Keane and Paul Ince started controlling the vital midfield area once again. They failed to add to their single goal but the final scoreline scarcely reflected United's superiority on the day.

It was Arsenal's first away defeat in the Premiership and it seemed that their midweek excursion to Europe had taken more of a toll on them than United's trip to Hungary in the European Cup.

League Record

	P	W	D	L	F	A	Pts	Pos
93-94 Premiership Record	8	5	1	2	11	6	16	2nd
All-time Premiership Record	50	20	12	18	51	44	72	
All-time League Record	3574	1557	882	1135	5895	4771		

	Home	Away	Total
League Attendances	113,065	112,438	225,503

Huddersfield Town
Arsenal

(0) 0
(2) 5

Tuesday 21st September 1993, Leeds Road

Att.: 14,275

HUDDERSFIELD TOWN

1	Steve	FRANCIS
2	Simon	TREVITT
3	*Chris*	*BILLY (†71)*
4	Phil	STARBUCK
5	Stuart	HICKS
6	Jonathan	DYSON
7	*Iain*	*DUNN (+61)*
8	Phil	ROBINSON
9	Andy	BOOTH
10	Chris	MARSDEN
11	Mark	WELLS

Subs

12	*Simon*	*COLLINS (†71)*
13	Kevin	BLACKWELL (gk)
14	*Ifem*	*ONUORA (+61)*

ARSENAL

1	David	SEAMAN
14	Martin	KEOWN
3	Nigel	WINTERBURN
4	Paul	DAVIS
5	Andy	LINIGHAN
6	Tony	ADAMS
17	*John*	*JENSEN (†78)*
8	Ian	WRIGHT
7	Kevin	CAMPBELL
10	*Paul*	*MERSON (+78)*
11	Eddie	McGOLDRICK

18	*David*	*HILLIER (†78)*
9	*Alan*	*SMITH (+78)*
13	Alan	MILLER (gk)

Match Facts

- The 5-0 win meant that Arsenal had not lost a cup match since January 1992, when they were defeated 2-1 by Wrexham in the FA Cup Third Round.
- Ian Wright's hat-trick brought an end to the run which had seen him fail to score in six previous meetings with Huddersfield.
- Wright's hat-trick was the third to be scored for the Gunners in a League Cup away tie – the others were David Jenkins (at Scunthorpe in 1968) and Michael Thomas (at Plymouth in 1989).

Score Sheet

I. WRIGHT 5 min – 0-1

K. CAMPBELL 15 min – 0-2

P. MERSON 57 min – 0-3

I. WRIGHT 63 min – 0-4

I. WRIGHT 82 min – 0-5

Referee:
Mr. J. Lloyd (Wrexham)

FA League Cup Second Round First Leg

39

A Wright Old Treble

Arsenal put the disappointment of their weekend defeat at Manchester United behind them with a spirited start to their Coca-Cola Cup defence. Inspired by a splendid hat-trick from Ian Wright – who had not scored in six previous encounters with the Terriers – they gave Second Division Huddersfield a footballing lesson.

Wright gave the Gunners the lead as early as the third minute when he slid in Eddie McGoldrick's pass. He was also involved in the second goal in the 16th minute when Kevin Campbell slotted home to practically kill off the game as a contest. Campbell himself turned provider for the third in the 57th minute, a loose ball driven home by Merson after a good reaction save by Francis.

Huddersfield, who had not won at home all season, rarely looked like keeping their hopes alive for the journey to London despite a brave rally in the first half when they had several chances to claw back a two-goal deficit. If Phil Starbuck or Andrew Booth had been more accurate from good shooting positions, Huddersfield might have made more of a game of it, but the gulf in class was always evident.

The difference between the two teams was emphasised by Ian Wright's second goal – Arsenal's fourth – midway through the second half. Spotting goalkeeper Steve Francis fractionally off his line, Wright produced an exquisite chip which even the opposition manager Neil Warnock was seen to applaud.

Wright completed his hat-trick, and the scoring, eight minutes from the end when Tony Adams got behind the tiring home defence and set up an easy tap-in. The victory ensured that a demanding seven-day programme for the Gunners, which had begun with the Cup-Winners' Cup trip to Odense, ended with a flourish and made the return leg at Highbury almost a formality.

League Cup Record

	P	W	D	L	F	A
League Cup Record 93-94	1	1	0	0	5	0
All-time League Cup Record	136	75	33	28	231	123

	Home	Away	Total
League Cup Attendances	–	14,275	14,275

Arsenal
Southampton

(1) 1
(0) 0

Saturday 25th September 1993, Highbury

Att.: 26,902

ARSENAL

1	David	SEAMAN
14	Martin	KEOWN
3	Nigel	WINTERBURN
4	*Paul*	*DAVIS (†83)*
5	Andy	LINIGHAN
6	Tony	ADAMS
17	John	JENSEN
8	Ian	WRIGHT
7	Kevin	CAMPBELL
10	Paul	MERSON
11	Eddie	McGOLDRICK

Subs

18	*David*	*HILLIER (†83)*
15	Anders	LIMPAR
13	Alan	MILLER (gk)

SOUTHAMPTON

1	Tim	FLOWERS
2	Jeff	KENNA
17	Kevin	MOORE
18	*Steve*	*WOOD (†59)*
20	Paul	MOODY
8	Glenn	COCKERILL
10	Neil	MADDISON
27	Paul	ALLEN
3	Micky	ADAMS
9	*Iain*	*DOWIE (+79)*
6	Ken	MONKOU

11	*Francis*	*BENALI (†59) – B'ked*
16	*Nicky*	*BANGER (+79)*
13	Ian	ANDREWS (gk)

Match Facts

- This was Arsenal's fourth consecutive win at Highbury following their opening day defeat against Coventry City.
- The 1-0 defeat was Southampton's eighth league defeat in nine games, with five of their total of seven goals coming in one match against Swindon Town.

Score Sheet

P. MERSON 45 min – 1-0

Referee:
K. Morton (Bury St Edmunds)

FA Carling Premiership

		P	W	D	L	F	A	Pts
1	Manchester United	9	7	1	1	19	6	22
2	**Arsenal**	**9**	**6**	**1**	**2**	**12**	**6**	**19**
3	Aston Villa	9	4	4	1	12	7	16
4	Leeds United	9	5	1	3	10	10	16
5	Norwich City	9	4	3	2	18	11	15

Result of this Season's Fixture

Arsenal
Southampton

Merson Makes Saints Suffer

Although too quick and powerful for a struggling Southampton side, Arsenal made hard work of beating a team who had lost seven of their first eight Premiership games. But, any side that wants to win championships has to be prepared to battle to win games like this. The Gunners once again displayed that they possess this vital quality to earn themselves all three points.

Faced by a very defensive Southampton line-up Arsenal had to wait until the stroke of half-time to score what turned out to be the winning goal. The build-up involved a cluster of players – including Wright, Davis, McGoldrick and Campbell – and it was finished acrobatically by a spectacular overhead kick from Paul Merson which took a slight deflection to leave Flowers stranded.

Merson was always Arsenal's most impressive player and he almost scored another two in the opening five minutes of the second half, once curling a shot inches over and once seeing the ball blocked by a desperate Southampton defender. Further chances fell to Jensen, Wright and Merson again before two moments of carelessness almost cost Arsenal the points.

In the 64th minute Paul Allen picked up a sloppy ball from Martin Keown, accelerated between Adams and Winterburn, and forced an outstanding save from David Seaman. Then Moody picked up an enormous clearance from goalkeeper Tim Flowers, outpaced Linighan but lobbed his shot too high. That was virtually Southampton's last chance and Arsenal continued to make and miss scoring opportunities.

It was a much relieved Gunners side that greeted the final whistle after a match that was never going to be a spectacular exhibition of all that is elegant in the game. More important than the performance was the three vital points that enabled them to maintain their championship challenge at the top of the Premiership.

League Record

	P	W	D	L	F	A	Pts	Pos
93-94 Premiership Record	9	6	1	2	12	6	19	2nd
All-time Premiership Record	51	21	12	18	52	44	75	
All-time League Record	3575	1558	882	1135	5896	4771		

	Home	Away	Total
League Attendances	139,967	112,438	252,405

Arsenal
Odense Boldklub

(0) 1
(0) 1

Wednesday 29th September 1993, Highbury   Att.: 25,689

ARSENAL

1	David	SEAMAN
2	Lee	DIXON
3	Nigel	WINTERBURN
4	Paul	DAVIS
5	Martin	KEOWN – *Booked*
6	Tony	ADAMS
7	John	JENSEN
8	*Ian*	*WRIGHT (†69)*
9	Kevin	CAMPBELL
10	Paul	MERSON
11	Anders	LIMPAR

Subs

12	*Alan*	*SMITH (†69)*
13	*Alan*	*MILLER (gk)*
14	Andy	LINIGHAN
15	Ian	SELLEY
16	Anders	LIMPAR

ODENSE BOLDKLUB

1	Lars	HOGH
2	Steen	NEDERGAARD
3	Michael	HEMMINGSEN
4	Brian	STEEN NIELSEN
5	Thomas	HELVEG
6	Allan	NIELSEN
7	*Per*	*HJORTH (†53)*
8	Carsten	DETHLEFSEN
9	Jess	THORUP
10	Alphonse	TCHAMI
11	*Brian*	*SKAARUP (+87)*

12	*Jens*	*MELVANG (†53)*
13	*John*	*DAMSTED (+87)*
14	Lars	BROGGER
15	Ulrik	PEDERSEN
16	Tom	STEROBO (gk)

Match Facts

• Kevin Campbell's first ever goal in the European Cup-Winners' Cup Competition.

• The only other English team Odense have met in the European competition are Liverpool who beat them 6-0 on aggregate in the 1982/83 European Cup, with Kenny Dalglish scoring a hat-trick.

Score Sheet

K. CAMPBELL 52 min – 1-0
A. NIELSEN 86 min – 1-1

Arsenal win 3-2 on aggregate

Referee:
Mr. H-J. Weber (Germany)

European Cup Winners' Cup – First Round, Second Leg

Gunners Fire Blanks

A disappointing 1-1 scoreline in the return leg of their European Cup-Winners' Cup first round match against Odense left Arsenal, and a very frustrated Highbury crowd, grateful for the slender one goal lead they had brought back from the first leg in Denmark.

Despite being almost permanently housed in the Odense half, Arsenal were unable to turn their domination into goals and this was a very unconvincing performance from a team regarded as one of the competition favourites at the start of the season. Although the players were probably feeling the affects of playing four games in eleven days, there was no doubt that the Danes' battling performance on the night gave them a deserved draw.

The best of the few chances that Arsenal created in a poor first half fell to Tony Adams after 31 minutes following a corner. Adams intercepted a poor clearance but, from 12 yards, failed to keep the ball down and shot over the bar. A goal at this stage of the match would surely have settled a few nerves and guaranteed much easier progress to the next round.

As it was, just after the break, Odense's Allan Nielsen had a glorious chance to give his side the lead after being put through but David Seaman – who had had little to do up to that point – saved his shot well and ensured that there would be no upset. Five minutes later, Nielsen was left to rue his missed chance as Kevin Campbell finally put the Gunners ahead. A Paul Davis free kick was pulled across the goalmouth and Campbell headed home from inside the six yard box.

Despite the goal advantage and the cushion of two away goals Arsenal failed to capitalise on their healthy position and it came as no real shock when Odense scored a deserved equaliser three minutes from time. Allan Nielsen made up for his earlier miss when following confusion in the Arsenal defence after his initial shot was saved he reacted more quickly to score from the rebound.

Despite there being little to cheer the Arsenal supporters on the night, the draw was enough to give the Gunners a 3-2 aggregate victory and a tie against Belgian side Standard Liege in the next round. Manager George Graham was as disappointed as the Highbury faithful with the performance, but realised that the hard work and attitude of the team in the first leg had been enough to get the club through what turned out to be a difficult tie.

ECWC Cup Record

	P	W	D	L	F	A
ECWC Record 93-94	2	1	1	0	3	2
All-time ECWC Record	11	5	5	1	16	7

	Home	Away	Total
ECWC Cup Attendances	25,689	9,580	35,269

Liverpool
Arsenal

(0) 0
(0) 0

Saturday 2nd October 1993, Anfield   Att.: 42,750

LIVERPOOL

1	Bruce	GROBBELAAR
2	Rob	JONES
3	Julian	DICKS
5	Mark	WRIGHT – *Booked*
25	Neil	RUDDOCK
7	Nigel	CLOUGH
8	Paul	STEWART – *Booked*
9	Ian	RUSH
15	Jamie	REDKNAPP
23	Robbie	FOWLER
6	Don	HUTCHISON

Subs

12	Ronnie	WHELAN
13	David	JAMES (gk)
17	Steve	McMANAMAN

ARSENAL

1	David	SEAMAN
2	Lee	DIXON
3	Nigel	WINTERBURN
4	Paul	DAVIS
5	Andy	LINIGHAN
6	Tony	ADAMS
17	John	JENSEN
8	Ian	WRIGHT
7	Kevin	CAMPBELL
10	Paul	MERSON
11	Eddie	McGOLDRICK

9	Alan	SMITH
13	Alan	MILLER (gk)
23	Ray	PARLOUR

Match Facts

- Robbie Fowler made his home debut for Liverpool. The draw brought an end to a run of four defeats for the Anfield club.

- For the fifth successive game Liverpool failed to score.

- Arsenal kept a clean sheet at Anfield for the second season running.

Score Sheet

Referee:
G. Ashby (Worcester)

FA Carling Premiership

		P	W	D	L	F	A	Pts
1	Manchester United	10	8	1	1	22	8	25
2	**Arsenal**	**10**	**6**	**2**	**2**	**12**	**6**	**20**
3	Leeds United	10	6	1	3	14	10	18
4	Norwich City	10	5	3	2	19	11	18
5	Blackburn Rovers	10	5	3	2	14	10	18

Result of this Season's Fixture

Liverpool
Arsenal

Unambitious Gunners

Arsenal treated a disappointing Liverpool team with too much respect and allowed Manchester United to increase their lead at the top of the Premiership to an ominous five points. Liverpool had suffered four successive defeats before this game and were definitely out of form.

Rarely in past clashes between these two clubs could Liverpool have looked so vulnerable, and so lacking in confidence, as they were in this game. Yet Arsenal failed to carry the game to their opponents, apparently believing that the old yardstick of avoiding defeat away from home is a solid base on which to mount a title campaign. It was pretty much on the cards that the game would remain goalless all afternoon – Liverpool had not scored for 410 minutes whilst the Arsenal defence had only conceded three goals in nine league matches.

Arsenal though, had to be grateful to an alert David Seaman for ensuring that they returned to Highbury with at least a point when he denied Don Hutchison twice in the first half with superb saves. He also foiled further efforts from Robbie Fowler and an enterprising 35-yarder from Neil Ruddock.

Liverpool's best chance came in the 66th minute when Fowler was put through with just Seaman to beat but the young striker learnt that the slightest hesitation at this level is a luxury that cannot be afforded and the Arsenal keeper was quick to block his attempted shot.

Arsenal's fewer chances were more sharply defined and came later on in the game when they started pressing for one of their traditional late winners. Ian Wright and Kevin Campbell had runs on the Liverpool goal stopped by clumsy challenges from Mark Wright and Paul Stewart which caused referee Gerald Ashby to caution both players. The Gunners could still have taken all three points in the last minute but, after being set-up by Eddie McGoldrick and Kevin Campbell with the perfect opportunity for a smash-and-grab winner, Paul Merson slipped in the act of shooting.

Consolation for Liverpool was that they avoided a dreaded fifth successive defeat whilst Arsenal probably realised that, but for their over-cautious approach to the game, they could have returned to Highbury with all the points.

League Record

	P	W	D	L	F	A	Pts	Pos
93-94 Premiership Record	10	6	2	2	12	6	20	2nd
All-time Premiership Record	52	21	13	18	52	44	76	
All-time League Record	3576	1558	882	1135	5896	4771		

	Home	Away	Total
League Attendances	139,967	155,188	295,155

Arsenal
Huddersfield Town

(0) 1
(1) 1

Tuesday 5th October 1993, Highbury   Att.: 18,789

ARSENAL

1	David	SEAMAN
2	Lee	DIXON
3	Nigel	WINTERBURN
23	Ray	PARLOUR
5	Andy	LINIGHAN
12	Steve	BOULD
17	John	*JENSEN (†77)*
9	Alan	SMITH
7	Kevin	CAMPBELL
15	Anders	LIMPAR
11	Eddie	*McGOLDRICK (+77)*

Subs

22	Ian	*SELLEY (†77)*
25	Neil	*HEANEY (+77)*
13	Alan	MILLER (gk)

HUDDERSFIELD TOWN

1	Steve	FRANCIS
2	Simon	TREVITT
3	Chris	*BILLY (†87)*
4	Phil	STARBUCK
5	Stuart	HICKS
6	Peter	JACKSON
7	Iain	DUNN
8	Phil	ROBINSON – *Booked*
9	Andy	BOOTH
10	Jonathan	DYSON
11	Mark	WELLS – *Booked*

12	Iwan	*ROBERTS (†87)*
13	Kevin	BLACKWELL
14	Ifen	ONUORA

Match Facts

• The crowd of 18,789 was the lowest home attendance at Highbury since the 10th February 1992 when a gate of 18,253 saw the visit of Wimbledon for a Premier League match.

• Alan Smith scored his first goal of the 1993/94 season.

• This was Arsenal's 11th Coca-Cola Cup match without defeat.

Score Sheet

I. DUNN 44 min – 0-1

A. SMITH 60 min – 1-1

Arsenal win 6-1 on aggregate

Referee:

Mr. K. Cooper (Mid-Glam)

FA League Cup Second Round Second Leg

Suffering Highbury

Ian Wright's absence after scoring a hat-trick, when Arsenal swept to a 5-0 win in the first leg of this Coca-Cola Cup second round tie, must have done wonders for Huddersfield Town's confidence as they approached this game.

With Adams and Merson also absent, the Terriers gave Arsenal a taste of their own medicine by defending tirelessly to ensure there were always plenty of men behind the ball and restricting the Gunners to a succession of hopeful long-range shots and earn themselves a creditable draw.

Although turning round a five goal deficit was an improbable task, the Second Division side looked capable of pulling off a sensational victory when Iain Dunn – a 21-year-old midfielder playing in the HFS Loans League with Goole Town the previous season – fired them ahead 90 seconds into first-half injury time. The recalled Steve Bould was at fault for the goal when attempting a tentative back pass which Dunn intercepted and coolly stabbed under the body of the advancing David Seaman.

Although Alan Smith spared the worst of Arsenal's blushes with a 63rd minute equaliser, an impatient Highbury crowd left no one in any doubt of their displeasure at the team's performance during the ninety minutes.

Five goals down from the first leg, Huddersfield manager Neil Warnock was pleased that his team restored their pride with a professional performance but George Graham was as disappointed as the Arsenal supporters with his own team's contribution to the tie.

League Cup Record

	P	W	D	L	F	A
League Cup Record 93-94	2	1	1	0	6	1
All-time League Cup Record	137	75	34	28	232	124

	Home	Away	Total
League Cup Attendances	18.789	14.275	33,064

Arsenal
Manchester City

(0) 0
(0) 0

Saturday 16th October 1993, Highbury   Att.: 29,567

ARSENAL

1	David	SEAMAN
2	Lee	DIXON
3	Nigel	WINTERBURN
4	Paul	DAVIS
5	Andy	LINIGHAN
6	Tony	ADAMS
25	*Neil*	*HEANEY (†82)*
8	Ian	WRIGHT
9	Alan	SMITH
23	Ray	PARLOUR
11	Eddie	McGOLDRICK

MANCHESTER CITY

1	Tony	COTON – *Booked*
22	Richard	EDGHILL
15	Alan	KERNAGHAN
5	Keith	CURLE
3	Terry	PHELAN
10	Gary	FLITCROFT
4	Steve	McMAHON
19	Fitzroy	SIMPSON
21	Steve	LOMAS
8	Mike	SHERON
9	Niall	QUINN

Subs

7	*Kevin*	*CAMPBELL (†82)*
14	Martin	KEOWN
26	Jim	WILL (gk)

24	Adrian	MIKE
18	David	BRIGHTWELL
25	Andy	DIBBLE (gk)

Match Facts

- Arsenal's third consecutive clean sheet in the Premiership.
- Neil Heaney made his first league appearance of the season.
- Arsenal dropped to third place in the Premiership.
- Arsenal have not conceded a league goal at Highbury in four matches.

Score Sheet

Referee:
Mr. R. Milford (Bristol)

FA Carling Premiership

		P	W	D	L	F	A	Pts
1	Manchester United	11	9	1	1	24	9	28
2	Norwich City	11	6	3	2	21	12	21
3	**Arsenal**	**11**	**6**	**3**	**2**	**12**	**6**	**21**
4	Leeds United	10	6	1	3	14	10	19
5	Tottenham Hotspur	11	5	3	3	18	12	18

Result of this Season's Fixture

Arsenal
Manchester City

49

Highbury Frustration

Arsenal's second successive goalless draw in the Premiership saw them slip further behind in the title race. They dropped to third place in the table after another disappointing game.

Tony Adams was a part of England's midweek defeat in Holland but he put that disappointment behind him and was one of the main reasons the game remained goalless. He was always the master of giant City striker Niall Quinn and his performance included clearing a Quinn header from an open goal five minutes from time.

City had the better of the opening exchanges with Adams straight into the action as he blocked a first minute shot from Mike Sheron. After a brief running battle with Ian Wright, Steve McMahon started to play some telling passes, and this gave City midfield supremacy – with Richard Edghill especially catching the eye. But it was no real surprise that the first half was goalless because Arsenal seemed reluctant to attack and City's finishing was poor.

The Highbury crowd certainly let their team know what they thought of their poor first half display when they went off at half-time and it was a very different Arsenal side that performed after the break. Ray Parlour went close with a rasping shot that stung Tony Coton's hands and City were grateful to their keeper again when he produced another fine save to deny Eddie McGoldrick.

The turning point of the game came on the hour when, with Wright chasing a long through ball from Adams, City defender Keith Curle headed a clearance into the hands of Tony Coton who was at least a yard outside the penalty area. Technically it was a red card offence but referee Roger Milford decided on a caution and Coton stayed on to watch Nigel Winterburn blast the free kick high over the bar.

After his let-off Coton continued to impress, saving well from McGoldrick, Heaney, Davis and Wright. But, with Tony Adams' goalline clearance denying Niall Quinn in the closing minutes, the game slowly ground to its almost inevitable conclusion with City the happier of the two teams, having taken their recent good run to just one defeat in eight games.

League Record

	P	W	D	L	F	A	Pts	Pos
93-94 Premiership Record	11	6	3	2	12	6	21	3rd
All-time Premiership Record	53	21	14	18	52	44	77	
All-time League Record	3577	1558	884	1135	5896	4771		

	Home	Away	Total
League Attendances	169,534	155,188	324,722

Arsenal
Standard Liege

(1) 3
(0) 0

Wednesday 20th October 1993, Highbury

Att.: 25, 258

ARSENAL			STANDARD LIEGE		
1	David	SEAMAN	1	Jacques	MUNARON
2	Lee	DIXON	2	Regis	GENAUX
3	Nigel	WINTERBURN	3	Patrick	VERVOORT – B'ked
4	Paul	DAVIS	4	Phillipe	LEONARD
5	Martin	KEOWN (+82)	5	Mircea	REDNIC – Booked
6	Tony	ADAMS	6	Thierry	PISTER
7	John	JENSEN	7	Guy	HELLERS
8	Ian	WRIGHT (†82) – B'ked	8	Mohamed	LASHAF
9	Alan	SMITH	9	Patrik	ASSELMAN (†49)
10	Paul	MERSON	10	Frans	Van ROOY
11	Eddie	McGOLDRICK	11	Marc	WILMOTS

Subs

12	Kevin	CAMPBELL (†82)	12	Michael	GOOSSENS (†49)
13	Alan	MILLER (gk)	13	Philippe	NUYENS
14	Andy	LINIGHAN (+82)	14	Paulo	BISCONTI
15	Anders	LIMPAR	15	Yves	SOUDAN
16	Ray	PARLOUR	16	Axel	SMEETS

Match Facts

• This was David Seaman's ninth clean sheet in 16 matches.

• Standard Liege's Patrick Vervoort's booking for a foul on Eddie McGoldrick was his second caution of the competition and puts him out of the second leg.

Score Sheet

I. WRIGHT 39 min – 1-0

P. MERSON 51 min – 2-0

I. WRIGHT 64 min – 3-0

Referee:
Mr. F. Kaupe (Austria)

European Cup Winners' Cup – Second Round, First Leg

Liege Gunned Down

Arsenal put their recent disappointments behind them to produce their best performance of the season so far. It enabled them to establish a commanding three-goal lead over Standard Liege in the first leg of their European Cup-Winners Cup second round tie.

The Gunners' emphatic win over such experienced European campaigners was fully warranted and the scoreline would have been even better had Paul Davis not hit the post and Kevin Campbell headed straight at goalkeeper Jacques Munaron a minute after coming on as substitute. Even John Jensen, whose failure to score for the Gunners since his arrival in the summer of 1992 had made him a somewhat of a folk hero with the Highbury crowd, went close twice.

Inevitably it was Ian Wright who led the Arsenal goal charge with two strikes of high quality. The first in the 39th minute came after a corner was not properly cleared. Martin Keown centred from the right and Wright beat Munaron with a firm header.

Paul Merson added a second in the 50th minute when he bent a free kick expertly over the Liege wall and past the outstretched arms of the diving Munaron. Wright completed the scoring in the 63rd minute, finishing off a fine move down the left between Nigel Winterburn and Merson, by chipping the ball over Munaron.

Such was Arsenal's domination of the match that David Seaman was forced to make just one save all evening and there was hardly any doubt that he would keep his ninth clean sheet in 16 matches. It was a night when Arsenal managed to combine their usual superb organisation with flair as Standard Liege were outplayed, over-run and generally made to look second best in every aspect of the game.

ECWC Record

	P	W	D	L	F	A
ECWC Record 93-94	3	2	1	0	6	2
All-time ECWC Record	12	6	5	1	19	7

	Home	Away	Total
ECWC Attendances	50,947	9,580	60,527

Oldham Athletic   **(0) 0**
Arsenal   **(0) 0**

Saturday 23rd October 1993, Boundary Park   Att.: 12,105

OLDHAM ATHLETIC

1	Paul	GERRARD
2	Craig	FLEMING
22	Chris	MAKIN
6	Steve	REDMOND
7	Gunnar	HALLE
20	*Mark*	*BRENNAN (†81)*
10	Mike	MILLIGAN
11	Paul	BERNARD
14	Graeme	SHARP
17	Darren	BECKFORD
25	Rick	HOLDEN – *Sent off*

ARSENAL

1	David	SEAMAN
2	Lee	DIXON – *Booked*
3	Nigel	WINTERBURN
4	Paul	DAVIS
5	Andy	LINIGHAN
6	Tony	ADAMS
18	*David*	*HILLIER (†74)*
8	Ian	WRIGHT
9	Alan	SMITH
10	Paul	MERSON
11	Eddie	McGOLDRICK

Subs

29	David	BERESFORD
26	Lance	KEY (gk)
15	*Andy*	*BARLOW (†81)*

7	*Kevin*	*CAMPBELL (†74)*
12	Steve	BOULD
13	Alan	MILLER (gk)

Match Facts

- Oldham's Rick Holden was sent off in his first match at Boundary Park since his return from Manchester City.
- Arsenal's third consecutive goalless draw in the Premiership.
- Oldham have now scored only eight goals in 12 Premiership games and have not won at home this season.

Score Sheet

Referee:
Mr. M. Reed (Birmingham)

FA Carling Premiership

		P	W	D	L	F	A	Pts
1	Manchester United	12	10	1	1	25	9	31
2	Norwich City	12	6	4	2	21	12	22
3	**Arsenal**	**12**	**6**	**4**	**2**	**12**	**6**	**22**
4	Leeds United	12	6	3	3	17	13	21
5	QPR	12	6	2	4	23	19	20

Result of this Season's Fixture

No Fixture

53

Predictable Tale

Before this game Oldham had scored only eight goals in 12 Premiership matches and had failed to win at home all season. Arsenal had managed just twelve themselves and came into this match on the back of two goalless draws. Almost inevitably, this game also ended scoreless.

Oldham, though, should have got a vital first home win under their belts. The fact that they didn't was probably due to the sending-off of Rick Holden who was playing his first game at Boundary Park since his return from Manchester City. For 37 minutes he threatened to win the game on his own, floating over so many almost-perfect centres that it seemed only a matter of time before one of his teammates managed to get on the end of at least one of them.

But Holden's clash with Lee Dixon resulted in referee Mike Reed showing him the red card for violent conduct, and his dismissal seemed to signal the end of any hopes Oldham might have had of securing all three points.

Up until that moment, David Seaman had kept the Gunners in the game with two good saves inside a minute to deny Darren Beckford and Mike Milligan. However, following Holden's dismissal, Arsenal came more into the game but continued to rely too much on playing safety first long balls.

In the second half, Arsenal's best chances fell to Ian Wright who, after receiving Paul Merson's perfect pass in the 53rd minute, shot just over the bar. He was then denied by Paul Gerrard five minutes later, who pushed away his shot at full stretch. In between Nigel Winterburn cleared off the line from Paul Bernard and David Seaman blocked a Graeme Sharp effort but neither team could break the goalless stalemate.

Arsenal did not really deserve to win and equally Oldham did not deserve to lose – between them they managed to get it right.

League Record

	P	W	D	L	F	A	Pts	Pos
93-94 Premiership Record	12	6	4	2	12	6	22	3rd
All-time Premiership Record	54	21	15	18	52	44	78	
All-time League Record	3578	1558	885	1135	5896	4771		

	Home	Away	Total
League Attendances	169,534	167,293	336,827

Arsenal
Norwich City

(0) 1
(1) 1

Tuesday 26th October 1993, Highbury   Att.: 24,539

ARSENAL

1	David	SEAMAN
2	Lee	DIXON
3	Nigel	WINTERBURN
23	Ray	PARLOUR
5	Andy	LINIGHAN
6	Tony	ADAMS – *Booked*
17	John	JENSEN
8	Ian	WRIGHT
9	Alan	SMITH
10	Paul	*MERSON (†73)*
11	Eddie	*McGOLDRICK (+82)*

Subs

7	Kevin	*CAMPBELL (†73)*
4	Paul	*DAVIS (+82)*
13	Alan	MILLER (gk)

NORWICH CITY

1	Bryan	GUNN
5	Ian	CULVERHOUSE
27	Spencer	PRIOR
17	Ian	BUTTERWORTH
2	Mark	BOWEN
3	Rob	NEWMAN
4	Ian	CROOK
11	Jeremy	GOSS
14	Ruel	FOX
20	Darren	EADIE
22	Chris	SUTTON

9	Gary	MEGSON
15	Daryl	SUTCH
13	Scott	HOWIE (gk)

Match Facts

- Arsenal's 20th Coca-Cola and FA Cup match without defeat.
- John Jensen still awaits his first goal since joining Arsenal in the summer of 1992.
- Arsenal have not lost at home in the competition since November 1990 when they were defeated 6-2 by Manchester United.

Score Sheet

I. CROOK 33 min – 0-1
I. WRIGHT 78 min – 1-1

Referee:
Mr. A. Gunn (South Chailey)

FA League Cup Third Round

55

Holders Hang On

Ian Wright, so often the saviour of Arsenal, rescued the Coca-Cola Cup holders with a 78th minute equaliser against an injury-hit Norwich side who had played by far the better football.

Norwich had taken the lead in the 34th minute when Arsenal failed to clear Ruel Fox's right-wing centre. The ball fell to Ian Crook – the game's most influential player – and he gave David Seaman no chance with a right-foot shot from 12 yards.

The Canaries played five men in defence and did the simple things well, restricting Arsenal largely to long-range shots. The closest Arsenal had come to scoring before their late equaliser, was when John Jensen's 24th minute half-volley was cleared off the line by Norwich defender Ian Culverhouse.

For the visitors, both Chris Sutton and Ruel Fox had shots well blocked by David Seaman and their attacking moves had far more purpose and variety than those of the cup holders. But, Arsenal's ability to snatch a good result even when they do not probably deserve it, was to prove Norwich's undoing as the Gunners finally made the vital breakthrough just 12 minutes from time.

Once again it was striker Ian Wright they had to thank for giving them another bite of the cherry in a replay at Carrow Road. The move started with Alan Smith who put Wright clear to the left of the Norwich goal and the England striker beat Bryan Gunn with a fiercely struck left-foot volley from 15 yards.

Manager George Graham's relief at getting a draw to stay in the competition – against what he considered were a very good side on the night – was evident. But the Highbury fans went home realising that their team would have to perform much better in the replay if they were to maintain their hold on the Coca-Cola Cup.

League Cup Record

	P	W	D	L	F	A
League Cup Record 93-94	3	1	2	0	7	2
All-time League Cup Record	138	75	35	28	233	125

	Home	Away	Total
League Cup Attendances	43,328	14,275	57,603

Arsenal
Norwich City

(0) 0
(0) 0

Saturday 30th October 1993, Highbury   Att.: 30,516

ARSENAL

1	David	SEAMAN
2	Lee	DIXON
3	*Nigel*	*WINTERBURN (†79) – Bkd*
4	Paul	DAVIS
12	Steve	BOULD – *Booked*
6	Tony	ADAMS
17	John	JENSEN
8	Ian	WRIGHT
9	*Alan*	*SMITH (+85)*
10	Paul	MERSON
15	Anders	LIMPAR

Subs

14	*Martin*	*KEOWN (†79)*
7	*Kevin*	*CAMPBELL (+85)*
13	Alan	MILLER (gk)

NORWICH CITY

1	Bryan	GUNN
5	Ian	CULVERHOUSE
3	Rob	NEWMAN
17	Ian	BUTTERWORTH
2	Mark	BOWEN
9	Gary	MEGSON
4	Ian	CROOK
20	Darren	EADIE
14	Ruel	FOX
27	Spencer	PRIOR
22	Chris	SUTTON – *Booked*

19	Andy	JOHNSON
26	Ade	AKINBIYI
13	Scott	HOWIE (gk)

Match Facts

- Arsenal's fourth consecutive goalless draw in the Premiership and their seventh draw of their last eight games in all competitions.
- In 13 Premiership games the Gunners have scored a total of 12 goals.
- David Seaman's ninth clean sheet in 13 league games.
- Norwich still unbeaten away from home.

Score Sheet

Referee:
Mr. L. Dilkes (Mossley)

FA Carling Premiership

		P	W	D	L	F	A	Pts
1	Manchester United	13	11	1	1	27	10	34
2	Norwich City	13	6	5	2	21	12	23
3	**Arsenal**	**13**	**6**	**5**	**2**	**12**	**6**	**23**
4	Blackburn Rovers	13	6	5	2	18	13	23
5	Aston Villa	13	6	5	2	15	10	23

Result of this Season's Fixture

Arsenal
Norwich City

Blankety-Blank

After their fourth successive goalless draw in the Premiership Arsenal must have been wondering when – or even whether – their goalscoring touch would ever return. They had three attempts cleared off the line in the second half and, during injury time, Ian Wright thumped a tremendous header against the bar.

Determined to bring an end to the dismal run which had brought them just one goal in five previous league matches, Arsenal tried to do their part in making it an attacking game by playing only three at the back – Bould, Adams and alternating full-backs. Even then, they were a bit overmanned in defence because Norwich usually had only Sutton up front in the hope that someone would give him the ball.

Straight from the kick-off the restored Anders Limpar was involved in a move which saw Merson shoot just wide. Then, a minute later, Limpar put Adams in for a shot that was well saved by the alert Bryan Gunn. But, from then on, the game lacked goalmouth incidents and that early excitement was a distant memory before Arsenal went seriously close again. Just before half time Wright, looking well off-side, was allowed to run on and shoot. It hit a defender and Gunn acrobatically got the ball away although he injured himself in the process in a collision against the post.

Norwich themselves had only the occasional dead-ball chance with Seaman saving well from Ian Crook. Bowen had a second effort blocked and Culverhouse was wide with a third. To no-one's surprise Norwich continued with their five-man defence in the second half which continued to frustrate the Gunners. When they did finally manage to break through the Canaries defensive blockade their luck was further out when they were thwarted by three goal-line clearances.

Norwich were, as ever, quick and eager to race upfield for occasional breakaways – usually engineered by their midfield play-maker Crook – the one man who seemed capable of finding time and creating space. But Ian Wright's crashing header against the bar in the final minute summed up the sort of luck Arsenal had all afternoon.

League Record

	P	W	D	L	F	A	Pts	Pos
93-94 Premiership Record	13	6	5	2	12	6	23	3rd
All-time Premiership Record	55	21	16	18	52	44	79	
All-time League Record	3579	1558	886	1135	5896	4771		

	Home	Away	Total
League Attendances	200,050	167,293	367,343

Standard Liege
Arsenal

(0) 0
(4) 7

Wednesday 3rd November 1993, Stade de Sclessin   Att.: 15,000

STANDARD LIEGE

1	Jacques	MUNARON
2	Regis	GENAUX
3	Phillipe	LEONARD
4	Guy	HELLERS
5	Andre	CRUX
6	Frans	Van ROOY
7	Thierry	PISTER
8	Marc	WILMOTS
9	Didier	BISCONTI – *Booked*
10	Michael	GOOSSENS
11	Patrick	ASSELMAN

Subs

12	Yves	SOUDAN
13	Axel	NUYENS (gk)
14	Max	ERNST
15	Axel	SMEETS
16	Daniel	KIMONI

ARSENAL

1	David	SEAMAN
2	Lee	DIXON
3	Nigel	WINTERBURN
4	Paul	DAVIS
5	*Martin*	*KEOWN (+45)*
6	Tony	ADAMS
7	John	JENSEN
8	Ian	SELLEY
9	*Alan*	*SMITH (†45)*
10	Kevin	CAMPBELL
11	Paul	MERSON

12	*Eddie*	*McGOLDRICK (†45)*
13	Alan	MILLER (gk)
14	*Steve*	*BOULD (†45)*
15	David	HILLIER
16	Anders	LIMPAR

Match Facts

- Arsenal recorded their biggest individual and aggregate victory in European football.
- This was only Standard Liege's seventh defeat in 60 home ties of European competition.
- Ian Selley scored his first goal for Arsenal.

Score Sheet

A. SMITH 2 min – 0-1

I. SELLEY 20 min – 0-2

T. ADAMS 37 min – 0-3

K. CAMPBELL 41 min – 0-4

P. MERSON 71 min – 0-5

K. CAMPBELL 79 min – 0-6

E. McGOLDRICK 81 min – 0-7

Arsenal win 10-0 on aggregate

Referee:

Mr. K. Natri (Finland)

European Cup Winners' Cup – Second Round, Second Leg

Seventh Heaven

Arsenal, who had failed to score in their previous four Premiership games, recorded their biggest individual and aggregate victory in ten seasons of European football by trouncing Standard Liege in this European Cup-Winners' Cup second round tie.

Manager George Graham gambled by leaving Ian Wright out of the team as he did not want to risk the chance of losing his star striker for the quarter-final because of a second yellow card. It was a gamble that paid off as Arsenal produced a breathtaking performance that took their run of cup-ties without defeat to a phenomenal 24 matches.

Alan Smith put Arsenal into the lead after just two minutes volleying home after a one-two between Paul Merson and Ian Selley. Selley himself scored his first goal for the Gunners in the 20th minute when he knocked in the rebound after goalkeeper Jacques Munaron had pushed out Paul Merson's shot. A fully deserved third goal came in the 36th minute when Kevin Campbell's header from a Paul Davis corner was only parried by Munaron and Tony Adams slammed home the loose ball. Four minutes before the interval Campbell added to the home side's night of woe when he made it 4-0 after Phillipe Leonard had missed David Seaman's long free-kick.

The second half was little more than a training session for Arsenal and it was not until the 67th minute that Seaman had a genuine shot to save when he was called into action to frustrate Michael Gossens.

Meanwhile Arsenal got on with what had suddenly become a very easy habit – scoring goals. Paul Merson got on the scoresheet in the 72nd minute when, unmarked, he side-footed a right-wing centre from Eddie McGoldrick past Munaron. Campbell scored his second of the night from McGoldrick's pass in the 79th minute and the slaughter was completed by the Irishman himself in the 81st minute when he beat Munaron with a magnificent rising shot from just inside the penalty area.

The Liege team and their supporters were stunned by the quality and power of Arsenal's performance and must have wondered how the Gunners had been struggling all season to score goals in the Premiership. It was Arsenal's most comprehensive win under manager George Graham during the seven years he had been in charge at Highbury.

ECWC Record

	P	W	D	L	F	A
ECWC Record 93-94	4	3	1	0	13	2
ECWC Record	13	7	5	1	26	7

	Home	Away	Total
ECWC Attendances	50,947	24,580	75,527

Arsenal
Aston Villa

Saturday, 6th November 1993, Highbury   Att.: 31,773

ARSENAL

1	David	SEAMAN
2	Lee	DIXON
3	Nigel	WINTERBURN
22	Ian	SELLEY
14	Martin	KEOWN
6	Tony	ADAMS
17	John	JENSEN – *Booked*
8	Ian	WRIGHT
7	Kevin	CAMPBELL
10	Paul	MERSON
15	Anders	LIMPAR

Subs

11	Eddie	McGOLDRICK
12	Steve	BOULD
13	Alan	MILLER (gk)

ASTON VILLA

13	*Mark*	*BOSNICH (†50)*
2	Earl	BARRETT
23	Bryan	SMALL
4	Shaun	TEALE
5	Paul	McGRATH
7	*Ray*	*HOUGHTON (+65)*
14	Andy	TOWNSEND
6	Kevin	RICHARDSON
9	Dean	SAUNDERS
10	Dalian	ATKINSON – *Booked*
11	Tony	DALEY

22	*Guy*	*WHITTINGHAM (+65)*
16	Ugo	EHIOGU
1	*Nigel*	*SPINK (gk) (†50)*

Match Facts

- Arsenal's first Premiership goal for 463 minutes avoided equalling their worst run (in 1910) of league games without a goal.
- Mark Bosnich saved his third successive penalty, pushing away Wright's spot-kick.
- Villa used their substitute goalkeeper Nigel Spink when Bosnich was forced to leave the field injured in the 50th minute.

Score Sheet

I. WRIGHT 58 min – 1-0

WHITTINGHAM 73 min – 1-1

A. TOWNSEND 90 min – 1-2

Referee:
Mr. M. Bodenham (Cornwall)

FA Carling Premiership

		P	W	D	L	F	A	Pts
4	Leeds United	14	7	4	3	24	17	25
5	Liverpool	14	7	2	5	22	12	23
6	**Arsenal**	**14**	**6**	**5**	**3**	**13**	**8**	**23**
7	QPR	14	7	2	5	25	21	23
8	Blackburn Rovers	14	6	5	3	18	14	23

Result of this Season's Fixture

Arsenal
Aston Villa

'Unlucky' Arsenal

Being called unlucky makes a change for Arsenal. Still rampant after their midweek scoring spree in Belgium they overran Aston Villa for much of this stirring contest and scored for the first time in five Premiership matches. Yet they still lost – beaten by an injury-time goal from Andy Townsend.

Led by Anders Limpar and Ian Wright and playing with verve and fluency Arsenal created chance after chance without finding the net. Wright should have headed the Gunners into an early lead from a Limpar centre long before the Swede released his team-mate after 42 minutes with a wonderful through pass.

Shaun Teale tapped Wright's ankles as he ran clear and the award of a penalty was perfectly justified. However, the Highbury crowd groaned in disappointment as Mark Bosnich hurled himself to his left to push Ian Wright's spot-kick away. It was the third penalty he had faced in the season and the third he had saved. However Bosnich hurt his hip keeping his 100 per cent record and had to give way to his deputy Nigel Spink five minutes into the second half.

Arsenal gave Spink plenty of opportunities to press his own claims for the number one shirt but his first act was to pick the ball out of the net after 58 minutes when Wright took a pass from Martin Keown, spun past Paul McGrath and buried a left-foot shot in the bottom corner. Spink then had to come off his line to deny Wright and Ian Selley while Teale cleared another Wright effort off the line with his goalkeeper beaten.

Then quite suddenly Atkinson pushed the ball through into Guy Whittingham's path after 73 minutes. He accelerated past Tony Adams and beat David Seaman with a shot that went in off both posts – it was his first touch of the ball since coming on as substitute a few minutes earlier.

As the proceedings came to a climax in a heart-stopping final 17 minutes Wright, Campbell and John Jensen went close to scoring with shots and headers at one end while Daley scraped the Arsenal crossbar with a lob at the other.

There was still time for a further sting in the tail though, and it came in the second minute of injury time. Whittingham headed on Spink's long clearance. Dean Saunders squared the ball across goal and Townsend broke Arsenal's hearts with a right-footed shot to give his side a fortuitous victory.

League Record

	P	W	D	L	F	A	Pts	Pos
93-94 Premiership Record	14	6	5	3	13	8	23	6th
All-time Premiership Record	56	21	16	19	53	46	79	
All-time League Record	3580	1558	886	1136	5897	4773		

	Home	Away	Total
League Attendances	231,823	167,293	399,116

Norwich City
Arsenal

(0) 0
(2) 3

Wednesday 10th November 1993, Carrow Road   Att.: 16,319

NORWICH CITY			ARSENAL		
1	Bryan	GUNN	1	David	SEAMAN
5	Ian	CULVERHOUSE	2	Lee	DIXON
3	Mark	BOWEN	14	Martin	KEOWN
17	Ian	BUTTERWORTH	22	Ian	SELLEY
10	John	POLSTON – *Booked*	5	Andy	LINIGHAN
3	Rob	NEWMAN	12	Steve	BOULD
20	*Darren*	*EADIE (†69)*	17	John	JENSEN
4	Ian	CROOK	8	Ian	WRIGHT
22	Chris	SUTTON	9	Alan	SMITH
14	Ruel	FOX	10	Paul	MERSON
11	Jeremy	GOSS	15	Anders	LIMPAR

Subs

9	Gary	MEGSON	7	Kevin	CAMPBELL
15	*Daryl*	*SUTCH (†69)*	21	Steve	MORROW
13	Scott	HOWIE (gk)	13	Alan	MILLER (gk)

Match Facts

- Arsenal extend their unbeaten run of cup-ties in all competitions to 25 games.
- Ian Wright's 100th league and cup game for Arsenal saw him score his 71st and 72nd goals for the club.
- Paul Merson scored his fifth goal in seven cup ties this season.
- Seaman's 13th clean sheet this season.

Score Sheet

I. WRIGHT 15 min – 0-1
P. MERSON 35 min – 0-2
I. WRIGHT 65 min – 0-3

Referee:
Mr. P. Foakes (Clacton)

FA League Cup Third Round Replay

Canaries Shot Down

Arsenal's best performance of the season saw them extend their unbeaten run of cup-ties to 25 as they reached the fourth round of the Coca-Cola Cup. This was an even better display than the remarkable 7-0 demolition of Standard Liege the week before in the European Cup-Winners' Cup. Arsenal were so professional that they made Norwich look ordinary – something that few teams had managed over the previous eighteen months.

Such was Arsenal's dominance that Norwich were restricted to just two worthwhile shots – from Ian Crook and Daryl Sutch – which goalkeeper David Seaman dealt with comfortably. The Gunners, even without Tony Adams, were well organised at the back and resourceful in midfield while Ian Wright, yet again, underlined what a lethal striker he is with his 71st and 72nd goals for the club.

Arsenal took the lead in the 14th minute when David Seaman's long clearance went between Ian Culverhouse and John Polston and fell to Wright who chipped over Bryan Gunn. The second goal after 34 minutes followed another huge clearance by Seaman. Alan Smith helped the ball on to Anders Limpar who found Wright. His shot was parried by Gunn and Merson was on hand to score from the rebound.

The Gunners made it 3-0 in the 65th minute when the referee played the advantage rule after Ian Butterworth had clattered Smith. Merson centred and the ball fell into the path of Wright who beat Bryan Gunn with a first-time shot.

George Graham had got his team's tactics on the night spot on. They nullified Norwich's danger men with Martin Keown particularly effective on Ruel Fox and Ian Selley subduing Crook. The Gunners had disappointed their fans too often in recent league matches but in one-off situations the club seemed to have few peers.

League Cup Record

	P	W	D	L	F	A
League Cup Record 93-94	4	2	2	0	10	2
All-time League Cup Record	139	76	35	28	236	125

	Home	Away	Total
League Cup Attendances	43,328	30,594	73,922

Chelsea
Arsenal

(0) 0
(2) 2

Saturday 20th November 1993, Stamford Bridge   Att.: 26,839

CHELSEA

1	Dimitri	KHARIN
6	Frank	SINCLAIR
4	David	LEE
5	*Erland*	*JOHNSEN (†54)*
15	*Mal*	*DONAGHY (+69) – B'ked*
2	Darren	BARNARD
10	Gavin	PEACOCK
11	Dennis	WISE
19	Neil	SHIPPERLEY
21	Mark	STEIN
12	Steve	CLARKE

Subs

27	*David*	*HOPKIN (†54)*
18	*Eddie*	*NEWTON (+69)*
13	Kevin	HITCHCOCK (gk)

ARSENAL

1	David	SEAMAN
2	Lee	DIXON
3	*Nigel*	*WINTERBURN (†77)*
4	Paul	DAVIS – *Booked*
5	Andy	LINIGHAN
12	Steve	BOULD
14	Martin	KEOWN – *Booked*
8	Ian	WRIGHT
9	Alan	SMITH
10	Paul	MERSON
22	Ian	SELLEY

7	Kevin	CAMPBELL
21	*Steve*	*MORROW (†77)*
13	Alan	MILLER (gk)

Match Facts

• Chelsea's sixth successive Premiership defeat.

• Arsenal's first league victory in five matches – since they beat Southampton on September 25th.

• Arsenal's win at Stamford Bridge makes their record there 19 wins, 19 draws and 19 defeats.

Score Sheet

A. SMITH 27 min – 0-1
I. WRIGHT 45 min Pen – 0-2

Referee:
Mr. P. Don (Middlesex)

FA Carling Premiership

		P	W	D	L	F	A	Pts
4	QPR	15	8	2	5	28	21	26
5	Leeds United	15	7	5	3	25	18	26
6	**Arsenal**	**15**	**7**	**5**	**3**	**15**	**8**	**26**
7	Blackburn Rovers	15	7	5	3	20	14	26
8	Liverpool	14	7	2	5	22	12	23

Result of this Season's Fixture

Chelsea
Arsenal

Chelsea Crumble

Much of the talk surrounding this game was centred on Chelsea's alarming slide into the relegation zone after six successive league defeats. Arsenal hardly needed to break sweat to beat a mediocre Chelsea team and secure their own first win in five matches.

The only exception in Chelsea's poor performance was Dennis Wise who, in the opening period of the game, was the only player to cause the Arsenal defence any problems. Two bad tackles on Wise were rewarded by bookings for Paul Davis and Martin Keown but, after that, Arsenal exploited the flaws in a very fragile Chelsea defence.

After 28 minutes Paul Merson's corner was flicked on by Andy Linighan and headed out from under the bar by Chelsea's Frank Sinclair. But there, waiting for the ball to drop, was Alan Smith and he drove it straight into the net to put the Gunners one up.

The goal sparked Arsenal's creative instincts and Paul Merson, Lee Dixon and Paul Davis built a fine move which saw Smith's goal-bound header cut out by Erland Johnsen. As the match moved into first-half injury time Ian Wright ran through and was tripped by a desperate David Lee. Wright himself scored from the spot-kick to make it 2-0.

Chelsea never recovered from that blow and their goal-scoring efforts gradually died to nothing. Indeed their best chance fell to centre-half David Lee but he spooned the ball wide after being put through. The rest of the game was comfortably controlled by Arsenal with the back four showing no sign of missing virus victim Tony Adams.

With the Gunners stronger and more skillful in every department Chelsea were reduced to knocking hopeful long balls into the penalty area and Arsenal had no trouble holding on to their two-goal advantage in the second period. The early-season optimism which had swept through Stamford Bridge with the appointment of Glenn Hoddle as manager in July had certainly disappeared after this sixth consecutive loss.

League Record

	P	W	D	L	F	A	Pts	Pos
93-94 Premiership Record	15	7	5	3	15	8	26	6th
All-time Premiership Record	57	22	16	19	55	46	82	
All-time League Record	3581	1559	886	1136	5899	4773		

	Home	Away	Total
League Attendances	231,823	194,132	425,955

West Ham United
Arsenal

(0) 0
(0) 0

Match 25

Wednesday 24th November 1993, Upton Park   Att.: 20,279

		WEST HAM UNITED			ARSENAL
1	Ludek	MIKLOSKO	1	David	SEAMAN – *Sent Off*
2	Tim	BREACKER	2	Lee	DIXON
33	David	BURROWS	3	Nigel	WINTERBURN
4	Steve	POTTS	14	Martin	KEOWN
12	Tony	GALE	5	Andy	LINIGHAN
16	Matt	HOLMES	12	Steve	BOULD
14	Ian	BISHOP	21	Steve	MORROW
8	Peter	BUTLER	8	*Ian*	*WRIGHT (+84)*
34	Mike	MARSH	9	Alan	SMITH
9	Trevor	MORLEY	10	Paul	MERSON
25	Lee	CHAPMAN	15	*Anders*	*LIMPAR (†46) – B'ked*

Subs

35	Jereom	BOERE	7	*Kevin*	*CAMPBELL (†46)*
18	Martin	ALLEN	4	Paul	DAVIS
13	Gerry	PEYTON (gk)	13	*Alan*	*MILLER (gk) (+84)*

Match Facts

- David Seaman became the first Arsenal player to be sent off in the 1993/94 season when he was dismissed for a professional foul in the 84th minute. • Arsenal's 15th clean sheet of the season and their 11th in the Premiership. • Substitute goalkeeper Alan Miller made his first appearance of the season when he came on in the 84th minute.

Score Sheet

Referee:
Mr. P. Durkin (Portland)

FA Carling Premiership

		P	W	D	L	F	A	Pts
4	Norwich City	15	7	6	2	24	14	27
5	Leeds United	16	7	6	3	26	19	27
6	**Arsenal**	**16**	**7**	**6**	**3**	**15**	**8**	**27**
7	QPR	16	8	2	6	28	22	26
8	Liverpool	15	7	2	6	22	15	23

Result of this Season's Fixture

West Ham Utd
Arsenal

Suffering Seaman

David Seaman left Upton Park probably preferring to forget his last eight days in football after being sent off for the first time in his career. His dismissal had come just a week after he had suffered the ignominy of conceding that eight second goal against San Marino as England were eliminated from the World Cup.

With Manchester United surprisingly dropping two home points against Ipswich Town, Arsenal squandered a rare opportunity to move closer to the leaders with this fifth goalless draw in their last seven games. But, given the departure of Seaman and a generally lacklustre performance, the Gunners were probably more than satisfied with a point at the end of the game.

Seaman was sent off for a professional foul five minutes from the end of this dour encounter when Trevor Morley, chasing Mike Marsh's through-ball, was body-checked by the England goalkeeper. Substitute goalkeeper Alan Miller immediately replaced Seaman with Ian Wright being taken off.

West Ham were awarded a free kick on the edge of the penalty area and, as if to sum up their evening, David Burrows' shot was cleared off the line by Nigel Winterburn. Arsenal's only two worthwhile chances in the match came from Anders Limpar and Kevin Campbell who both went close with good efforts, but a re-shuffled midfield was guilty all evening of failing to create enough for the front men.

Changes in the side were forced upon George Graham by a flu bug that was sweeping around Highbury and the handy habit of picking up points when you're not at your best was never more in evident for the Gunners than after this match.

League Record

	P	W	D	L	F	A	Pts	Pos
93-94 Premiership Record	16	7	6	3	15	8	27	7th
All-time Premiership Record	58	22	17	19	55	46	83	
All-time League Record	3582	1559	887	1136	5899	4773		

	Home	Away	Total
League Attendances	231,823	214,411	446,234

Arsenal
Newcastle United

(1) 2
(0) 1

Saturday 27th November 1993, Highbury   Att.: 36,091

ARSENAL			NEWCASTLE UNITED		
1	David	SEAMAN	30	Mike	HOOPER
2	Lee	DIXON	2	Barry	VENISON
3	Nigel	WINTERBURN	5	Kevin	SCOTT
21	Steve	MORROW – *Booked*	19	Steve	WATSON
12	Steve	BOULD – *Booked*	26	*Robbie*	*ELLIOTT* (†59)
14	Martin	KEOWN	7	Robert	LEE
17	John	JENSEN	4	Paul	BRACEWELL
8	Ian	WRIGHT – *Booked*	11	Scott	SELLARS
9	Alan	SMITH	10	*Lee*	*CLARK* (+59)
10	Paul	MERSON	9	Andy	COLE
11	Eddie	McGOLDRICK	8	Peter	BEARDSLEY

Subs

	Paul	DAVIS	6	*Steve*	*HOWEY* (†59)
4	Paul	DAVIS	6	*Steve*	*HOWEY* (†59)
7	Kevin	CAMPBELL	14	*Alex*	*MATHIE* (+59)
13	Alan	MILLER (gk)	1	Pavel	SRNICEK (gk)

Match Facts

- The all-seated Clock End was fully open for the first time and the crowd of 36,091 was Arsenal's biggest of the season.

- Newcastle's Andy Cole made his first appearance at Highbury since his transfer to Bristol City in March 1992.

Score Sheet

I. WRIGHT 15 min – 1-0

A. SMITH 60 min – 2-0

P. BEARDSLEY 61 min – 2-1

Referee:
Mr. A. Gunn (Sussex)

FA Carling Premiership

		P	W	D	L	F	A	Pts
1	Manchester United	17	14	2	1	34	13	44
2	Leeds United	17	8	6	3	29	19	30
3	**Arsenal**	**17**	**8**	**6**	**3**	**17**	**9**	**30**
4	Blackburn Rovers	17	8	5	4	22	16	29
5	Aston Villa	16	8	5	3	18	13	29

Result of this Season's Fixture

Arsenal
Newcastle Utd

A Wright Magic Day

The biggest home attendance of the season so far saw Arsenal and newly-promoted Newcastle United produce a thrilling match on the day the new all-seated Highbury was unveiled. It was also billed as the clash of the goal-scoring heavyweights – Arsenal's Ian Wright versus United's Andy Cole. Cole was making his first appearance at Highbury since his move to Bristol City in March 1992. On the day Wright took the honours, laying on a display of subtle skills and pace that the young – and still learning – United forward would have learnt a lot from. Arsenal's power and more direct paths to goal ultimately proved too much for a sometimes inspired Newcastle side who conceded both goals to set pieces. Newcastle looked well beaten when they went two down after just an hour but then scored themselves almost immediately to set up a thrilling final half hour. Before going ahead Arsenal were forced on the defensive by Newcastle's superior movement and Steve Bould and Martin Keown, at the centre of the defence, always looked likely to be outwitted by Cole and Beardsley. But once the Gunners got into their stride it was the Newcastle back four that looked the more vulnerable.

Arsenal might have scored in the 13th minute when Lee Dixon's cross was met by a firm header from Paul Merson but Mike Hooper saved well. A minute later a late rescuing tackle from Dixon stopped Andy Cole from putting United one up and the young forward went close again only a minute later after being put through by Peter Beardsley.

Arsenal took the lead after 15 minutes when Steve Morrow's corner was headed on by Bould. Ian Wright nodded past Hooper as Steve Watson stood transfixed on the line. Their second goal was a replica of the first. This time Merson took the corner to the near post, Bould flicked on and Alan Smith rose to head strongly home. Newcastle hit back just a minute later with Cole providing the pass that allowed Beardsley to skip past his marker and beat David Seaman with a rising drive. Ian Wright produced the best moment of the game in the 68th minute when he picked the ball up just inside the Newcastle half, beat three defenders and almost released Eddie McGoldrick with an audacious back heel. Not to be outdone Cole nearly equalised with an acrobatic overhead kick as Newcastle rallied near the end. George Graham was more than satisfied with his own side's performance and was full of praise for United but Kevin Keegan reckoned his team had not played up to their usual high standards – a measure of how much the expectations of United had risen in the eighteen months that Keegan had been in charge.

League Record

	P	W	D	L	F	A	Pts	Pos
93-94 Premiership Record	17	8	6	3	17	9	30	3rd
All-time Premiership Record	59	23	17	19	57	47	86	
All-time League Record	3583	1560	887	1136	5901	4774		

	Home	Away	Total
League Attendances	267,914	214,411	482,325

Arsenal
Aston Villa

(0) 0
(1) 1

Tuesday 30th November 1993, Highbury   Att.: 26,453

ARSENAL

1	David	SEAMAN
2	*Lee*	*DIXON (†70)*
3	Nigel	WINTERBURN
21	Steve	MORROW
14	Martin	KEOWN
12	Steve	BOULD
17	*John*	*JENSEN (+70)*
8	Ian	WRIGHT
9	Alan	SMITH
10	Paul	MERSON
11	Eddie	McGOLDRICK

ASTON VILLA

13	Mark	BOSNICH
2	Earl	BARRETT
4	Shaun	TEALE
5	Paul	McGRATH
17	Neil	COX
7	Ray	HOUGHTON
6	Kevin	RICHARDSON
14	Andy	TOWNSEND
8	Garry	PARKER
9	*Dean*	*SAUNDERS (†89)*
10	Dalian	ATKINSON

Subs

4	*Paul*	*DAVIS (†70)*
7	*Kevin*	*CAMPBELL (+70)*
13	Alan	MILLER (gk)

11	*Tony*	*DALEY (†89)*
22	Guy	WHITTINGHAM
1	Nigel	SPINK (gk)

Match Facts

• Arsenal's first defeat in 26 cup-ties and their first in the League Cup since October 1991 when they lost 1-0 at Coventry City in the third Round of the competition.

• Steve Morrow made his first Coca-Cola appearance since breaking his elbow in the after-match celebrations following his winning goal against Sheffield Wednesday in the 1993 final.

Score Sheet

D. ATKINSON 4 min – 0-1

Referee:
Mr. R. Gifford (Mid-Glam)

FA League Cup Fourth Round

Coca Cola Fizzles Out

Arsenal – the double cup winners in the 1992/93 season – were knocked out of this year's Coca-Cola Cup competition by an Aston Villa side who outplayed and out-thought the holders. It was Arsenal's first defeat in 26 cup ties and certainly spoiled George Graham's 49th birthday celebrations.

Ron Atkinson brought back Shaun Teale after injury but, in a surprising tactical switch, played him at left back moving Earl Barrett into the middle of defence to counteract the pace of Ian Wright. It worked a treat and with Villa's midfield – led by ex-Arsenal player Kevin Richardson – all energy and purpose, the visitors dominated the game from start to finish to earn a deserved place in the last eight.

Dalian Atkinson's 10th goal of the season after just four minutes set Villa on the road to victory. Steve Bould and Martin Keown were both caught square by Dean Saunders who slipped the ball to Atkinson. The Villa striker beat Nigel Winterburn before shooting past David Seaman from 15 yards.

Arsenal's efforts were mainly restricted to two late shots from Ian Wright which were blocked by Villa defenders and a 25 yard drive from Steve Morrow, five minutes from time, which Mark Bosnich in the Villa goal managed to push away for a corner. Apart from this Arsenal did not really pressurise the Villa defence and Bosnich was hardly extended all evening.

George Graham was philosophical about the defeat admitting that Villa deserved their win on the night. After a below-par performance from several of their players the Arsenal supporters left no-one in doubt that they were unhappy not only with the defeat but the manner of it, whilst Aston Villa manager Ron Atkinson headed back to Birmingham having won his second tactical battle at Highbury inside a month.

League Cup Record

	P	W	D	L	F	A
League Cup Record 93-94	5	2	2	1	10	3
All-time League Cup Record	140	76	35	29	236	126

	Home	Away	Total
League Cup Attendances	69,781	30,594	100,375

Coventry City
Arsenal

(0) 1
(0) 0

Saturday 4th December 1993, Highfield Road   Att.: 12,722

COVENTRY CITY			ARSENAL		
1	Steve	OGRIZOVIC	1	David	SEAMAN
4	Peter	ATHERTON	2	Lee	DIXON – *Booked*
3	Steve	MORGAN	3	Nigel	WINTERBURN – *B'ked*
6	David	RENNIE	4	Paul	DAVIS
20	Phil	BABB	14	Martin	KEOWN
16	Willie	BOLAND	6	*Tony*	*ADAMS (†75)*
18	Sean	FLYNN	22	Ian	SELLEY – *Booked*
25	Julian	DARBY	8	Ian	WRIGHT – *Booked*
17	Roy	WEGERLE	9	Alan	SMITH
10	Mick	QUINN	10	Paul	MERSON
12	Peter	NDLOVU	11	*Eddie*	*McGOLDRICK (+75)*

Subs

7	John	WILLIAMS	12	*Steve*	*BOULD (†75)*
21	Chris	MARSDEN	7	*Kevin*	*CAMPBELL (+75)*
23	Jonathan	GOULD (gk)	13	Alan	MILLER (gk)

Match Facts

• Arsenal lost and conceded a goal away for the first time in eight outings since Sept. 19th, when Eric Cantona scored Manchester United's winner at Old Trafford.

• Quinn's fourth goal of the season against Arsenal following his opening day hat-trick.

• Coventry's first goal at home against Arsenal for five games.

Score Sheet

M. QUINN 78 min – 1-0

Referee:
Mr. R. Hart (Darlington)

FA Carling Premiership

		P	W	D	L	F	A	Pts
2	Leeds United	18	9	6	3	32	21	33
3	Newcastle United	18	9	4	5	34	18	31
4	**Arsenal**	**18**	**8**	**6**	**4**	**17**	**10**	**30**
5	Aston Villa	18	8	6	4	21	17	30
6	Blackburn Rovers	17	8	5	4	22	16	29

Result of this Season's Fixture

Coventry City
Arsenal

Quinn Strikes Again

How Coventry City striker Mick Quinn must love playing against Arsenal. On the season's opening day he scored a hat-trick at Highbury as his side won 3-0. In this game he was on target again scoring the winner as Arsenal lost and conceded a goal away from home for the first time in eight outings since September 19th when Eric Cantona scored Manchester United's winner at Old Trafford.

For Quinn and Coventry it was a well-merited result which could have been a lot higher but for a series of outstanding saves from goalkeeper David Seaman including three from his tormentor Quinn before he was finally beaten 11 minutes from time. The goal was the product of a catalogue of errors from Arsenal's point of view. Nigel Winterburn was dispossessed on the left flank by Sean Flynn who promptly crossed towards Quinn, lurking on the edge of the six-yard box. It was not an easy chance but Quinn eased in front of the statue-like Martin Keown to flick the ball past Seaman.

Coventry had wasted other good chances. Lee Dixon blocked a Roy Wegerle shot after four minutes and Seaman saved well after Quinn was granted a free header following a perfect cross from Peter Atherton.

Most of the action was contained in the middle third of the pitch with Arsenal struggling to put together any sort of decent move. The second half saw Coventry exert non-stop pressure on the Arsenal goal and the defence were forced to repel wave upon wave of City attacks. Flynn, in particular, was in lively form as was Wegerle who forced Seaman to another full-length save in the final minutes of the game.

Dumped out of the Coca-Cola Cup in midweek and falling even further behind in the Premiership, manager George Graham hinted at changes for the forthcoming North London derby against Tottenham at Highbury.

League Record

	P	W	D	L	F	A	Pts	Pos
93-94 Premiership Record	18	8	6	4	17	10	30	4th
All-time Premiership Record	60	23	17	20	57	48	86	
All-time League Record	3584	1560	887	1137	5901	4775		

	Home	Away	Total
League Attendances	267,914	227,133	495,047

Arsenal   (0) 1
Tottenham Hotspur (1) 1

Monday 6th December 1993, Highbury   Att.: 35,669

ARSENAL

1	David	SEAMAN
2	Lee	DIXON
6	Tony	ADAMS
12	Steve	BOULD
14	Martin	KEOWN
22	Ian	SELLEY – *Booked*
17	John	JENSEN
8	Ian	WRIGHT
9	*Alan*	*SMITH (†82)*
10	Paul	MERSON
15	Anders	LIMPAR

Subs

7	*Kevin*	*CAMPBELL (†82)*
21	Steve	MORROW
13	Alan	MILLER (gk)

TOTTENHAM HOTSPUR

1	Erik	THORSTVEDT
22	David	KERSLAKE
5	Colin	CALDERWOOD
14	Steve	SEDGELEY
3	Justin	EDINBURGH
20	*Darren*	*CASKEY (†67)*
16	Micky	HAZARD – *Booked*
4	*Vinny*	*SAMWAYS (+86) – B'kd*
12	Jason	DOZZELL
9	Darren	ANDERTON
23	Sol	CAMPBELL

25	*John*	*HENDRY (†67)*
2	*Dean*	*AUSTIN (+86)*
13	Ian	WALKER (gk)

Match Facts

• Tottenham's ninth league game without a win. • From their last 12 games Arsenal have taken just 15 points. • Arsenal's aggregate attendances passed 500,000 with the gate of 35,669 at Highbury. • This was the 25th draw in 114 league meetings between the two clubs.

Score Sheet

D. ANDERTON 25 min – 0-1
I. WRIGHT 65 min – 1-1

Referee:
Mr. P. Don (Middlesex)

FA Carling Premiership

		P	W	D	L	F	A	Pts
3	Blackburn Rovers	19	10	5	4	26	17	35
4	Newcastle United	19	9	5	5	35	19	32
5	**Arsenal**	**19**	**8**	**7**	**4**	**18**	**11**	**31**
6	QPR	20	9	4	7	34	28	31
7	Aston Villa	20	8	7	5	23	20	31

Result of this Season's Fixture

Arsenal
Tottenham H

The Wright Reward

A cracking derby with honours rightfully shared but a point was hardly enough to satisfy any aspirations Arsenal had of gaining ground on a fast disappearing Manchester United in the Premiership. Yet another draw also meant that Arsenal had taken just 15 points from their last 12 league games although they had conceded just six goals in the same sequence.

Lacking any sort of midfield ingenuity in the first half Arsenal were fortunate to find themselves trailing only to Darren Anderton's 25th minute goal but, after the break, they were transformed, driving Spurs back relentlessly with the power game they play so well when the mood is upon them.

Anderton's goal in the 25th minute saw him collect the ball just inside the Arsenal half from Jason Dozzell's knock-down and gallop past Tony Adams before picking his spot wide of David Seaman. Spurs might have had a second, five minutes after Anderton's goal, but Darren Caskey, having just failed to make contact with a cross from Campbell, then sent a twisting header just wide of the upright as Anderton played the ball back into the middle.

Undeterred by this miss, Tottenham continued to carry the game to Arsenal looking for the goal that would kill off the Gunners and David Seaman was forced to produce an outstanding save just before the interval to deny Vinny Samways.

For all Arsenal's pressure throughout the second half, clear-cut opportunities were at a premium. One chance presented itself to Wright in the 56th minute but the angle was too acute. Ten minutes later, an upfield punt by Seaman was flicked on by Smith to Limpar and, as his lob cleared Colin Calderwood's head, it dropped invitingly over the shoulder of Wright who rifled the ball just inside the post for the equaliser.

Lee Dixon, impressive in the counter-attack, and Paul Merson both came close to stealing victory for Arsenal but there were few complaints from either camp about the final result at the end of the game.

League Record

	P	W	D	L	F	A	Pts	Pos
93-94 Premiership Record	19	8	7	4	18	11	31	4th
All-time Premiership Record	61	23	18	20	58	49	87	
All-time League Record	3585	1560	888	1137	5902	4776		

	Home	Away	Total
League Attendances	303,583	227,133	530,716

Arsenal
Sheffield Wednesday

(0) 1
(0) 0

Match 30

Sunday 12th December 1993, Highbury   Att.: 22,026

ARSENAL			SHEFFIELD WEDNESDAY		
13	Alan	MILLER	13	Kevin	PRESSMAN
2	Lee	DIXON	2	Roland	NILSSON
14	*Martin*	*KEOWN (†56)*	28	Simon	COLEMAN
6	Tony	ADAMS	4	Carlton	PALMER
21	Steve	MORROW	17	Des	WALKER
17	John	JENSEN	14	*Chris*	*BART-WILLIAMS (†89)*
22	Ian	SELLEY	16	Graham	HYDE
8	Ian	WRIGHT	21	Ryan	JONES
9	Alan	SMITH	3	Nigel	WORTHINGTON
10	*Paul*	*MERSON (+79)*	19	*Nigel*	*JEMSON (+79)*
15	Anders	LIMPAR	10	Mark	BRIGHT

Subs

12	*Steve*	*BOULD (†56)*	12	*Andy*	*PEARCE (†89)*
7	*Kevin*	*CAMPBELL (+79)*	7	Adam	*PORIC (+79)*
26	Jim	WILL (gk)	23	Lance	KEY (gk)

Match Facts

- Due to Seaman's suspension, Alan Miller made his first full appearance of the season.
- This was the sixth meeting of the clubs during 1993 – Arsenal winning four and losing just one of the clashes. • Sheffield Wednesday's first defeat in 14 matches.
- Wright's goal was Arsenal's 100th goal in home games against Sheffield Wednesday.

Score Sheet

I. WRIGHT 90 min – 1-0

Referee:
Mr. D. Gallagher (Banbury)

FA Carling Premiership

		P	W	D	L	F	A	Pts
3	Leeds United	19	10	6	3	33	21	36
4	Blackburn Rovers	19	10	5	4	26	17	35
5	**Arsenal**	**20**	**9**	**7**	**4**	**19**	**11**	**34**
6	Norwich City	19	9	5	5	35	19	32
7	QPR	20	9	4	7	34	28	31

Result of this Season's Fixture

Arsenal
Sheffield Wed

Leaving It Late

Ian Wright scored the winning goal of this game some 75 seconds into injury time. It was his only chance of the game as Arsenal's domination of Sheffield Wednesday in 1993 continued. The visitors should have registered their second win in football's 10-hour mini-series but instead they slipped to their first defeat in 14 matches.

Wright had been so closely marked by Des Walker throughout the game that it would have surprised no-one had the Wednesday captain followed the striker into the Arsenal dressing room at half time. But, such is the quality of Wright, that he needed only one opportunity to win the game. Steve Morrow's long ball was flicked on by Alan Smith and Wright, for once free of Walker's shackles, scored with a low shot from 12 yards.

While Wednesday should have won – if chances created are the yardstick – the visitors only had themselves to blame for leaving empty-handed. Seconds before Wright's winner Mark Bright shot inches wide from close range after Adam Poric had made the opening. In such moments are games won and lost. Before that Nigel Worthington, Nigel Jemson and Bright all had chances to put the game well beyond Arsenal's reach and when Jemson missed from Bart-Williams' centre in the 65th minute, it looked easier to score.

Bart-Williams in fact was the most impressive player on view as, too often, both the passing and finishing were poor from either side. Alan Miller, making only his fourth full appearance in place of the suspended David Seaman, did well but the lack of creativity in the Arsenal midfield was evident to all at Highbury.

For Arsenal it was encouraging to see them get back to winning ways despite a poor performance – but where would they be without their phenomenal goalscorer Ian Wright?

League Record

	P	W	D	L	F	A	Pts	Pos
93-94 Premiership Record	20	9	7	4	19	11	34	4th
All-time Premiership Record	62	24	18	20	59	49	90	
All-time League Record	3586	1561	888	1137	5903	4776		

	Home	Away	Total
League Attendances	325.609	227,133	552,742

Leeds United
Arsenal

(1) 2
(1) 1

Saturday 18th December 1993, Elland Road   Att.: 37,515

LEEDS UNITED

13	Mark	BEENEY
22	Gary	KELLY
18	David	WETHERALL
16	Jon	NEWSOME – *Booked*
3	Tony	DORIGO
10	Gary	McALLISTER
5	Chris	FAIRCLOUGH
14	Steve	HODGE
7	*Gordon*	*STRACHAN (†86)*
9	Brian	DEANE
8	Rod	WALLACE

Subs

20	Kevin	SHARP
15	*David*	*ROCASTLE (†86)*
1	John	LUKIC (gk)

ARSENAL

1	David	SEAMAN
2	*Lee*	*DIXON (+90)*
3	Nigel	WINTERBURN
6	Tony	ADAMS
12	Steve	BOULD
17	John	JENSEN
22	Ian	SELLEY
7	Kevin	CAMPBELL
8	Ian	WRIGHT
9	*Alan*	*SMITH (†49)*
15	Anders	LIMPAR – *Booked*

23	*Ray*	*PARLOUR (†49)*
21	*Steve*	*MORROW (+90)*
13	Alan	MILLER (gk)

Match Facts

- This was only Leeds United's second success against Arsenal in the last 14 meetings.
- Kevin Campbell's first league goal since his hat-trick against Ipswich Town on September 11th.

Score Sheet

G. McALLISTER 21 min – 0-1
K. CAMPBELL 27 min – 1-1
T. ADAMS 60 min o.g. – 1-2

Referee:
Mr. K. Burge (Tonypandy)

FA Carling Premiership

		P	W	D	L	F	A	Pts
3	Blackburn Rovers	20	11	5	4	28	17	38
4	Newcastle United	20	10	5	5	37	19	35
5	**Arsenal**	**20**	**9**	**7**	**4**	**19**	**11**	**34**
6	Norwich City	19	8	7	4	30	21	31
7	Liverpool	20	9	4	7	33	26	31

Result of this Season's Fixture

Leeds United
Arsenal

Adams Nods Leeds to Victory

The combination of Gary McAllister's guile and an own goal by Tony Adams lifted Leeds to second place in the Premiership and possibly removed Arsenal from title contention.

Arsenal had contributed to the salvation of a contest that barely rose above the mundane in the early stages and had, in Anders Limpar, a player with the vision to destabilise the Leeds defence. Arsenal fashioned the chances to put the points beyond reach and yet Leeds too squandered opportunities when they were on top.

It was the impressive Gary McAllister, in the 21st minute, who helped inspire Leeds' belief that they could sustain their challenge for the championship. Steve Hodge's ball in from the left broke loose to McAllister patrolling the edge of the penalty area. As Arsenal's back line advanced McAllister calmly flicked the ball into the space behind them and with equal composure curled his shot around David Seaman and in off the far post.

It took Arsenal only six minutes to equalise. Kevin Campbell surged down the middle and fed Wright. His cross was headed out by Newsome straight to John Jensen who returned it goalwards and Campbell applied the final header.

Leeds goalkeeper, Beeney, was relieved to see Limpar's instant long-range shot land off-target after his punch-out, and was similarly grateful when Campbell failed to trouble him from Limpar's through ball. Campbell again found himself goalside of the Leeds defence just before half time but, once again, the chance was spurned.

The introduction of Ray Parlour gave Arsenal better balance in the second half with Wright moving into the middle and Anders Limpar given the freedom to move into the gaps previously plugged in front of him. However there was to be no happy ending and, once again, Gary McAllister was the cause of Arsenal's downfall.

On the hour McAllister's perfectly flighted in-swinging free kick struck the head of Tony Adams and was deflected into his own net for what turned out to be the winning goal. An excellent stop by Beeney from Limpar protected Leeds' lead and Wallace might have scored a third for the home side after Gordon Strachan's sorcery prised an opening in the Arsenal defence a few minutes from time. Although Arsenal had the chances to win the game, it was one of those days when unfortunately none fell to Ian Wright.

League Record

	P	W	D	L	F	A	Pts	Pos
93-94 Premiership Record	21	9	7	5	20	13	34	5th
All-time Premiership Record	63	24	18	21	60	51	90	
All-time League Record	3587	1561	888	1138	5904	4778		

	Home	Away	Total
League Attendances	325,609	264,648	590,257

Swindon Town (0) 0
Arsenal (2) 4

Monday 27th December 1993, County Ground   Att.: 17,651

SWINDON TOWN

1	Fraser	DIGBY
26	Terry	FENWICK
16	Kevin	HORLOCK
14	Adrian	WHITBREAD
6	Shaun	TAYLOR
11	Craig	MASKELL
7	John	MONCUR – *Booked*
10	Martin	LING
3	*Paul*	*BODIN (†63)*
27	Keith	SCOTT
25	*Andy*	*MUTCH (+72)*

Subs

2	*Nicky*	*SUMMERBEE (†63)*
9	*Jan Aage*	*FJORTOFT (+72)*
23	Nicky	HAMMOND (gk)

ARSENAL

1	David	SEAMAN
2	Lee	DIXON
3	Nigel	WINTERBURN
23	*Ray*	*PARLOUR (+83)*
12	Steve	BOULD
6	*Tony*	*ADAMS (†83)*
17	John	JENSEN
18	David	HILLIER – *Booked*
8	Ian	WRIGHT – *Booked*
7	Kevin	CAMPBELL
11	Eddie	McGOLDRICK

14	*Martin*	*KEOWN (†83)*
10	*Paul*	*MERSON (+83)*
13	Alan	MILLER (gk)

Match Facts

• Kevin Campbell's second hat-trick of the season. • David Hillier's booking was Arsenal's 30th of the season. • Swindon remain bottom of the Carling Premiership. • Ian Wright scored his 20th league and cup goal of the present campaign.

Score Sheet

K. CAMPBELL 19 min – 0-1
K. CAMPBELL 26 min – 0-2
K. CAMPBELL 65 min – 0-3
I. WRIGHT 89 min – 0-4

Referee:
Mr. S. Lodge (Barnsley)

FA Carling Premiership

		P	W	D	L	F	A	Pts
3	Leeds United	22	11	7	4	37	25	40
4	Blackburn Rovers	21	11	6	4	29	18	39
5	**Arsenal**	**22**	**10**	**7**	**5**	**24**	**13**	**37**
6	Newcastle United	21	10	6	5	38	20	36
7	Norwich City	20	9	7	4	33	22	34

Result of this Season's Fixture

No Fixture

Gunners Romp Home

Kevin Campbell went some way to dismissing the myth that Arsenal have a one-man strike-force with his second hat-trick of the season in a superlative display at the County Ground. But, once again, he was upstaged by Ian Wright in the last minute who scored with an exquisite 35-yard lob. Wright made the first three goals and his audacious strike rounded off an impressive contribution to an Arsenal performance that shattered any hopes Swindon might have had of rising from the foot of the Premiership.

With Alan Smith injured and Paul Merson recovering from flu, George Graham saw his side, using Ray Parlour and Eddie McGoldrick on the flanks, take full advantage of Swindon's suicidal offside trap.

Arsenal threatened to overrun Swindon in the first half, and Wright had already forced Digby to save before he set up the opening goal. Parlour's long ball found Wright, who carried it 25 yards before rolling it across for Campbell to convert comfortably. The second goal, seven minutes later, was again engineered by Wright. His long forward ball dropped perfectly for Campbell to control and finish from 15 yards.

Even John Jensen – still goalless since his arrival at Highbury in 1992 – looked like scoring but he wasted one effort failing to control the ball properly and when he did manage to strike the ball well Digby produced an excellent save. Campbell collected his hat-trick in the 69th minute. Wright and Parlour combining before he tapped home his 12th goal of the season.

Swindon threatened briefly with Craig Maskell planting a firm header into David Seaman's arms before Wright completed an impressive afternoon's performance from Arsenal. With Fraser Digby only five yards off his line, Wright summed up his options, aimed and fired. His lob sailed over the goalkeeper. Digby arched to palm the ball but succeeded only in helping the striker collect a goal described by George Graham as one of pure genius. Few at the County Ground would have argued.

League Record

	P	W	D	L	F	A	Pts	Pos
93-94 Premiership Record	22	10	7	5	24	13	37	4th
All-time Premiership Record	64	25	18	21	64	51	93	
All-time League Record	3588	1562	888	1138	5908	4778		

	Home	Away	Total
League Attendances	325,609	282.299	607.908

Arsenal
Sheffield United

(2) 3
(0) 0

Wednesday 29th December 1993, Highbury   Att.: 27,035

ARSENAL			SHEFFIELD UNITED		
1	David	SEAMAN	1	Alan	KELLY
2	Lee	DIXON	17	Carl	BRADSHAW
3	Nigel	WINTERBURN	26	Jamie	HOYLAND – *Booked*
23	*Ray*	*PARLOUR (†76)*	16	Paul	BEESLEY
12	Steve	BOULD	24	*Jonas*	*WIRMOLA (†45)*
6	Tony	ADAMS	33	*Roger*	*NILSEN (+55)*
18	David	HILLIER	8	Paul	ROGERS
17	John	JENSEN	18	Dane	WHITEHOUSE
8	*Ian*	*WRIGHT (+87)*	12	Jostein	FLO
7	Kevin	CAMPBELL	27	Bobby	DAVISON
11	Eddie	McGOLDRICK	22	Andy	SCOTT

Subs

10	*Paul*	*MERSON (†76)*	10	*Glyn*	*HODGES (†45)*
14	*Martin*	*KEOWN (+87)*	21	*Alan*	*CORK (+55)*
13	Alan	MILLER (gk)	30	Carl	MUGGLETON (gk)

Match Facts

- Kevin Campbell took his tally to five goals in 48 hours following his hat-trick at Swindon.
- Sheffield United have now gone six games without a goal – their only scoring effort in nine matches coming from a deflection against Chelsea.
- Kevin Campbell's 14th goal of the season.

Score Sheet

K. CAMPBELL 11 min – 1-0

I. WRIGHT 40 min – 2-0

K. CAMPBELL 55 min – 3-0

Referee:
Mr. R. Milford (Bristol)

FA Carling Premiership

		P	W	D	L	F	A	Pts
3	Blackburn Rovers	22	12	6	4	31	18	42
4	Leeds United	23	11	8	4	38	26	41
5	**Arsenal**	**23**	**11**	**7**	**5**	**27**	**13**	**40**
6	Newcastle United	22	10	6	6	38	21	36
7	Norwich City	21	9	7	5	34	24	34

Result of this Season's Fixture

No Fixture

Blades Blunted

For the second time in three days Arsenal swept aside struggling opposition with consummate ease and, also for the second time in that period, Kevin Campbell led the rout – this time with two goals. Another similarity to the previous victory was the scintillating goal which Ian Wright added to his immaculate collection, sandwiched in between Campbell's brace.

Apart from the form of Wright and Campbell, George Graham would have been pleased with the performance of David Hillier, creator of Arsenal's first two goals. The game was 11 minutes old when Hillier's piercing through ball set up Campbell who got beyond Jamie Hoyland and found the net off Alan Kelly's left-hand post.

United threatened briefly before Arsenal scored again with Wright dispatching another memorable goal. Hillier's long pass from inside his own area sent Wright chasing with three defenders to beat. The angle seemed too acute but he turned Paul Beesley before driving sweetly into the far corner.

United had been overrun in midfield in the first half but the introduction of Glyn Hodges for Jonas Wirmola did little to improve their performance. Within two minutes Campbell hit the side netting before making amends in the 55th minute when David Seaman launched a long kick. Ray Parlour tried but failed to control the ball and it bounced invitingly to Campbell, whose pace took him beyond his marker before he sent a low shot under Kelly's body.

The Yorkshire side had managed to score just one goal in their last nine games – a deflected effort against Chelsea – and Arsenal should have finished the game with a healthier advantage. United short of goals and points looked and played like a team struggling to avoid the drop.

League Record

	P	W	D	L	F	A	Pts	Pos
93-94 Premiership Record	23	11	7	5	27	13	40	4th
All-time Premiership Record	65	26	18	21	67	51	96	
All-time League Record	3589	1563	888	1138	5911	4778		

	Home	Away	Total
League Attendances	352,644	282,299	634,943

Wimbledon
Arsenal

(0) 0
(2) 3

Saturday 1st January 1994, Selhurst Park   Att.: 16,584

WIMBLEDON			ARSENAL		
1	Hans	SEGERS	1	David	SEAMAN
2	Warren	BARTON	2	*Lee*	*DIXON (+78)*
33	Gary	ELKINS	3	Nigel	WINTERBURN
5	Dean	BLACKWELL	23	Ray	PARLOUR
6	Scott	FITZGERALD	12	Steve	BOULD
26	Neil	ARDLEY	6	Tony	ADAMS
4	Vinny	JONES	17	*John*	*JENSEN (+85)*
8	Robbie	EARLE	18	David	HILLIER
24	*Peter*	*FEAR (+45)*	8	Ian	WRIGHT
9	John	FASHANU	7	Kevin	CAMPBELL
10	Dean	HOLDSWORTH	11	Eddie	McGOLDRICK

Subs

7	*Andy*	*CLARKE (+45)*	10	*Paul*	*MERSON (+85)*
23	Neil	SULLIVAN (gk)	14	*Martin*	*KEOWN (+78)*
21	Chris	PERRY	13	Alan	MILLER (gk)

Match Facts

• Kevin Campbell's seventh goal in four games and his total of fifteen for the season equals his best ever for the club.

• Wimbledon's biggest home gate of the season – 16,584 – a week after this season's Premiership lowest, 4,739 when they lost to Coventry City.

Score Sheet

K. CAMPBELL 18 min – 0-1
R. PARLOUR 23 min – 0-2
I. WRIGHT 55 min – 0-3

Referee:
Mr. G. Ashby (Worcester)

FA Carling Premiership

		P	W	D	L	F	A	Pts
1	Manchester United	24	17	6	1	49	20	57
2	Blackburn Rovers	23	13	6	4	32	18	45
3	**Arsenal**	**24**	**12**	**7**	**5**	**30**	**13**	**43**
4	Leeds United	24	11	9	4	38	26	42
5	Newcastle United	23	11	6	6	40	21	39

Result of this Season's Fixture

Wimbledon
Arsenal

Wimbledon Wiped Out

Was this the same team that had failed to score a single goal in October when they had been involved in four successive goalless draws? After hitting just 20 goals in their previous twenty Premiership matches, Arsenal took their total in their three holiday games to ten with this 3-0 defeat of Wimbledon at Selhurst Park. Equally significant was the fact that they kept three more clean sheets.

Wimbledon presented a far tougher challenge than their two previous opponents, Swindon and Sheffield United, yet they were swept aside by a team suddenly bristling with a swaggering confidence. Under intense pressure for the first 10 minutes, Arsenal's defence, and Steve Bould in particular, stood firm against the powerful running of John Fashanu. From the moment Kevin Campbell opened the scoring in the 18th minute, they rarely looked troubled.

The goal was created by Arsenal's most effective player, Ray Parlour, who headed Nigel Winterburn's cross from the left across the Wimbledon goalmouth allowing Campbell to steal in and nod home from close range. Four minutes later Parlour himself struck when Eddie McGoldrick's corner was only half-cleared allowing Parlour to drill a left foot shot past Hans Segers from the edge of the area.

The form of Kevin Campbell over the past three matches had also relieved the pressure on Ian Wright and. liberated from a purely goal-scoring role, his touches and darting runs off the ball were a joy to watch. It was hardly noticed that he failed to carve out a single chance for himself in the first half. He was not to be denied his place on the scoresheet. however. and nine minutes after the break he poked home his 22nd goal of the season from close in after Hans Segers could only block a fierce Ray Parlour shot.

Wimbledon had earlier had two good chances to reduce the arrears through Dean Blackwell and Dean Holdsworth and their best opportunity fell to Fashanu with seven minutes remaining when he dispossessed McGoldrick in the penalty area only to shoot wide. Arsenal continued to press and Wright should have scored a second when Campbell's flick put him clear but his shot was blocked by an alert Segers at the near post.

Arsenal. despite still trailing leaders Manchester United by 14 points, had done nothing over the holiday period to suggest that they were ready to concede the Premiership title halfway through the season.

League Record

	P	W	D	L	F	A	Pts	Pos
93-94 Premiership Record	24	12	7	5	30	13	43	3rd
All-time Premiership Record	66	27	18	21	70	51	99	
All-time League Record	3590	1564	888	1138	5914	4778		

	Home	Away	Total
League Attendances	352.644	298,883	651,527

Arsenal   (0) 0
Queens Park Rangers (0) 0

Monday 3rd January 1994, Highbury   Att.: 34,935

ARSENAL

1	David	SEAMAN
2	Lee	DIXON
3	Nigel	WINTERBURN
23	Ray	PARLOUR
12	Steve	BOULD
6	Tony	ADAMS
18	David	HILLIER
17	*John*	*JENSEN (†71)*
8	Ian	WRIGHT – *Booked*
7	Kevin	CAMPBELL
11	Eddie	McGOLDRICK

Subs

14	*Martin*	*KEOWN (†71)*
10	Paul	MERSON
13	Alan	MILLER (gk)

QUEENS PARK RANGERS

13	Jan	STEJSKAL
2	David	BARDSLEY
3	Clive	WILSON
24	Steve	YATES
5	Darren	PEACOCK
11	Trevor	SINCLAIR
14	Simon	BARKER
4	Ray	WILKINS
22	Mike	MEAKER
12	Gary	PENRICE – *Booked*
9	Les	FERDINAND

7	Andy	IMPEY
15	Rufus	BENNETT
1	Tony	ROBERTS (gk)

Match Facts

- Arsenal's sixth goalless draw of the season.
- This was the fourth successive goalless draw between the two teams – Paul Merson being the last player to score in the fixture on the opening day of the 1991/92 season.
- Arsenal's 20th clean sheet of the season in 35 competitive matches.

Score Sheet

Referee:
Mr. J. Borrett (Suffolk)

FA Carling Premiership

		P	W	D	L	F	A	Pts
1	Manchester United	25	17	7	1	52	23	58
2	Blackburn Rovers	23	13	6	4	32	18	45
3	**Arsenal**	**25**	**12**	**8**	**5**	**30**	**13**	**44**
4	Newcastle United	24	12	6	6	42	22	42
5	Leeds United	24	11	9	4	38	26	42

Result of this Season's Fixture

Arsenal

QPR

Goals Dry Up Again

The scoring power that had swept Arsenal through the holiday period in a flurry of goals deserted them against Queens Park Rangers at Highbury. It was hardly a surprise – this was the fourth successive goalless draw between the two teams and was certainly one of the least eventful.

After running in ten goals in three games without reply, the Gunners were unable to claim the one that would have taken them to second place in the table. It was a game where no-one could spark their goalscorers. Ian Wright, the scorer of five goals in their previous six matches, and Kevin Campbell, with seven in four, both drew blanks.

There were only two notable incidents in a poor first half and both involved Kevin Campbell. Rangers' defence had been negligent in leaving him unmarked after only three minutes and were grateful to see a firm header from Eddie McGoldrick's corner clip the top of the bar. Ten minutes later Parlour touched on Steve Bould's high ball and Campbell was denied by goalkeeper Jan Stejskal's knees.

The second half saw gaps begin to develop in the Rangers defence and Ray Parlour, in his new position on the right of midfield, began exploiting the space on his flank to good effect. Four times he whipped in low crosses that players on either side could have diverted into the net. Rangers defender Steve Yates hit the first of them against his own bar, Darren Peacock scraped the second one away, McGoldrick flicked another wide and, with three minutes left, had his shot from six yards well saved by Stejskal.

Rangers, though never overwhelmed, managed only one shot at David Seaman – Les Ferdinand forcing the Arsenal goalkeeper to plunge to his left to keep out a half-volley from 25 yards. Four Premiership games in eight days had certainly taken their toll on both teams.

League Record

	P	W	D	L	F	A	Pts	Pos
93-94 Premiership Record	25	12	8	5	30	13	44	3rd
All-time Premiership Record	67	27	19	21	70	51	100	
All-time League Record	3591	1564	889	1138	5914	4778		

	Home	Away	Total
League Attendances	387,579	298,883	686,462

Millwall
Arsenal

(0) 0
(0) 1

Monday 10th January 1994, New Den   Att.: 20,093

MILLWALL

1	Kasey	KELLER
2	Richard	HUXFORD
3	Ben	THATCHER
4	Andy	ROBERTS
5	Pat	Van den HAUWE
6	Keith	STEVENS
7	Alex	RAE
8	Etienne	VERVEER
9	Dave	MITCHELL – *Booked*
10	Jon	GOODMAN
11	Phil	BARBER

Subs

12	Andy	MAY
13	Carl	EMBERSON (gk)
14	Jamie	MORALEE

ARSENAL

1	David	SEAMAN
2	Lee	DIXON
3	Nigel	WINTERBURN
18	*David*	*HILLIER (+89)*
12	Steve	BOULD – *Booked*
6	Tony	ADAMS
14	Martin	KEOWN
23	Ray	PARLOUR
8	*Ian*	*WRIGHT (†70) – B'ked*
7	Kevin	CAMPBELL
11	Eddie	McGOLDRICK

10	*Paul*	*MERSON (†70)*
17	*John*	*JENSEN (+89)*
13	Alan	MILLER (gk)

Match Facts

• The crowd of 20,093 was Millwall's record attendance at the New Den.

• Ian Wright's booking took him over the 21 disciplinary points mark and an automatic two-game suspension which includes the fourth Round tie.

• Arsenal's ninth FA Cup game without defeat – they were last beaten in the third Round by Wrexham back in January 1992.

Score Sheet

T. ADAMS 89 min – 0-1

Referee:
Mr. P. Durkin (Portland)

FA Cup Third Round

The Late Late Show

Arsenal won the 1993 FA Cup with a last-minute goal in a replay against Sheffield Wednesday. They started their defence of the trophy in similar fashion at Millwall, when Tony Adams bundled the ball over the line in the 89th minute, after an Eddie McGoldrick corner was not collected by Lions goalkeeper Kasey Keller.

It was a messy goal which gave the Gunners a scarcely deserved victory in what was a disappointing game but their attitude, tactics and style showed why they are the premier cup team.

It was Millwall who set the early pace, and they almost took the lead in the first minute when a shot from Dave Mitchell was deflected wide by Martin Keown. Sadly, the explosive start was not a sign of things to come and neither goalkeeper was particularly extended. Arsenal reorganised themselves and, from then on, an air of inevitability regarding the result was never far away.

The nearest Arsenal came to breaking the first half deadlock was from a mis-kick, when Eddie McGoldrick's centre hit Ben Thatcher and almost squeezed in on the near post. Apart from that, Kevin Campbell and Ian Wright had half-chances, as did Millwall's Mitchell and Goodman, but it was hardly a night of vintage football.

The frenzied midfield action of the opening forty-five minutes continued unabated in the second half with both teams prepared to battle and scrap for any sort of opening. Ray Parlour almost put Arsenal ahead with a volley from David Hillier's cross and Phil Barber, after swapping passes with Mitchell, drove narrowly over the top of the bar.

No-one really expected a goal, least of all Millwall's Kasey Keller who had hardly been troubled all evening. He tried desperately to react, after his initial mistake from McGoldrick's corner, only to see the ball go into the net off his shoulder. Millwall had deserved a replay at Highbury but Arsenal captain Tony Adams, who led by example all evening, deserved the credit not only for his winning goal but for his superb leadership.

FA Cup Record

	P	W	D	L	F	A
FA Cup Record 93-94	1	1	0	0	1	0
All-time FA Cup Record	356	185	83	88	649	391

	Home	Away	Total
FA Cup Attendances	–	20,093	20,093

Manchester City (0) 0
Arsenal (0) 0

Saturday 15th January 1994, Maine Road   Att.: 25,642

MANCHESTER CITY

1	Tony	COTON
22	Richard	EDGHILL
3	Terry	PHELAN
15	Alan	KERNAGHAN
6	Michel	VONK
18	David	BRIGHTWELL (+75)
7	David	ROCASTLE
20	Alfons	GROENENDIJK (†58)
11	Carl	GRIFFITHS
26	Kaare	INGEBRIGTSEN – B'ked
21	Steve	LOMAS

Subs

10	Gary	FLITCROFT (†58)
8	Mike	SHERON (+75)
25	Andy	DIBBLE (gk)

ARSENAL

1	David	SEAMAN
2	Lee	DIXON
3	Nigel	WINTERBURN – B'ked
18	David	HILLIER
12	Steve	BOULD
6	Tony	ADAMS
17	John	JENSEN (+80)
7	Kevin	CAMPBELL
8	Ian	WRIGHT
23	Ray	PARLOUR
11	Eddie	McGOLDRICK (†12)

10	Paul	MERSON (†12)
14	Martin	KEOWN (+80)
13	Alan	MILLER (gk)

Match Facts

- Manchester City's fourth consecutive league match against Arsenal without scoring a goal. • Arsenal's sixth successive clean sheet and their seventh goalless draw of the season. • The second goalless draw between the two clubs in the Premiership this season. • David Seaman's 20th clean sheet of the season in all competitions.

Score Sheet

Referee:
Mr. D. Allison (Lancaster)

FA Carling Premiership

		P	W	D	L	F	A	Pts
1	Manchester United	26	18	7	1	53	23	61
2	Blackburn Rovers	24	14	6	4	34	19	48
3	**Arsenal**	**26**	**12**	**9**	**5**	**30**	**13**	**45**
4	Leeds United	25	11	10	4	38	26	43
5	Newcastle United	24	12	6	6	42	22	42

Result of this Season's Fixture

Manchester City
Arsenal

Predictably Pointless

With Manchester City low on confidence after 15 league matches without a win and a continuing boardroom battle at Maine Road, the scoreline was almost predictable. But it was a confrontation that both teams felt they could have won and Arsenal, in particular, had cause to curse their misfortune after dominating the second half.

It was City who had the chances to win the game in the first period with Michel Vonk, the central defender turned striker, unsettling the Arsenal defence with his aerial power and unflinching commitment. It was he who had City's best chance, midway through the half, when David Rocastle robbed John Jensen in midfield, fed Carl Griffiths and his cross found Vonk who drove his shot against the legs of David Seaman.

Arsenal created little in the first half but Ian Wright could have put the Gunners ahead just after the start of the second period when he rounded Alan Kernaghan, cut back inside but hit his shot against the post from an acute angle. Ray Parlour did at last find the net with a left foot shot in the 62nd minute but, to the disappointment of the travelling Arsenal fans, the goal was disallowed for offside against Kevin Campbell.

David Rocastle, the former Arsenal midfield player, was central to City's brighter moments but, at times, over-indulged himself in an apparent attempt to prove a point. Terry Phelan, revelling in an advanced role on the left side, frequently pierced the Arsenal cover with his blistering pace but the Gunners defence held firm.

The upshot of it all was that Arsenal kept their fifth successive clean sheet but hardly bolstered their belief that they could threaten Manchester United's charge for the Premiership title. Whilst the point for City provided little insurance in their endeavours to pull back from the brink of the relegation mire into which they had slowly been slipping over the past two months.

League Record

	P	W	D	L	F	A	Pts	Pos
93-94 Premiership Record	26	12	9	5	30	13	45	4th
All-time Premiership Record	68	27	20	21	70	51	101	
All-time League Record	3592	1564	890	1138	5914	4778		

	Home	Away	Total
League Attendances	387,579	324,525	712,104

Arsenal
Oldham Athletic

(1) 1
(1) 1

Saturday 22nd January 1994, Highbury   Att.: 26,524

ARSENAL

1	David	SEAMAN
2	Lee	DIXON
3	Nigel	WINTERBURN
18	David	HILLIER
12	Steve	BOULD
6	Tony	ADAMS
17	John	*JENSEN (+65)*
8	Ian	WRIGHT
7	Kevin	CAMPBELL
23	Ray	PARLOUR
11	Eddie	*McGOLDRICK (†65)*

Subs

10	Paul	*MERSON (†65)*
14	Martin	*KEOWN (+65)*
13	Alan	MILLER (gk)

OLDHAM ATHLETIC

13	Jon	HALLWORTH
2	Craig	FLEMING
22	Chris	MAKIN
3	Neil	*POINTON (†82)*
5	Richard	JOBSON
6	Steve	REDMOND
11	Steve	BERNARD
14	Graeme	SHARP
21	Sean	McCARTHY
10	Mike	*MILLIGAN (+84)*
25	Rick	HOLDEN

16	Tore	*PEDERSON (†82)*
19	Roger	*PALMER (+84)*
1	Paul	GERRARD (gk)

Match Facts

- Arsenal's run of six successive clean sheets came to an end with Sharp's fourth minute goal and it was the first goal they had conceded at Highbury since the 6th of December.

- Graeme Sharp's goal was only Oldham's seventh away from home.

Score Sheet

G. SHARP 4 min – 0-1
I. WRIGHT 45 min Pen – 1-1

Referee:
Mr. P. Foakes (Clacton)

FA Carling Premiership

		P	W	D	L	F	A	Pts
1	Manchester United	27	19	7	1	54	23	64
2	Blackburn Rovers	24	14	6	4	34	19	48
3	**Arsenal**	**27**	**12**	**10**	**5**	**31**	**14**	**46**
4	Newcastle United	26	13	6	7	45	25	45
5	Liverpool	26	12	7	7	44	32	43

Result of this Season's Fixture

No Fixture

Missing Masters

Arsenal, with the meanest defence in the Premiership, handed a draw to struggling Oldham when they gave away a goal virtually from the kick-off. They then took just one of the endless number of opportunities they created for themselves.

The Gunners had previously gone over nine hours without conceding a goal but found themselves one down after just four minutes. A free kick just outside the penalty area was rolled to Graeme Sharp by Rick Holden and the ball flew into the top right hand corner as David Seaman advanced off his line.

Oldham promptly posted five defenders in front of goalkeeper Jon Hallworth and Arsenal spent the rest of the half trying to break down a resolute defence. Ray Parlour ran the show in midfield, setting up many chances that were wasted by his forwards with, for once, Ian Wright the main culprit. The best chance fell to Wright after 15 minutes when Parlour danced 30 yards down the right touchline and sent in a dipping ball to the near post. It looked as though Wright running in could not miss but somehow – and surprisingly – he managed it.

Wright eventually equalised, deep into first half injury-time, when Arsenal were awarded a hotly disputed penalty after Neil Pointon was judged to have handled the ball in the penalty area. Wright found the target with a firm shot past Hallworth from the spot.

Arsenal's agony was far from over. Most of the second half was taken up by them missing more opportunities, their final misery coming two minutes from time when Kevin Campbell hit a fierce shot against the bar. Wright was on to the rebound in an instant but his volley went flashing wide of the post.

Although it had been a frustrating afternoon for the usually so lethal striker, Wright was at least pleased that he had got himself into the right positions to miss the numerous chances that had come his way. A day when Arsenal almost perfected the art of missing chances.

League Record

	P	W	D	L	F	A	Pts	Pos
93-94 Premiership Record	27	12	10	5	31	14	46	3rd
All-time Premiership Record	69	27	21	21	71	52	102	
All-time League Record	3593	1534	891	1138	5915	4779		

	Home	Away	Total
League Attendances	414,103	324,525	738,628

Bolton Wanderers (1) 2
Arsenal (0) 2

Monday 31st January 1994, Burnden Park   Att.: 18,891

BOLTON WANDERERS			ARSENAL		
1	Aiden	DAVISON	1	David	SEAMAN
2	Phil	BROWN	2	Lee	DIXON
3	Jimmy	PHILLIPS	3	Nigel	WINTERBURN
4	Alan	STUBBS	18	David	HILLIER
5	Mark	WINSTANLEY	12	Steve	BOULD
6	Jason	McATEER	6	Tony	ADAMS
7	David	LEE	14	Martin	KEOWN
8	Tony	KELLY	7	Kevin	CAMPBELL
9	Owen	COYLE	8	Ian	WRIGHT
10	John	McGINLAY	10	Paul	MERSON
11	*Mark*	*PATTERSON (†64)*	23	*Ray*	*PARLOUR (†86)*

Subs

12	*Andy*	*WALKER (†64)*	9	*Alan*	*SMITH (†86)*
13	Russell	HOULT (gk)	17	John	JENSEN
14	David	BURKE	13	Alan	MILLER (gk)

Match Facts

- Arsenal's 10th FA Cup game without defeat.
- Owen Coyle kept up his record of scoring in every round of the FA Cup this season.
- Ian Wright scored his 25th goal of the season.
- Referee Terry Holbrook was replaced by Barry Priest at half-time because of injury.

Score Sheet

J. McATEER 31 min – 0-1
I. WRIGHT 51 min – 1-1
T. ADAMS 62 min – 1-2
O. COYLE 86 min – 2-2

Referee:
Mr. T. Holbrook (Walsall)

FA Cup Fourth Round

Hanging On

Bruce Rioch's Bolton Wanderers again demonstrated their fighting qualities by taking holders Arsenal to a replay after this fluctuating FA Cup Fourth Round tie. In the previous year Bolton had claimed the scalps of Liverpool and in the Third Round had ousted Everton. It needed all of Arsenal's renowned cup-fighting resilience to survive this severe examination after Jason McAteer had given the First Division side a deserved half time lead.

Even before they went a goal down the Arsenal defence had been in danger of collapsing several times and David Seaman had had to make three crucial saves in succession. Having scrambled away a shot from McGinlay, Seaman did well to block another dangerous attempt from Coyle before beating away a close-range header from Phil Brown after Tony Kelly's near-post flick. Finally Bolton took the lead they deserved in the 32nd minute when Jason McAteer, running powerfully on to a pass from McGinlay, shot comfortably past David Seaman. The Gunners had posed little threat before this, their only real chance falling to Martin Keown who headed Ian Wright's cross weakly into the side netting.

In the second half, though, Arsenal's response to the threat of elimination was immediate and Bolton were soon knocked out of their confident stride by an impressive comeback from the Gunners. Paul Merson hit the post and Campbell headed wide before Ian Wright brought Arsenal level in the 51st minute when he anticipated a deflection from a Paul Merson shot and beat goalkeeper Aidan Davison with a low drive.

The Bolton goalkeeper was similarly exposed in the 62nd minute when Tony Adams was left unmarked from Nigel Winterburn's free kick and allowed the freedom of the six-yard box to head home from close range. Kevin Campbell had the chance to put the tie beyond Bolton's reach when he was put clear by Ian Wright but with just Davison to beat he shot wide.

But, with just four minutes to go, Bolton hit back with a dramatic equaliser to earn themselves a replay at Highbury. Owen Coyle pounced onto a superbly-placed header by John McGinlay, to beat David Seaman with a volley from five yards. Even then the home side might have pinched it and the Arsenal team and their supporters were relieved to see David Seaman deny Tony Kelly in injury time. Arsenal weren't going to give up the FA Cup without a fight.

FA Cup Record

	P	W	D	L	F	A
FA Cup Record 93-94	2	1	1	0	3	2
All-time FA Cup Record	357	185	84	88	651	393

	Home	Away	Total
FA Cup Attendances	–	38,984	38,984

Arsenal
Bolton Wanderers

(1) 1
(1) 3

Wednesday 9th February 1994, Highbury　　　　Att.: 33,863

ARSENAL

1	David	SEAMAN
2	Lee	DIXON
3	Nigel	WINTERBURN
18	David	HILLIER (†33)
12	Steve	BOULD
6	Tony	ADAMS
7	Kevin	CAMPBELL
8	Ian	WRIGHT (+69)
9	Alan	SMITH
10	Paul	MERSON
23	Ray	PARLOUR

Subs

14	Martin	KEOWN (†33) – Sent Off
11	Eddie	McGOLDRICK (+69)
13	Alan	MILLER (gk)

BOLTON WANDERERS

1	Aidan	DAVISON
2	Phil	BROWN
3	Jimmy	PHILLIPS
4	Tony	KELLY
5	Mark	SEAGRAVES
6	Alan	STUBBS
7	David	LEE
8	Jason	McATEER
9	Owen	COYLE
10	John	McGINLAY – Booked
11	Mark	PATTERSON (†72)
12	Andy	WALKER (†72)
13	Russell	HOULT (gk)
14	David	BURKE

Match Facts

● Arsenal's first defeat in the FA Cup since they lost to Wrexham in the Third Round in January 1992.

● Including replays, this was the ninth meeting between the two clubs in the FA Cup – the result meant that each club had won three times with three games drawn.

Score Sheet

J. McGINLAY 20 min – 0-1

A. SMITH 36 min – 1-1

J. McATEER 99 min – 1-2

A. WALKER 115 min – 1-3

Referee:

Mr. G. Ashby (Worcester)

FA Cup Fourth Round Replay

Cup Of Woe

Bolton Wanderers completed a memorable FA Cup hat-trick by knocking out holders Arsenal in this Fourth Round replay at Highbury. The previous season Bolton had won at Liverpool in a Third Round replay. In this season's Third Round they defeated Everton – also in a replay – and their win over Arsenal in this replay brought them a thoroughly deserved place in the Fifth Round.

Arsenal only had themselves to blame. They had the chances to win – Kevin Campbell missed sitters in the fifth and final minutes and Paul Merson seemed to hit every part of Highbury except the Bolton goal.

It was Bolton who took the lead in the 20th minute, when Tony Kelly headed on Mark Patterson's corner. Ray Parlour's weak clearance fell to Phil Brown who hoisted it back into the Arsenal goalmouth where John McGinlay headed home.

Arsenal equalised ten minutes before half-time when Lee Dixon's throw-in was helped on by Tony Adams and Aidan Davison, under pressure from Ian Wright, failed to collect leaving Alan Smith to score from 12 yards.

No further goals were forthcoming in the second half and the game went into extra-time. Ten minutes into the extra period Nigel Winterburn's attempted back-pass was intercepted by Owen Coyle. His shot struck an upright but Jason McAteer made no mistake with the rebound. Five minutes later, Arsenal's grip on the FA Cup was finally relinquished when a slip by Lee Dixon let in substitute Andy Walker who beat Seaman with a low shot.

Further problems befell Arsenal in the final minute of extra time. With their supporters calling for a fourth goal, Bolton were awarded a free-kick on the edge of the penalty area. Tony Kelly curled the ball into the net but referee Gerald Ashby disallowed the effort because Keown, previously booked for a foul, had encroached. This was perceived as a second bookable offence and Keown was sent off and the goal struck off – an action which completed a night of misery for Arsenal.

There was no doubt that Bolton had deserved their win. They had played all the good football and had defended intelligently, tackled crisply in midfield and counter-attacked with speed and purpose. For their part, Arsenal seemed too ponderous and predictable and they now knew that success in the European Cup-Winners' Cup was their only hope of glory this season.

FA Cup Record

	P	W	D	L	F	A
FA Cup Record 93-94	3	1	1	1	4	5
All-time FA Cup Record	358	185	84	89	652	396

	Home	Away	Total
FA Cup Attendances	33,863	38,984	72,847

Norwich City
Arsenal

(0) 1
(1) 1

Sunday 13th February 1994, Carrow Road   Att.: 17,667

NORWICH CITY

1	Bryan	GUNN
2	Mark	BOWEN
5	Ian	CULVERHOUSE
8	*Colin*	*WOODTHORPE (+45)*
10	John	POLSTON
3	Rob	NEWMAN
4	Ian	CROOK
9	*Gary*	*MEGSON (†74)*
7	Efan	EKOKU
22	Chris	SUTTON
11	Jeremy	GOSS

Subs

16	*Lee*	*POWER (†74)*
20	*Darren*	*EADIE (+45)*
13	Scott	HOWIE (gk)

ARSENAL

1	David	SEAMAN
2	Lee	DIXON
3	Nigel	WINTERBURN
4	Paul	DAVIS
12	Steve	BOULD
6	Tony	ADAMS
17	John	JENSEN
7	Kevin	CAMPBELL
9	Alan	SMITH
10	Paul	MERSON
23	Ray	PARLOUR

14	Martin	KEOWN
22	Ian	SELLEY
13	Alan	MILLER (gk)

Match Facts

• This was a fourth consecutive league draw for both teams. • Norwich fail to beat Arsenal in four attempts this season. • This was the third successive league draw between the clubs. • Since joining Arsenal in September 1991 this was the 24th match Ian Wright had missed – of these the Gunners had won just six.

Score Sheet

K. CAMPBELL 33 min – 1-0
E. EKOKU 57 min – 1-1

Referee:
Mr. R. Dilkes (Mossley)

FA Carling Premiership

		P	W	D	L	F	A	Pts
1	Manchester United	28	20	7	1	57	25	67
2	Blackburn Rovers	27	17	6	4	41	20	57
3	**Arsenal**	**28**	**12**	**11**	**5**	**32**	**15**	**47**
4	Newcastle United	27	13	6	8	47	29	45
5	Liverpool	27	12	8	7	46	34	44

Result of this Season's Fixture

Norwich City
Arsenal

Campbell Back on Song

At the end of ninety minutes no-one was surprised that this game had ended in a draw. Both teams went into the match having drawn their previous three League games and, with Arsenal missing Ian Wright as well, a draw was the best that Carrow Road could have hoped for.

Kevin Campbell, who had been the subject of some merciless barracking four days earlier in the FA Cup defeat by Bolton, returned to London with his dignity restored after scoring in the 33rd minute. Lee Dixon floated the ball to the far post, Alan Smith headed it back and, with Bryan Gunn hesitating, Campbell had the easiest of chances side-footing home from a few feet.

Earlier, Arsenal had survived when Jeremy Goss fed Chris Sutton and the Norwich striker held off the challenge of Steve Bould, looked up and delivered a tremendous shot which David Seaman matched by arching back to push it on to the crossbar.

Norwich altered things at half time, replacing Colin Woodthorpe with Darren Eadie and the young winger began to suggest that he could alter the balance of play. However, Arsenal might have extended their lead in the 48th minute when a free kick from Paul Davis came off John Polston and unluckily bounced onto the top of the crossbar.

Norwich equalised in the 57th minute when a long clearance from Bryan Gunn was headed on by the impressive Sutton to Efan Ekoku who eluded Steve Bould before shooting smartly past the stranded David Seaman. Arsenal had what appeared to be justifiable claims for a penalty turned down after Rob Newman had brought down Ray Parlour. Similarly, Ekoku had a chance to clinch all three points for City after being set up by Sutton again but his diving header went just wide.

After their midweek cup defeat by Bolton, Arsenal returned home reasonably pleased with the draw but Norwich City's dismal home form continued – just three wins at Carrow Road so far in the season.

League Record

	P	W	D	L	F	A	Pts	Pos
93-94 Premiership Record	28	12	11	5	32	15	47	3rd
All-time Premiership Record	70	27	22	21	72	53	103	
All-time League Record	3594	1564	892	1138	5916	4780		

	Home	Away	Total
League Attendances	414,103	342,192	756,295

Everton (0) 1
Arsenal (0) 1

Saturday 19th February 1994, Goodison Park   Att.: 19,891

EVERTON

1	Neville	SOUTHALL
2	Matthew	JACKSON
3	Andy	HINCHCLIFFE
25	Neil	MOORE
5	Dave	WATSON
4	Ian	SNODIN
16	*Pedrag*	*RADOSAVIJEVIC (†62)*
8	Graham	STUART
15	*Paul*	*RIDEOUT (+71)*
22	Brett	ANGELL
11	Peter	BEAGRIE

Subs

10	*Barry*	*HORNE (†62)*
9	*Tony*	*COTTEE (+71)*
13	Jason	KEARTON (gk)

ARSENAL

1	David	SEAMAN
2	Lee	DIXON
3	Nigel	WINTERBURN
4	Paul	DAVIS
12	Steve	BOULD
6	*Tony*	*ADAMS (†76)*
7	Kevin	CAMPBELL
17	*John*	*JENSEN (+88)*
9	Alan	SMITH
10	Paul	MERSON
23	Ray	PARLOUR

14	*Martin*	*KEOWN (†76)*
18	*David*	*HILLIER (+88)*
13	Alan	MILLER (gk)

Match Facts

- Arsenal's fifth successive league draw and their 12th of the season.
- Paul Merson's first goal since the 10th of November and his first in the Premiership since September 25th.

Score Sheet

P. MERSON 56 min – 1-0

T. COTTEE 81 min – 1-1

Referee:
Mr. D. Allison (Lancaster)

FA Carling Premiership

		P	W	D	L	F	A	Pts
1	Manchester United	28	20	7	1	57	25	67
2	Blackburn Rovers	28	18	6	4	42	20	60
3	**Arsenal**	**29**	**12**	**12**	**5**	**33**	**16**	**48**
4	Leeds United	28	12	10	6	41	29	46
5	Newcastle United	28	13	6	9	47	30	45

Result of this Season's Fixture

Everton
Arsenal

Marvellous Merson

Despite dominating the game throughout, and creating numerous chances, Arsenal only had a spectacular strike from Paul Merson and one point to show for all their efforts in this drawn game at Everton. Merson, playing in a free role just behind the Arsenal front two, was superb throughout and capped an excellent display with an exquisite lob in the 54th minute.

Everton had defender Dave Watson to thank for still being in the game by the time Merson scored and their fragile defence was even more grateful for the woeful finishing of Alan Smith and Kevin Campbell. Smith had a poor afternoon and should have done a lot better with his 11th minute far post header from Lee Dixon's cross.

The home side did not have a chance of getting on target until the 22nd minute when a Paul Rideout lay-off found Brett Angell coming in late, and he rattled the Arsenal crossbar with a splendid first-time shot. Preki also had a chance early in the second half but he headed wide.

Arsenal had created enough chances of their own to sew up the game by the time Merson put them a goal up. Ray Parlour put two good chances wide, while Kevin Campbell twice allowed Dave Watson to make goal-saving tackles after he was clear. Merson's goal, when it came, was worth waiting for as he beat Neville Southall from the corner of the penalty area with a marvellous chip.

The introduction of substitute Tony Cottee in the 72nd minute proved to be the turning point of the game and the striker set about his work as though he had something to prove to Mike Walker, Everton's new manager. He put a new sense of purpose into the Everton side and it was no surprise when he equalised in the 81st minute. Some uncharacteristic defending from Arsenal saw the defence fail to clear the ball in the six-yard box and Cottee revealed his inherent scoring knack by driving the loose ball home.

Once again Arsenal had paid the price for not converting the numerous chances they had created and the absence of the injured Ian Wright was proving very costly indeed.

League Record

	P	W	D	L	F	A	Pts	Pos
93-94 Premiership Record	29	12	12	5	33	16	48	3rd
All-time Premiership Record	71	27	23	21	73	54	104	
All-time League Record	3595	1564	893	1138	5917	4781		

	Home	Away	Total
League Attendances	414,103	362,083	776,186

Arsenal
Blackburn Rovers

(0) 1
(0) 0

Saturday 26th February 1994, Highbury   Att.: 35,050

ARSENAL

1	David	SEAMAN
2	Lee	DIXON
3	Nigel	WINTERBURN
4	Paul	DAVIS
12	Steve	BOULD
6	Tony	ADAMS
17	John	JENSEN
7	Kevin	CAMPBELL
9	Alan	SMITH
10	Paul	MERSON
23	Ray	PARLOUR

Subs

18	David	HILLIER
5	Andy	LINIGHAN
26	Jim	WILL (gk)

BLACKBURN ROVERS

26	Tim	FLOWERS
20	Henning	BERG
6	Graeme	LE SAUX
2	David	MAY
21	*Kevin*	*MORAN (†83)*
23	David	BATTY
7	Stuart	RIPLEY
12	Nicky	MARKER
11	Jason	WILCOX
9	Alan	SHEARER
8	*Kevin*	*GALLACHER (+26)*

18	*Andy*	*MORRISON (†83)*
22	*Mark*	*ATKINS (+26)*
1	Bobby	MIMMS (gk)

Match Facts

• Blackburn's first defeat in 13 league matches.

• Arsenal's first victory in six Premiership matches but their ninth without defeat.

Score Sheet

P. MERSON 73 min – 1-0

Referee:
Mr. J. Worrall (Warrington)

FA Carling Premiership

		P	W	D	L	F	A	Pts
1	Manchester United	29	20	8	1	59	27	68
2	Blackburn Rovers	30	18	7	5	44	23	61
3	**Arsenal**	**30**	**13**	**12**	**5**	**34**	**16**	**51**
4	Newcastle United	29	14	6	9	51	30	48
5	Liverpool	30	13	8	9	49	40	47

Result of this Season's Fixture

Arsenal
Blackburn Rvrs

Blackburn Crash

Arsenal's deserved win over Blackburn inflicted serious damage on Rovers' brave attempt to overhaul Manchester United in the Premiership. The final margin of victory was small but Paul Merson's second-half goal hardly reflected Arsenal's superiority. But for Tim Flowers and a stroke of luck Blackburn's first defeat in 13 League matches would have been much more painful. Adding to their problems was the loss through injury of Kevin Gallacher who was carried off with a fractured leg.

Alan Smith, replacing the still-injured Ian Wright, more than justified his inclusion. His mastery in the air was always a principal threat to Blackburn and he played a major role in their downfall. Smith, who had nodded wide Arsenal's only real chance of the first half, brought his team to life after 24 minutes of the second half by meeting Lee Dixon's cross so powerfully with his head that Flowers had to fling himself acrobatically to his left to turn the ball away to safety.

In the 73rd minute Smith, under pressure, succeeded in crossing the ball from a narrow angle to the left of goal. His centre so wrong-footed the Blackburn defence that Merson had time to pick his spot in the roof of the net and score at the far post.

As Arsenal overran Blackburn in the closing minutes Flowers pulled off a tremendous reflex save to stop Merson scoring again with a pile-driving shot. The goalkeeper was fortunate a minute later though, when the shot which Ray Parlour cheekily pushed through his legs, took just enough of a deflection to trickle wide.

All Blackburn could do at that stage was reflect on a couple of chances missed by Gallacher and David Batty in the first 15 minutes and the header Alan Shearer directed straight at David Seaman from a Graeme Le Saux cross shortly before the interval.

Arsenal set off for their European Cup-Winners' Cup quarter-final tie in Italy in good heart after their second half display. Blackburn's defeat left their manager still unbowed and clearly with no intention of abandoning his team's relentless chase of Manchester United.

League Record

	P	W	D	L	F	A	Pts	Pos
93-94 Premiership Record	30	13	12	5	34	16	51	3rd
All-time Premiership Record	72	28	23	21	74	54	107	
All-time League Record	3596	1565	893	1138	5918	4781		

	Home	Away	Total
League Attendances	449,133	362,083	811,216

Torino
Arsenal

(0) 0
(0) 0

Wednesday 2nd March 1994, Delle Alpi Stadium   Att.: 32,480

TORINO			ARSENAL		
1	Giovanni	GALLI	1	David	SEAMAN
7	*Andrea*	*SOTTILL (†63)*	2	Lee	DIXON
3	Robert	JARNI	3	Nigel	WINTERBURN
4	Sandro	COIS	4	*Paul*	*DAVIS (†83)*
5	Angelo	GREGUCCI	5	Steve	BOULD
6	Luca	FUSI	6	Tony	ADAMS
7	Roberto	MUSSI	7	John	JENSEN
8	Daniele	FORTUNATO	8	Kevin	CAMPBELL
2	*Andrea*	*SILENZI (+67)*	9	Alan	SMITH
10	Enzo	FRANCESCOLI	10	Paul	MERSON
11	Giorgio	VENTURIN	11	David	HILLIER

Subs

12	*Marco*	*SINIGAGLIA (†63)*	12	Martin	KEOWN
13	*Benito*	*CARBONE (+67)*	13	Alan	MILLER (gk)
14	Raffaele	SERGIO	14	*Ian*	*SELLEY (†83)*
15	Paolo	POGGI	15	Anders	LIMPAR
16	Luca	PASTINE (gk)	16	Eddie	McGOLDRICK

Match Facts

- Arsenal's third successive European match without conceding a goal.
- Arsenal's 24th clean sheet of the season.

Score Sheet

Referee:
Mr. J. Quiniou (France)

European Cup Winners' Cup – Quarter Final, First Leg

Italian Dream

A typically disciplined professional display by Arsenal in the Delle Alpi Stadium saw them restrict Torino to only two half-chances and emerge as favourites to qualify for the European Cup-Winners' Cup semi-finals. As away performances go in Europe this must rate alongside the best. Torino were made to look decidedly ordinary and struggled to break down a formation superbly organised by George Graham.

Both sides had two half-chances in the first 45 minutes. In the 29th minute Paul Davis' right-wing corner was returned to him and he centred into the penalty box where Kevin Campbell flicked on for Adams, sliding in at the far post. But the ball was always running away from the Arsenal captain and his effort was wide. Three minutes later, Lee Dixon's deflected shot brought anxiety to Torino before it was cleared.

Four minutes before the interval, Daniele Fortunato headed wide from Robert Jarni's left wing centre then David Seaman needed two attempts to hold a stinging Jarni drive from 25 yards. Apart from this the game struggled to flow as there were so many stoppages for offside and petty fouls. Arsenal did the simple things very well and John Jensen and David Hillier must have set personal records for the tackles they won in midfield, whilst Paul Merson worked tirelessly down the left.

With all the stoppages the match never really had a chance to develop a pattern. Arsenal were quite happy to play a safety first game and they smothered Torino so comprehensively that the Italian side had little or no answer. The Italians had just one corner and, even then, Francescoli's kick landed 10 yards from anyone.

With the crowd on their backs, Torino fared even worse during the second half when, no matter what they tried, the ball seemed to end up being cleared by Arsenal. The Gunners had played result football to near perfection and the sound of whistling and jeering from the frustrated home supporters was music to the ears of the visitors. In the end they were probably a little disappointed not to return with a victory under their belts.

Euro Cup-Winners' Cup Record

	P	W	D	L	F	A
ECWC Record 93-94	5	3	2	0	13	2
All-time ECWC Record	14	7	6	1	26	7

	Home	Away	Total
ECWC Attendances	50,947	57,060	108,007

Ipswich Town **(0) 1**
Arsenal **(3) 5**

Saturday 5th March 1994, Portman Road   Att.: 18,656

IPSWICH TOWN

13	Clive	BAKER
2	Mick	STOCKWELL
3	Neil	THOMPSON
5	John	WARK – *Booked*
6	*David*	*LINIGHAN (†45)*
7	Geraint	WILLIAMS
10	Ian	MARSHALL
11	Chris	KIWOMYA
16	Eddie	YOUDS
18	Steve	PALMER
21	Stuart	SLATER

Subs

4	*Paul*	*MASON (†45)*
9	Bontcho	GUENTCHEV
26	Phillip	MORGAN (gk)

ARSENAL

1	David	SEAMAN
2	Lee	DIXON
3	Nigel	WINTERBURN
12	Steve	BOULD
6	Tony	ADAMS
18	*David*	*HILLIER (+89)*
22	Ian	SELLEY
15	*Anders*	*LIMPAR (†76)*
9	Alan	SMITH
8	Ian	WRIGHT
23	Ray	PARLOUR

10	*Paul*	*MERSON (†76)*
14	*Martin*	*KEOWN (+89)*
13	Alan	MILLER (gk)

Match Facts

- Ipswich keeper Craig Forrest was injured in the pre-match warm up and was replaced by Clive Baker.
- Ian Wright's first hat-trick since May 1992 – his third was his 28th goal of the season.
- Ipswich have now conceded nine goals against Arsenal this season.

Score Sheet

I. WRIGHT 17 min – 0-1
E. YOUDS 23 min o.g. – 0-2
I. WRIGHT 40 min – 0-3
R. PARLOUR 51 min – 0-4
L. DIXON 69 min o.g. – 1-4
I. WRIGHT 86 min – 1-5

Referee:
Mr. K. Barrett (Coventry)

FA Carling Premiership

		P	W	D	L	F	A	Pts
1	Manchester United	30	20	8	1	59	28	68
2	Blackburn Rovers	31	19	7	5	44	23	64
3	**Arsenal**	**31**	**14**	**12**	**5**	**39**	**17**	**54**
4	Newcastle United	30	15	6	9	52	30	51
5	Aston Villa	30	13	10	7	38	28	49

Result of this Season's Fixture

Ipswich Town
Arsenal

A Wright Good Return

Ian Wright erased the frustration of being left out of Arsenal's midweek European Cup-Winners' Cup first leg tie against Torino by hitting a hat-trick against a poor Ipswich side suffering from losing their FA Cup replay against Wolves. Never mind the quality of the opposition – Wright was in the mood to show the world that he was definitely back after his hamstring injury.

Ipswich had been forced to make a last-minute goalkeeping change when Clive Baker had to replace Craig Forrest who injured himself in the pre-match warm up. Baker probably wished he could have stayed on the bench all afternoon with Wright in this sort of goal-scoring mood. Wright scored Arsenal's first in the 17th minute, finishing off a solo run by Lee Dixon down the right flank. Then Ipswich defender Eddie Youds scrambled the ball into his own net after he had been given time to clear an Anders Limpar shot.

Ipswich could scarcely raise a worthwhile attacking move until Lee Dixon headed into his own net in the 69th minute but, by then, Arsenal were 4-1 ahead – Wright scoring from a penalty in the 40th minute – and Ray Parlour heading in David Hillier's cross in the 51st minute. Wright's third goal – and Arsenal's fifth – came in the 85th minute when he ran on to Tony Adams' through-pass and slotted the ball past a hapless Baker. That goal finally ended Ipswich's on-field torture although it carried on off-field for manager Mick McGiven, who was the subject of a demonstration by frustrated home supporters after the final whistle.

Ipswich, falling fast down the table, found themselves just nine points above the relegation places after this defeat. In contrast, Arsenal could look forward to the second leg of their Cup-Winners' Cup match against Torino at Highbury with a great deal of confidence.

League Record

	P	W	D	L	F	A	Pts	Pos
93-94 Premiership Record	31	14	12	5	39	17	54	3rd
All-time Premiership Record	73	29	23	21	79	55	110	
All-time League Record	3597	1566	893	1138	5923	4782		

	Home	Away	Total
League Attendances	449,133	380,739	829,872

Arsenal
Torino

(0) 1
(0) 0

Tuesday 15th March 1994, Highbury

Att.: 34,678

ARSENAL

1	David	SEAMAN
2	Lee	DIXON
3	Nigel	WINTERBURN
4	Paul	DAVIS
5	Steve	BOULD
6	Tony	ADAMS
7	*John*	*JENSEN (+87)*
8	Ian	WRIGHT
9	Alan	SMITH
10	Paul	MERSON
11	*David*	*HILLIER (†14)*

Subs

12	Kevin	CAMPBELL
13	Alan	MILLER (gk)
14	*Martin*	*KEOWN (+87)*
15	*Ian*	*SELLEY (†14) – B'ked*
16	Anders	LIMPAR

TORINO

1	Giovanni	GALLI
2	Roberto	MUSSI
3	Enrico	ANNONI
4	Sandro	COIS
5	Angelo	GREGUCCI – *Sent Off*
6	Luca	FUSI
7	Marco	SINIGAGLIA (†72)
8	Daniele	FORTUNATO
9	Andrea	SILENZI
10	Enzo	FRANCESCOLI
11	*Giorgo*	*VENTURIN (†25)*

12	*Robert*	*JARNI (†25)*
13	*Paolo*	*POGGI (+72)*
14	Delli	CARRI
15	Andrea	SOTTILL
16	Luca	PASTINE (gk)

Match Facts

- David Seaman's 24th clean sheet in 45 matches.
- Arsenal's fourth successive European Cup-Winners' Cup game without conceding a goal.
- Tony Adams' fourth goal of the season – but none scored in the Premiership.

Score Sheet

T. ADAMS 66 min – 1-0

Referee:
J. Blankenstein (Holland)

European Cup Winners' Cup – Quarter Final, Second Leg

Adams Books Place in Last Four

A superbly-taken headed goal by Tony Adams was enough to earn Arsenal a place in the semi-finals of the European Cup-Winners' Cup after an absorbing tie at Highbury. It quickly became obvious that one goal would decide the outcome of a game in which both defences were dominant.

Much of the game was played in midfield and, if there were few chances, the likelihood that one goal would be decisive gave the game an added edge. One or two tackles were over-enthusiastic and Ian Selley was lucky to be shown just the yellow card for his challenge on Fortunato in the 19th minute. Angelo Gregucci was not so fortunate. Cautioned for a foul on Wright in the 37th minute, the defender was sent off for a second bookable offence against the same player two minutes from the end.

Gregucci also gave away the free kick for a foul on Alan Smith which led to Arsenal's goal in the 66th minute. Paul Davis took the kick and Tony Adams rose to head past Giovanni Galli – his fourth and most important goal of the season.

The only time David Seaman was really troubled was when a back-pass by Steve Bould was left by Adams and the goalkeeper did well to save with his legs and deny Andrea Silenzi. Despite their lack of goalscoring opportunities, this was a far more adventurous performance from Torino and the Italians looked a significantly better side at Highbury than they did on their own ground two weeks previously. Even so, over the two games, Torino created practically nothing against a brilliantly organised Arsenal side.

Three years ago, Arsenal had gone to Lisbon in the European Cup and drawn 1-1 against Benfica but had lost at Highbury 3-1 in the second leg after being given a European footballing lesson by the Portuguese team. The lessons had been learnt well and Arsenal were fast becoming the teachers themselves.

Euro Cup-Winners' Cup Record

	P	W	D	L	F	A
ECWC Record 93-94	6	4	2	0	14	2
All-Time ECWC Record	15	8	6	1	27	7

	Home	Away	Total
ECWC Attendances	85,625	57,060	142,685

Southampton
Arsenal

(0) 0
(2) 4

Saturday 19th March 1994, The Dell   Att.: 16,790

SOUTHAMPTON		
1	Dave	BEASANT
2	Jeff	KENNA
14	Simon	CHARLTON
18	*Steve*	*WOOD (+65)*
6	Ken	MONKOU – *Booked*
11	Francis	BENALI
4	Jim	MAGILTON
9	Iain	DOWIE
7	Matthew	Le TISSIER
10	Neil	MADDISON
8	*Craig*	*MASKELL (†65)*

ARSENAL		
1	David	SEAMAN
2	Lee	DIXON
3	Nigel	WINTERBURN
14	Martin	KEOWN
5	Andy	LINIGHAN
6	Tony	ADAMS
23	Ray	PARLOUR
8	Ian	WRIGHT
7	Kevin	CAMPBELL
22	Ian	SELLEY
15	*Anders*	*LIMPAR (†81) – B'ked*

Subs

16	*Nicky*	*BANGER (†65)*
13	Ian	ANDREWS (gk)
27	*Paul*	*ALLEN (+65) – B'ked*

9	*Alan*	*SMITH (†81)*
21	Steve	MORROW
13	Alan	MILLER (gk)

Match Facts

- Ian Wright's second successive Premiership hat-trick.
- On his debut for Arsenal, Wright also scored a hat-trick at Southampton.
- Arsenal's 11th league match without defeat.
- Southampton's first home defeat under new manager Alan Ball.

Score Sheet

I. WRIGHT 18 min – 0-1

I. WRIGHT 30 min – 0-2

I. WRIGHT 68 min Pen– 0-3

K. CAMPBELL 84 min – 0-4

Referee:
Mr. D. Frampton (Poole)

FA Carling Premiership

		P	W	D	L	F	A	Pts
2	Blackburn Rovers	31	19	7	5	44	23	64
3	Newcastle United	32	17	6	9	63	33	57
4	**Arsenal**	**32**	**15**	**12**	**5**	**43**	**17**	**57**
5	Leeds United	33	14	13	6	47	32	55
6	Liverpool	33	15	8	10	53	44	53

Result of this Season's Fixture

Southampton

Arsenal

111

Suffering Saints

Ian Wright scored his second hat-trick in successive Premiership games as Arsenal overwhelmed Southampton with an exhilarating brand of football. Anders Limpar also starred for the Gunners, demonstrating both vision and passion and having a hand in all of Wright's goals.

Limpar, given a roving commission, made his first decisive intervention after 17 minutes, releasing Campbell with a long pass. Campbell laid back to Ian Selley who, having spotted Wright slip behind Jeff Kenna, found him with a first-time cross that the diving Wright headed low to Dave Beasant's right. Fourteen minutes later, Limpar broke free on the left and chipped across for Wright to volley a shot past Beasant with awesome power.

Wright, who had scored a hat-trick at the Dell on his Arsenal debut two seasons ago, got his third from a penalty after 69 minutes following another Limpar run. The Swede had already sprinted 40 yards, being chased by Ken Monkou, when he reached the penalty area. Monkou's only consolation for the clumsy challenge that brought Limpar down was that he was not booked for a second time. For the fourth goal Wright turned provider, Kevin Campbell scoring from his cross after Beasant got in a tangle.

But it was not all Arsenal. Southampton created several clear chances and David Seaman, apart from one fluffed clearance, was outstanding making excellent saves at crucial times from Jeff Kenna low to his left, from a Neil Maddison point-blank header and from Craig Maskell.

Southampton, considering their lowly position in the table, were outfought, outworked and outplayed by an Arsenal team out of the Premiership title race but still highly motivated – no doubt by the competition for places at Highbury as their run in the European Cup-Winners' Cup continued.

League Record

	P	W	D	L	F	A	Pts	Pos
93-94 Premiership Record	32	15	12	5	43	17	57	4th
All-time Premiership Record	74	30	23	21	83	55	113	
All-time League Record	3598	1567	893	1138	5927	4782		

	Home	Away	Total
League Attendances	449,133	397,529	846,662

Arsenal
Manchester United

(1) 2
(1) 2

Tuesday 22nd March 1994, Highbury   Att.: 36,203

ARSENAL

1	David	SEAMAN
2	Lee	DIXON
3	Nigel	WINTERBURN
4	*Paul*	*DAVIS (†68)*
12	Steve	BOULD
6	Tony	ADAMS
17	John	JENSEN
8	Ian	WRIGHT
9	Alan	SMITH
10	Paul	MERSON – *Booked*
22	Ian	SELLEY

Subs

14	Martin	KEOWN
7	*Kevin*	*CAMPBELL (†68)*
13	Alan	MILLER (gk)

MANCHESTER UNITED

1	Peter	SCHMEICHEL
2	Paul	PARKER
3	Denis	IRWIN
4	Steve	BRUCE
5	*Lee*	*SHARPE (†81)*
6	Gary	PALLISTER
7	Eric	CANTONA – *Sent Off*
8	Paul	INCE
16	Roy	KEANE – *Booked*
10	Mark	HUGHES
11	Ryan	GIGGS

9	*Brian*	*McCLAIR (†81)*
12	Bryan	ROBSON
13	Les	SEALEY (gk)

Match Facts

- Eric Cantona's dismissal was his second in four days and his third of the season.
- Arsenal's highest attendance at Highbury so far this season and their eighth Premiership home match without defeat.
- Paul Merson's third consecutive goal in his last three full appearances for the first team.

Score Sheet

L. SHARPE 10 min – 0-1
PALLISTER 36 min o.g. – 1-1
L. SHARPE 53 min – 1-2
P. MERSON 78 min – 2-2

Referee:
Mr. V. Callow (Solihull)

FA Carling Premiership

		P	W	D	L	F	A	Pts
1	Manchester United	33	21	10	2	68	32	73
2	Blackburn Rovers	32	20	7	5	48	24	67
3	**Arsenal**	**33**	**15**	**13**	**5**	**45**	**19**	**58**
4	Newcastle United	32	17	6	9	63	33	57
5	Leeds United	33	14	13	6	47	32	55

Result of this Season's Fixture

Arsenal
Manchester Utd

United Charge Held Up

Manchester United lived up to their reputation for mixing skill with steel in this pulsating encounter at Highbury which saw them drop two valuable points and have Eric Cantona sent off for the second successive game.

It was United who got off to a flying start when they took the lead following a rare error by David Seaman. Roy Keane fed Paul Parker, whose cross was met by Mark Hughes, but Seaman dropped his shot and Lee Sharpe, returning after injury, responded by knocking the loose ball home from eight yards. A bout of unpleasantness then took over with Paul Ince lucky to escape a caution for a late tackle on Ian Selley and Roy Keane being booked for kicking Paul Davis.

Arsenal equalised in the 36th minute thanks to an own goal from United defender Gary Pallister. United had complained that Steve Bruce had been harshly penalised for handling when the ball seemed to strike him on the shoulder. But Merson's free kick curled in against the swirling wind, dropped in amongst a forest of players and bounced behind Schmeichel off Pallister's shin.

Football skills took over from the misbehaviour for most of an enthralling second half and United regained their lead within nine minutes of the restart. Ryan Giggs fed Cantona, his return ball struck the Welshman and came neatly into the path of Lee Sharpe. The Arsenal appeals for offside were rejected and Sharpe drove the ball past David Seaman for the second time.

Arsenal fought back again with Schmeichel saving well from Steve Bould and Selley's shot being blocked by Parker before they equalised in the 78th minute. Dixon put Paul Merson through and he hesitated slightly before driving home a volley in off the top left stanchion from an awkward angle.

However, the drama was not over as United, once again, finished with only ten men. Cantona's high, late challenge left Selley in a heap and then, a few minutes later, he was adjudged to have come in late on Nigel Winterburn. Although the second booking appeared somewhat harsh, Cantona did not wait for referee Vic Callow to raise the card and left straight for the dressing room.

The result damaged United's title aspirations and they left Highbury knowing that their nearest rivals Blackburn Rovers could draw level with them on points at the top of the Premiership if they won their next two games.

League Record

	P	W	D	L	F	A	Pts	Pos
93-94 Premiership Record	33	15	13	5	45	19	58	3rd
All-time Premiership Record	75	30	24	21	85	57	114	
All-time League Record	3599	1567	894	1138	5929	4784		

	Home	Away	Total
League Attendances	485,336	397,529	882,865

Arsenal
Liverpool

(0) 1
(0) 0

Saturday 26th March 1994, Highbury   Att.: 35,556

ARSENAL

1	David	SEAMAN
2	Lee	DIXON
14	Martin	KEOWN
12	Steve	BOULD
5	Andy	LINIGHAN
17	*John*	*JENSEN (†66)*
22	Ian	SELLEY
7	Kevin	CAMPBELL
8	*Ian*	*WRIGHT (+79)*
10	Paul	MERSON
23	Ray	PARLOUR

Subs

21	*Steve*	*MORROW (†66)*
9	*Alan*	*SMITH (+79)*
13	Alan	MILLER (gk)

LIVERPOOL

13	David	JAMES
2	Rob	JONES
3	Julian	DICKS
5	*Mark*	*WRIGHT (†28)*
25	Neil	RUDDOCK
17	Steve	McMANAMAN
15	Jamie	REDKNAPP
12	Ronnie	WHELAN
10	John	BARNES
9	Ian	RUSH
23	*Robbie*	*FOWLER (+71)*

4	*Steve*	*NICOL (†28)*
16	*Michael*	*THOMAS (+71)*
1	Bruce	GROBBELAAR (gk)

Match Facts

- Highbury attendances in the Premiership pass the half million mark.
- Paul Merson's 11th goal of the season.
- Arsenal's 13th Premiership game without defeat.
- Liverpool's ninth away defeat of the season.

Score Sheet

P. MERSON 47 min – 1-0

Referee:
Mr. R. Hart (Darlington)

FA Carling Premiership

		P	W	D	L	F	A	Pts
1	Manchester United	33	21	10	2	68	32	73
2	Blackburn Rovers	32	20	7	5	48	24	70
3	**Arsenal**	**34**	**16**	**13**	**5**	**4**	**19**	**61**
4	Newcastle United	33	18	6	9	65	33	60
5	Leeds United	34	14	13	7	47	33	55

Result of this Season's Fixture

Arsenal
Liverpool

Jekyll and Hyde

Spying on his European Cup-Winners' Cup opponents, the coach of Paris St. Germain, Artur Jorge, must have left Highbury a very puzzled man. After having overrun Liverpool for the best part of 70 minutes, Arsenal were fortunate to hang on to a 1-0 win. Such was the transformation that overtook the game in the last 20 minutes that Liverpool might have scored three or four times.

Paul Merson, revelling in the free role he had been granted in recent games, had the ball in the net as early as the 11th minute but was denied a goal by a late and questionable offside flag. Arsenal themselves were saved shortly afterwards by an intervention from Andy Linighan who got his body in the way of a first-time shot from Robbie Fowler to block an otherwise certain goal.

The first half was a series of raids on the Liverpool goal. Merson twice wasted shooting opportunities and David James had to make good saves to deny Kevin Campbell and Ian Wright. It looked even worse for Liverpool after 28 minutes when Mark Wright suffered a knee injury and was replaced by Steve Nicol.

Things did not stay that way for long in the second half. Two minutes after the restart, Ian Selley released Paul Merson through the Liverpool defence and, despite looking suspiciously offside, he beat David James with a shot into the far corner. Ian Wright should have made it 2-0 soon afterwards but he thought about his shot too long and did little more than shoot at a grateful James. James then pulled off an acrobatic save to deny Kevin Campbell a few minutes later.

Such was Arsenal's domination that it came as a complete surprise when Steve McManaman suddenly left Jamie Redknapp with just David Seaman to beat in the 70th minute. Seaman did well to foil the Liverpool midfielder with his feet, followed by two other excellent saves he made as his defensive cover disappeared.

The introduction of Michael Thomas increased Liverpool's forward momentum and Seaman had to dash off his line when a Steve Bould error offered Ian Rush a sight of goal. The best of all Liverpool's late chances fell to Steve McManaman nine minutes from the end. In yards of space he shot tamely at Seaman, then failed to atone for the miss a minute later with a shot that screamed over the bar.

George Graham had used 18 different players in Arsenal's last seven games and had come to the conclusion that the inconsistencies with his selections had brought about more consistent results – his case seemed proven – Arsenal had now gone 13 Premiership matches without defeat.

League Record

	P	W	D	L	F	A	Pts	Pos
93-94 Premiership Record	34	16	13	5	46	19	61	3rd
All-time Premiership Record	76	31	24	21	86	57	117	
All-time League Record	3600	1568	894	1138	5930	4784		

	Home	Away	Total
League Attendances	520,892	397,529	918,421

Paris St. Germain (0) 1
Arsenal (1) 1

Tuesday 29th March 1994, Parc des Princes   Att.: 46,000

PARIS ST. GERMAIN

1	Bernard	LAMA
2	*Francis*	*Llacher (†45)*
3	Patrick	COLLETER
4		RICARDO
5	Jean-Luc	SASSUS
6	Paul	LE GUEN
7	Laurent	FOURNIER
8	Vincent	GUERIN
9		VALDO
10	George	WEAH
11	David	GINOLA

Subs

12	*Daniel*	*BRAVO (†45)*
13	Antoine	KOMBOERARE
14	Jose	COBOS
15	Xavier	GRAVELAINE
16	Luc	BORELLI (gk)

ARSENAL

1	David	SEAMAN
2	Lee	DIXON
3	Nigel	WINTERBURN
4	*Paul*	*DAVIS (†84)*
5	Steve	BOULD
6	Tony	ADAMS – *Booked*
7	John	JENSEN
8	Ian	WRIGHT
9	*Alan*	*SMITH (+84)*
10	Paul	MERSON – *Booked*
11	Ian	SELLEY

12	*Martin*	*KEOWN (†84)*
13	Alan	MILLER (gk)
14	*Kevin*	*CAMPBELL (+84)*
15	Steve	MORROW
16	Eddie	McGOLDRICK

Match Facts

- PSG's unbeaten record in all competitions now stretches to 36 games.
- Excluding the Charity Shield the 46,000 crowd was the largest to watch Arsenal so far this season.
- The bookings of Paul Merson and Tony Adams mean that eight Arsenal players go into the second leg on one yellow card.

Score Sheet

I. WRIGHT 35 min – 0-1
D. GINOLA 50 min – 1-1

Referee:
Mr. L. Sundell (Sweden)

European Cup Winners' Cup – Semi-Final, First Leg

Perfect in Paris

Another superb display in the European Cup-Winners' Cup gave Arsenal an excellent chance of reaching the final after gaining a valuable away score-draw in this semi-final first leg. Arsenal had improved steadily in the competition as they had advanced to the last four and this was another performance full of patience and professionalism.

George Graham was more adventurous than he had been in previous European games playing Wright and Merson in an advanced wide role in a five-man midfield, with Alan Smith the lone striker. With John Jensen and Ian Selley inspirational in midfield, and the defence, led by Tony Adams, dealing comfortably with everything thrown at it, David Seaman was hardly troubled.

Jensen, in fact, nearly gave the Gunners the lead in the 23rd minute but his well-struck 25-yard shot was brilliantly saved by Lama in the St. Germain goal. But, inevitably, it was Ian Wright who put Arsenal one up when he headed Paul Davis' free-kick past the diving Lama in the 35th minute. Having given his side the lead though, Wright almost undid his good work two minutes before the break. Defending is not one of his stronger points and he rashly tried to dribble on the edge of his own penalty area. Valdo dispossessed him and it was fortunate for Arsenal that Ginola's header from the Brazilian's centre was blocked.

Ginola – the French Footballer of the Year – troubled Arsenal with his pace and control but the defence stuck manfully to the their task and kept him at bay until the 50th minute when he headed home the equaliser from Valdo's corner. A warning of the danger of St. Germain at corners should have been heeded two minutes earlier when Nigel Winterburn had cleared off the line from Ricardo after a left-wing corner.

Arsenal continued to battle on, and Alan Smith had the chance in the 73rd minute to win the game for the Gunners. Paul Merson created the opening and Smith found himself free on the edge of the six-yard box, just to the right of goal. However, the striker shot straight at a grateful Lama – a moment when the tie could have been put beyond PSG's reach.

A draw though was probably a fair result in a game which was far more open and exciting than most had expected given the defensive policies of both teams. At the end of the match, Paris St. Germain were still unbeaten in 36 games and Arsenal knew there was a lot of hard work to be done at Highbury if they were to reach the final.

Euro Cup-Winners' Cup Record

	P	W	D	L	F	A
ECWC Record 93-94	7	4	3	0	15	3
All-time ECWC Record	16	8	7	1	28	8

	Home	Away	Total
ECWC Attendances	85,625	103,060	188,685

Arsenal
Swindon Town

(1) 1
(1) 1

Saturday 2nd April 1994, Highbury   Att.: 31,634

ARSENAL

1	David	SEAMAN
2	Lee	DIXON
14	Martin	KEOWN
4	Paul	DAVIS
5	Andy	LINIGHAN
6	Tony	ADAMS
17	John	JENSEN (+75)
8	Ian	WRIGHT
9	Alan	SMITH
10	Paul	MERSON (†75)
23	Ray	PARLOUR

Subs

7	Kevin	CAMPBELL (†75)
11	Eddie	McGOLDRICK (+75)
13	Alan	MILLER (gk)

SWINDON TOWN

1	Nicky	HAMMOND
2	Nicky	SUMMERBEE
3	Paul	BODIN
5	Luc	NIJHOLT
6	Shaun	TAYLOR
14	Adrian	WHITBREAD
31	Brian	KILCLINE
7	John	MONCUR
27	Keith	SCOTT (†78)
9	Jan Aage	FJORTOFT (+85)
33	Lawrie	SANCHEZ

16	Kevin	HORLOCK (†78)
32	Frank	McAVENNIE (+85)
34	Paul	HEALD (gk)

Match Facts

• Arsenal's 14th league match without defeat. • Swindon have still not won an away game in the Premiership. • Alan Smith's third league goal of the season. • Arsenal have conceded just 20 goals in the Premiership compared to Swindon's 86.

Score Sheet

A. SMITH 4 min – 0-1
P. BODIN 29 min Pen – 1-1

Referee:
Mr. B. Hill (Kettering)

FA Carling Premiership

		P	W	D	L	F	A	Pts
2	Blackburn Rovers	35	22	7	6	54	29	73
3	Newcastle United	35	19	7	9	69	34	64
4	**Arsenal**	**35**	**16**	**14**	**5**	**47**	**20**	**62**
5	Leeds United	35	14	14	7	48	34	56
6	Liverpool	36	15	8	13	54	48	53

Result of this Season's Fixture

No Fixture

119

Going Down Fighting

Say what you like about Swindon Town – they have been struggling at the bottom of the Premiership all season – but not only do they try and entertain, they also allow the opposition to follow suit and, for a quarter of this match, Arsenal sprayed the ball around Highbury seemingly without a care in the world.

They scored after just four minutes. Tony Adams chipped neatly up the right flank for Lee Dixon who battled to the by-line, fed Ray Parlour inside and his lofted cross was met at the far post by Alan Smith. The goal betrayed the familiar defensive frailty of Swindon and everyone sat back to wait for the slaughter.

It never came. Try as they might, Arsenal were unable to convert all their purpose into penetration. Swindon suddenly started defending a little bit like Arsenal and then went and pinched an equaliser in the 29th minute when Paul Davis brought down John Moncur. Paul Bodin gratefully drove his penalty kick past David Seaman.

Having committed themselves wholeheartedly to defence, Swindon had to take what they could on the break but they continually found Martin Keown eager to impress at left back. A lone charge by Jan Aage Fjortoft took him from the halfway line to the edge of the area but he failed to get in his shot.

Arsenal, after their bright opening start, struggled to break down the resolute Swindon defence and, when they did get within sight of goal, keeper Nicky Hammond dealt well with everything that came his way. Ian Wright should have made sure of all three points with just five minutes to go, but his shot was again well saved by Hammond.

Despite their fighting performance in getting a creditable draw, Swindon dropped further behind the other strugglers at the foot of the Premiership as all their rivals won. Unwilling to sacrifice their principles they looked doomed for the drop after just one season in the Premiership.

League Record

	P	W	D	L	F	A	Pts	Pos
93-94 Premiership Record	35	16	14	5	47	20	62	4th
All-time Premiership Record	77	31	25	21	87	58	118	
All-time League Record	3601	1568	895	1138	5931	4785		

	Home	Away	Total
League Attendances	552,526	397,529	950,055

Sheffield United (0) 1
Arsenal (0) 1

Monday 4th April 1994, Bramall Lane   Att.: 20,019

SHEFFIELD UNITED

13	Simon	TRACEY
17	Carl	BRADSHAW
33	Roger	NILSSON
14	David	TUTTLE
16	Paul	BEESLEY
10	Glyn	HODGES
8	Paul	ROGERS
4	John	GANNON
18	Dane	WHITEHOUSE – *B'ked*
12	Jostein	FLO
9	*Adrian*	*LITTLEJOHN (†41)*

Subs

15	Charlie	HARTFIELD
30	*Nathan*	*BLAKE (†41)*
31	Salvatore	BIBBO (gk)

ARSENAL

1	David	SEAMAN
14	*Martin*	*KEOWN (†79)*
3	Nigel	WINTERBURN
22	Ian	SELLEY
12	Steve	BOULD
6	Tony	ADAMS
7	Kevin	CAMPBELL
8	Ian	WRIGHT
9	Alan	SMITH
23	Ray	PARLOUR
11	*Eddie*	*McGOLDRICK (+79)*

2	*Lee*	*DIXON (†79)*
10	*Paul*	*MERSON (+79)*
13	Alan	MILLER (gk)

Match Facts

• Sheffield United's eighth game without defeat but they have now conceded 32 points at home. • Since their promotion in 1990 United have failed to beat Arsenal in eight attempts. • Arsenal's 15th league game without defeat. • Kevin Campbell's 14th league goal of the season.

Score Sheet

P. ROGERS 54 min – 1-0
K. CAMPBELL 69 min – 1-1

Referee:
Mr. D. Frampton (Poole)

FA Carling Premiership

		P	W	D	L	F	A	Pts
2	Blackburn Rovers	36	23	7	6	57	29	76
3	Newcastle United	37	19	8	10	70	36	65
4	**Arsenal**	**36**	**16**	**15**	**5**	**48**	**21**	**63**
5	Leeds United	36	15	14	7	52	34	59
6	Sheffield Wed	37	15	12	10	67	50	57

Result of this Season's Fixture

No Fixture

Blades Battle On

Sheffield United's latest exercise in escapology suffered a setback when they were held to a draw at Bramall Lane by Arsenal. Dave Bassett's side had led after 54 minutes through a Paul Rogers goal but were denied victory when Kevin Campbell levelled 15 minutes later.

In the first half, United created the better chances with David Seaman denying Dane Whitehouse and saving at Adrian Littlejohn's feet. The goalkeeper was lucky to escape further punishment when his poor clearance allowed Littlejohn to send in a cross, from which Jostein Flo's back-post effort was deflected off Tony Adams' boot as he made a crucial tackle.

Rogers, with a header, and Glyn Hodges went near while, at the other end, only a timely intervention by the impressive David Tuttle prevented Campbell profiting from an Adams long ball which had deceived Paul Beesley. Whilst Ray Parlour, put clear by Eddie McGoldrick's clever lob, just failed to get enough power on his shot to trouble Simon Tracey.

United's goal nine minutes into the second half was untidy but precious. Roger Nilsen's long throw sailed over Flo's head at the near post but Paul Rogers raced on to the ball and squeezed it in off an upright and the body of Steve Bould. Arsenal hit back. Ian Selley struck a post and Ian Wright forced a good save from Tracey before they finally equalised in the 69th minute when Campbell met Eddie McGoldrick's corner kick and put a glancing header across the goalkeeper and into the net.

Another poor clearance by Seaman led to a goalmouth scramble but United were unable to find the penetration to get the much-needed winner. It was typical of their lack of quality where it mattered when Rogers burst clear down the left only to deliver his cross straight to Seaman, when three team-mates had found themselves in rare space in the penalty area.

League Record

	P	W	D	L	F	A	Pts	Pos
93-94 Premiership Record	36	16	15	5	48	21	63	4th
All-time Premiership Record	78	31	26	21	88	59	119	
All-time League Record	3602	1568	896	1138	5932	4786		

	Home	Away	Total
League Attendances	552,526	417,548	970,074

Arsenal
Paris St. Germain

(1) 1
(0) 0

Tuesday 12th April 1994, Highbury

Att.: 34,212

ARSENAL

1	David	SEAMAN
2	Lee	DIXON
3	Nigel	WINTERBURN (+87)
4	Paul	DAVIS (†76)
5	Steve	BOULD
6	Tony	ADAMS
7	John	JENSEN
8	Ian	WRIGHT – Booked
9	Alan	SMITH
10	Kevin	CAMPBELL
11	Ian	SELLEY

Subs

12	Martin	KEOWN (+87)
13	Alan	MILLER (gk)
14	David	HILLIER (†76)
15	Ray	PARLOUR
16	Eddie	McGOLDRICK

PARIS ST. GERMAIN

1	Bernard	LAMA
2	Alain	ROCHE
3	Patrick	COLLETER – Booked
4		RICARDO
5	Jean-Luc	Sassus (†79)
6	Paul	LE GUEN
7	Laurent	FOURNIER
8	Vincent	GUERIN
9		RAI (†77)
10		VALDO
11	David	GINOLA

12	Francis	LLACER (+79)
13	Xavier	GRAVELAINE (†77)
14	Antoine	KOMBOUARE
15	Jose	COBOS
16	Luc	BORRELLI (gk)

Match Facts

• Ian Wright's second yellow card of the tournament meant he would miss the final.

• It was Arsenal's eighth match in this season's European Cup-Winners' Cup without defeat – they have conceded just three goals and David Seaman has kept five clean sheets.

• Arsenal have not lost one of the 17 ties they have played in the competition – their only reversal was by a penalty shoot-out against Valencia in 1980.

Score Sheet

K. CAMPBELL 5 min – 1-0

Referee:
Mr. P. Mikkelsen (Sweden)

European Cup Winners' Cup – Semi-Final, Second Leg

Campbell Clinches Final Place

Arsenal reached the final of the European Cup-Winners' Cup when they overcame Paris St. Germain in an emotional semi-final. However, they will have to face Parma in Copenhagen without leading goalscorer Ian Wright who was booked for the second time in the competition.

Paris St. Germain outplayed Arsenal for long periods of the match but the inner spirit, determination and organisation that had become the hallmark of the team saw them through to a memorable victory, sealed by Kevin Campbell's sixth-minute goal. That decisive moment saw Lee Dixon take a throw-in down the right, take a return pass from Alan Smith and his centre was met by Campbell whose deft header beat Lama, although the goalkeeper got his left hand to the ball.

Instead of pressing home their advantage Arsenal allowed Paris St. Germain to control the tempo and it was difficult to believe that the visitors were still behind at the interval given their possession. Their best chance in the first half came when David Seaman threw the ball straight to Valdo who should have shot but instead he passed to Rai. His effort was well blocked by a timely tackle from Tony Adams, who had his usual magnificent game in the heart of Arsenal's defence.

The French team had a further chance in the 72nd minute when a mistake by the tiring Ian Selley saw David Ginola in possession 12 yards from the Arsenal goal unmarked. The ball was on his weaker right foot but even so he should at least have forced a save from David Seaman – instead he shot wide.

It was their last chance. Arsenal kept their shape and, more importantly, their nerve and held on to their one goal advantage. A wonderful night for Highbury when the only disappointment had been the rather harsh booking of Ian Wright for a foul on Roche. Although Paris St. Germain had played very well they were unable to finish off their excellent midfield movements and paid the penalty.

Euro Cup-Winners' Cup Record

	P	W	D	L	F	A
ECWC Record 93-94	8	5	3	0	16	3
All-time ECWC Record	17	9	7	1	29	8

	Home	Away	Total
ECWC Attendances	119,837	103,060	222,897

Arsenal
Chelsea

Saturday 16th April 1994, Highbury   Att.: 34,314

ARSENAL

1	David	SEAMAN
2	Lee	DIXON
21	Steve	MORROW
18	*David*	*HILLIER (†45)*
14	Martin	KEOWN – *Booked*
6	Tony	ADAMS
22	Ian	SELLEY
8	Ian	WRIGHT
7	Kevin	CAMPBELL
23	Ray	PARLOUR
11	Eddie	McGOLDRICK

Subs

5	Andy	LINIGHAN
9	*Alan*	*SMITH (†45)*
13	Alan	MILLER (gk)

CHELSEA

1	Dimitri	KHARIN
12	Steve	CLARKE
18	Eddie	NEWTON
35	Jakob	KJELDBJERG
4	David	LEE
6	Frank	SINCLAIR
15	Mal	DONAGHY
27	David	HOPKIN
7	John	SPENCER
10	Gavin	PEACOCK
11	Dennis	WISE

2	Darren	BARNARD
17	Nigel	SPACKMAN
13	Kevin	HITCHCOCK

Match Facts

- Ian Wright's 21st Premiership goal while the defence kept their 21st clean sheet of the season. • Arsenal's unbeaten run in the Premiership stretches to 16 games.
- Chelsea's 12th away defeat of the season – along with Everton the worst in the league.
- Over one million spectators have watched Arsenal in the Premiership this season.

Score Sheet

I. WRIGHT 72 min – 1-0

Referee:
A. Wilkie (Chester-le-Street)

FA Carling Premiership

		P	W	D	L	F	A	Pts
2	Blackburn Rovers	38	24	7	7	59	32	79
3	Newcastle United	38	20	8	10	72	36	68
4	**Arsenal**	**37**	**17**	**15**	**5**	**49**	**21**	**66**
5	Leeds United	36	15	14	7	52	34	59
6	Sheffield Wed	38	15	13	10	68	51	58

Result of this Season's Fixture

Arsenal
Chelsea

Wright Has the Last Laugh

Chelsea fans spent the afternoon taunting Ian Wright over him missing the final of the forthcoming European Cup-Winners' Cup in Copenhagen in May. But it was the Arsenal striker who had the last laugh with a 72nd minute goal that gave the Gunners a fully deserved win. It maintained their bid for a place in the Premiership's top three.

For the umpteenth time that afternoon Arsenal launched an offensive down the right flank and Eddie McGoldrick picked out Wright with his centre towards the near post. Wright's fine header left goalkeeper Dimitri Kharin grasping thin air and finally silenced the jeers of the Chelsea supporters.

Until then, this all-London clash had been a disappointment and the match was curiously tame and subdued. Kevin Campbell had a couple of half chances and Wright beat Kharin with a flicked shot shortly before the interval only to see Chelsea defender Frank Sinclair race back and clear off the line.

Arsenal steeped up the tempo in the second half. They brought on Alan Smith for the injured David Hillier and he was on target inside three minutes but his snap shot was well saved by Kharin. The Gunners could have won it more convincingly had Wright and Parlour shown a little more composure in the closing stages.

As it was, they came close to throwing it away. Goalkeeper David Seaman did well to keep out a close-range header from David Hopkin and then Eddie Newton almost grabbed an equaliser when he hit the post in the last minute. Apart from that late scare, Chelsea had hardly troubled Arsenal all afternoon. With Chelsea through to the final of the FA Cup it was pretty obvious that both teams had half an eye on their respective cup finals coming up in the next month.

League Record

	P	W	D	L	F	A	Pts	Pos
93-94 Premiership Record	37	17	15	5	49	21	66	4th
All-time Premiership Record	79	32	26	21	89	59	122	
All-time League Record	3603	1569	896	1138	5933	4786		

	Home	Away	Total
League Attendances	586,840	417,548	1,004,388

Arsenal
Wimbledon

(0) 1
(1) 1

Tuesday 19th April 1994, Highbury   Att.: 21,192

ARSENAL

1	David	SEAMAN
2	Lee	DIXON
14	Martin	KEOWN
4	*Paul*	*DAVIS (†68)*
12	Steve	BOULD
6	Tony	ADAMS
7	Kevin	CAMPBELL
8	Ian	WRIGHT
9	Alan	SMITH
23	Ray	PARLOUR
22	Ian	SELLEY

Subs

24	*Mark*	*FLATTS (†68)*
5	Andy	LINIGHAN
13	Alan	MILLER (gk)

WIMBLEDON

1	Hans	SEGERS
2	Warren	BARTON
33	Gary	ELKINS
19	Stewart	CASTLEDINE
5	Dean	BLACKWELL
15	John	SCALES – *Booked*
20	Marcus	GAYLE
8	Robbie	EARLE
9	John	FASHANU
10	Dean	HOLDSWORTH
24	Peter	FEAR

7	Andy	CLARKE
21	Chris	PERRY
23	Neil	SULLIVAN (gk)

Match Facts

- Steve Bould's first goal of the season marked the Gunners' 50th league goal.

- Arsenal extend their unbeaten league run to 17 matches – their last defeat being at home to Leeds United on the 18th of December 1992.

- Highbury's lowest league crowd of the season.

Score Sheet

R. EARLE 37 min – 0-1

S. BOULD 51 min – 1-1

Referee:
Mr. R. Gifford (Mid-Glam)

FA Carling Premiership

		P	W	D	L	F	A	Pts
2	Blackburn Rovers	38	24	7	7	59	32	79
3	Newcastle United	38	20	8	10	72	36	68
4	**Arsenal**	**38**	**17**	**16**	**5**	**50**	**22**	**67**
5	Leeds United	37	16	14	7	54	34	62
6	Sheffield Wed	38	15	13	10	68	51	58

Result of this Season's Fixture

Arsenal
Wimbledon

Bould Strike

Arsenal extended their unbeaten league run to 17 games and, but for a rare goal from defender Steve Bould, would have become the latest victims of Wimbledon's recent success. In fact Wimbledon should have capitalised on a strangely uncomfortable defensive performance by the meanest rearguard in the division and could even have won the game.

Stewart Castledine had an early chance to put Wimbledon ahead when the Arsenal defence allowed themselves to be pushed deep. Castledine's shot tested David Seaman to the full. Soon afterwards the Arsenal goalkeeper failed to respond as effectively. In the 37th minute a corner from the impressive Gary Elkins tricked Seaman into committing himself early, the ball tipped the top of his glove and Robbie Earle powered a header home into the top corner.

The start of the second half saw Wimbledon have further chances to put the game beyond Arsenal's reach. Warren Barton's free kick hit the side netting and Dean Holdsworth again brought out the best in David Seaman before Arsenal finally levelled in the 51st minute. Ian Selley cornered from the left, Ray Parlour headed on and Tony Adams added a touch before Steve Bould volleyed home his first league goal for twenty months.

Further chances fell to both teams in the closing stages. David Seaman stretched to deny Castledine and Peter Fear missed in front of an open goal after collecting a magnificent cross-field pass from Gary Elkins. Before the end Arsenal took over with Lee Dixon hitting the post and Ian Wright forcing an excellent save from goalkeeper Hans Segers.

In the end it was the performances of both goalkeepers that had prevented further goals in a game which began slowly but finally provided enough entertainment to appease Arsenal's lowest league crowd of the season. Wimbledon, for their part, had shown glimpses of the form that had accounted for Manchester United, Blackburn, Newcastle and Leeds over the previous few weeks.

League Record

	P	W	D	L	F	A	Pts	Pos
93-94 Premiership Record	38	17	16	5	50	22	67	4th
All-time Premiership Record	80	32	27	21	90	60	123	
All-time League Record	3604	1569	897	1138	5934	4787		

	Home	Away	Total
League Attendances	608,132	417,548	1,025,680

Aston Villa
Arsenal

(0) 1
(1) 2

Saturday 23rd April 1994, Villa Park   Att.: 31,580

ASTON VILLA

1	Nigel	SPINK
2	Earl	BARRETT
17	Neil	COX
4	Shaun	TEALE
16	Ugo	EHIOGU
6	Kevin	RICHARDSON
7	Ray	HOUGHTON
14	Andy	TOWNSEND
10	Dalian	ATKINSON
25	Graham	FENTON
21	Dave	FARRELL

Subs

9	Dean	SAUNDERS
19	Stefan	BEINLICH
30	Michael	OAKES (gk)

ARSENAL

1	David	SEAMAN
2	Lee	DIXON
14	Martin	KEOWN
4	*Paul*	*DAVIS – Booked (†80)*
5	Andy	LINIGHAN
12	Steve	BOULD
21	Steve	MORROW
7	Kevin	CAMPBELL
8	Ian	WRIGHT
9	Alan	SMITH
24	Mark	FLATTS

23	*Ray*	*PARLOUR (†80)*
11	Eddie	McGOLDRICK
13	Alan	MILLER (gk)

Match Facts

• 18 matches in the Premiership without defeat for the Gunners.

• 35 goals for Ian Wright in all competitions.

• Villa's eighth defeat at home in the Premiership.

Score Sheet

I. WRIGHT 30 min Pen– 0-1

R. HOUGHTON 57 min – 1-1

I. WRIGHT 90 min – 1-2

Referee:
Mr. K. Cooper (Pontypridd)

FA Carling Premiership

		P	W	D	L	F	A	Pts
2	Blackburn Rovers	38	24	7	7	59	32	79
3	Newcastle United	39	21	8	10	75	38	71
4	**Arsenal**	**39**	**18**	**16**	**5**	**52**	**23**	**70**
5	Leeds United	38	16	15	7	55	35	63
6	Sheff Wed	39	16	13	10	73	51	61

**Result of this
Season's Fixture**

Aston Villa

Arsenal

Wright's Timely Strike

Ian Wright proved his value to Arsenal yet again with a high-class, two-goal display to sink Coca-Cola Cup winners Aston Villa. Wright was a constant threat to a Villa team who failed to get into gear in a first half dominated by Arsenal from start to finish.

Wright twice went close in the opening 20 minutes of the game before Arsenal made a deserved breakthrough on the half hour. Villa right back Neil Cox pulled down Wright in the area and the striker got up to easily beat Nigel Spink from the spot.

Whatever Ron Atkinson had to say in the Villa dressing room at half-time certainly had the desired effect as his team began the second half in a much more positive fashion. Dave Farrell almost grabbed a 49th minute equaliser with an 18 yard drive, before Ray Houghton brought them level in the 57th minute. Houghton found himself in acres of space and chipped the ball over goalkeeper David Seaman from 30 yards.

It was Villa who came closest to securing all three points in the 89th minute when David Seaman did well to deny Dalian Atkinson with his legs. There was still time for a sting in the tail, however, and it was Ian Wright who provided it in the 90th minute. Arsenal surged forward, Wright picked up a pass from Kevin Campbell and drove the ball past Nigel Spink from six yards.

George Graham was more than pleased with his side's display and it helped extend their unbeaten run in the Premiership to eighteen games. Ron Atkinson was certainly not happy with the performance of his players – so infuriated in fact that he left his seat in the directors' box after just 19 minutes to take a place in the dug-out. Not much had gone right for Villa since their Coca-Cola Cup win over Manchester United.

League Record

	P	W	D	L	F	A	Pts	Pos
93-94 Premiership Record	39	18	16	5	52	23	70	4th
All-time Premiership Record	81	33	27	21	92	61	126	
All-time League Record	3605	1570	897	1138	5936	4778		

	Home	Away	Total
League Attendances	608,132	449,128	1,057,260

Queens Park Rangers (1) 1
Arsenal (0) 1

Wednesday 27th April 1994, Loftus Road   Att.: 11,442

QUEENS PARK RANGERS

1	Tony	ROBERTS
2	David	BARDSLEY
3	Clive	WILSON
18	Karl	READY – *Booked*
4	Ray	WILKINS
24	Steve	YATES
7	Andrew	IMPEY
8	Ian	HOLLOWAY
14	Simon	BARKER
19	*Devon*	*WHITE (†45)*
12	Gary	PENRICE

Subs

10	*Bradley*	*ALLEN (†45)*
15	Rufus	BREVETT
13	Jan	STEJSKAL

ARSENAL

1	David	SEAMAN
2	Lee	DIXON
14	*Martin*	*KEOWN (+72)*
5	Andy	LINIGHAN
6	Tony	ADAMS
21	Steve	MORROW
24	*Mark*	*FLATTS (+45)*
8	Ian	WRIGHT
9	Alan	SMITH
10	Paul	MERSON
23	Ray	PARLOUR

11	*Eddie*	*McGOLDRICK (+72)*
22	*Ian*	*SELLEY (†45)*
13	Alan	MILLER (gk)

Match Facts

- Arsenal's ninth away draw of the season.
- QPR have not beaten Arsenal in their last eight meetings and the last six fixtures between the clubs have been drawn.
- Before Penrice scored in the fifth minute Rangers had not scored against Arsenal since November 1990 when Roy Wegerle scored from the penalty spot in a 3-1 defeat.

Score Sheet

G. PENRICE 5 min – 1-0

P. MERSON 46 min – 1-1

Referee:
Mr. I. Borrett (Gt. Yarmouth)

FA Carling Premiership

		P	W	D	L	F	A	Pts
2	Blackburn Rovers	39	24	8	7	60	33	80
3	Newcastle United	40	22	8	10	80	39	74
4	**Arsenal**	**40**	**18**	**17**	**5**	**53**	**24**	**71**
5	Leeds United	39	16	15	8	55	37	63
6	Sheff Wed	39	16	13	10	73	51	61

Result of this Season's Fixture

QPR

Arsenal

Rangers Rage

A Paul Merson goal just after the start of the second half preserved Arsenal's 19-match unbeaten run in the Premiership. But most post-match talk surrounded referee Ian Borrett, who controversially turned down two penalty appeals from Rangers.

It was the home side who took the lead as early as the fifth minute when Gary Penrice rose unchallenged to head home a pinpoint cross from Simon Barker. Rangers dominated the rest of the first half but were unable to take advantage of some uncharacteristically jittery defending from Arsenal and increase their goal advantage.

A tactical switch at half time by George Graham brought about a change in fortunes for the Gunners. Paul Merson was released from the rigours of midfield and put into a free role behind the striking pair of Wright and Smith. The effect was immediate with Merson dashing at the Rangers defence, jinking past three defenders and rifling home an unstoppable left-foot shot off the underside of the crossbar after 46 minutes for the equaliser.

On the hour came the first of the controversial penalty incidents when Steve Morrow seemed to clearly foul David Bardsley in the area but the incident went unpunished by the referee. Then, with seven minutes to go, Rangers' appeals for another penalty were turned away when Lee Dixon appeared to have handled.

The reactions of the managers at the end of the game were, as you might expect, entirely different. Rangers boss Gerry Francis was incensed by the decisions and he had to be restrained by the police as he approached the referee after the final whistle. George Graham, despite losing Martin Keown through injury, confidently looked forward to the final of the European Cup-Winners' Cup the following week.

League Record

	P	W	D	L	F	A	Pts	Pos
93-94 Premiership Record	40	18	17	5	53	24	71	4th
All-time Premiership Record	82	33	28	21	93	62	127	
All-time League Record	3606	1570	898	1138	5937	4789		

	Home	Away	Total
League Attendances	608,132	460,570	1,068,702

Arsenal
West Ham United

(0) 0
(0) 2

Saturday 30th April 1994, Highbury

Att.: 33,701

ARSENAL

13	Alan	MILLER
11	*Eddie*	*McGOLDRICK (†47)*
3	Nigel	WINTERBURN
4	Paul	DAVIS
12	Steve	BOULD
5	Andy	LINIGHAN
23	Ray	PARLOUR
8	Ian	WRIGHT
7	Kevin	CAMPBELL
10	*Paul*	*MERSON (+75)*
22	Ian	SELLEY

Subs

21	*Steve*	*MORROW (†47)*
27	*Paul*	*DICKOV (+75)*
26	Jim	WILL (gk)

WEST HAM UNITED

1	Ludek	MIKLOSKO
2	Tim	BREACKER
33	*David*	*BURROWS (†88)*
4	Steve	POTTS
15	Kenny	BROWN
12	Tony	GALE
14	Ian	BISHOP
18	Martin	ALLEN
28	Matthew	RUSH
34	Mike	MARSH
9	Trevor	MORLEY – *Booked*

20	*Danny*	*WILLIAMSON (†88)*
25	Lee	CHAPMAN
13	Gary	KELLY (gk)

Match Facts

- Arsenal's unbeaten run of 19 Premiership matches comes to an end. • Alan Miller's second full league appearance of the season. • Arsenal cannot finish any higher than fourth in the table. • West Ham's seventh away win of the season. • Arsenal started their season at Highbury with a defeat and ended it with a defeat.

Score Sheet

T. MORLEY 77 min – 0-1

M. ALLEN 88 min – 0-2

Referee:
Mr. R. Milford (Bristol)

FA Carling Premiership

		P	W	D	L	F	A	Pts
2	Blackburn Rovers	40	25	8	7	62	34	83
3	Newcastle United	41	22	8	11	80	41	74
4	**Arsenal**	**41**	**18**	**17**	**6**	**53**	**26**	**71**
5	Leeds United	40	17	15	8	58	37	66
6	Wimbledon	41	18	11	12	54	50	65

Result of this Season's Fixture

Arsenal
West Ham Utd

Limping to Copenhagen

Arsenal ended their Highbury campaign on a low note with this defeat against West Ham. It was their first defeat in the Premiership in 1994 and was hardly the ideal result before their Cup-Winners' Cup final match against Parma.

Alan Miller, in for the injured David Seaman, had kept his team in the game with some stunning saves in a first half which was dominated by West Ham. He was called into action straight away when Martin Allen snaked out a right foot to shoot from a difficult angle. The goalkeeper responded well to turn the ball over the bar. Trevor Morley then went close before Ian Bishop spotted Miller off his line and chipped from 30 yards. Miller, back-pedalling, just managed to touch the ball over.

Arsenal's defence was clearly missing Adams, and Miller again came to the rescue with a superb stop at point-blank range to deny Gale. He then made his third great save to prevent Morley breaking the deadlock. But, however poorly Arsenal are playing, there is always the chance that Ian Wright will pull something out of the bag. It almost happened towards the end of the first half when he flicked the ball over Potts and Brown only for Miklosko to pluck the ball bravely off his foot as he was about to shoot.

The tempo slowed in the second half but Campbell should have put Arsenal ahead when he was released by Merson but Miklosko again did well to block his shot. Then West Ham hit Arsenal with two goals in the last 12 minutes. First, Trevor Morley pounced on Linighan's poor back-pass and slotted the ball under Miller and then, two minutes from time, Martin Allen finished off a swift West Ham break with a superb 25-yard drive.

It was Arsenal's first Premiership defeat in 19 matches but, with Adams, Dixon and Smith being rested and Seaman out injured, George Graham knew it would be a different story against Parma with practically a full squad to choose from.

League Record

	P	W	D	L	F	A	Pts	Pos
93-94 Premiership Record	41	18	17	6	53	26	71	4th
All-time Premiership Record	83	33	28	22	93	64	127	
All-time League Record	3607	1570	898	1139	5937	4791		

	Home	Away	Total
League Attendances	641,833	460,570	1,102,403

Arsenal
Parma

(1) 1
(0) 0

Wednesday 4th May 1994, Parken Stadium, Copenhagen Att.: 33,765

ARSENAL

1	David	SEAMAN
2	Lee	DIXON
3	Nigel	WINTERBURN
4	Paul	DAVIS
5	Steve	BOULD
6	Tony	ADAMS – *Booked*
7	Kevin	CAMPBELL – *Booked*
8	Steve	MORROW
9	Alan	SMITH
10	*Paul*	*MERSON (†86)*
11	Ian	SELLEY – *Booked*

Subs

12	Andy	LINIGHAN
13	Alan	MILLER (gk)
14	*Eddie*	*McGOLDRICK (†86)*
15	Ray	PARLOUR
16	Paul	DICKOV

PARMA

1	Luca	BUCCI
2	Antonio	BENARRIVO
3	Alberto	Di CHIARA
4	*Gabriele*	*PIN (†70)*
5	Luigi	APOLLONI – *Booked*
6	Lorenzo	MINOTTI
7	Massimo	CRIPPA
8	Nestor	SENSINI
9	Faustina	ASPRILLA – *Booked*
10	Gianfranco	ZOLA
11	Tomas	BROLIN

12	*Alessandro*	*MELLI (†70)*
13	Marco	BALLOTTA (gk)
14	Roberto	MALTIGLIATI
15	David	BALLERI
16	Daniele	ZORATTO

Match Facts

- Arsenal become the seventh English team to win the European Cup -Winners' Cup.

- Alan Smith's strike was Arsenal's fourth successive goal from a set-piece in the competition.

- It was the 24th victory of 36 European finals in which English teams have appeared.

- Apart from their penalty shoot-out defeat against Valencia in the 1980 Final Arsenal have still to lose an actual match in the competition.

Score Sheet

A. SMITH 19 min – 1-0

Referee:
V. Krondl (Czech Republic)

European Cup Winners' Cup – Final

Arsenal's European Triumph

A superb display of discipline, organisation, professionalism and technique brought Arsenal a deserved win in the final of the European Cup-Winners' Cup in Copenhagen against the holders Parma. The victory brought George Graham his sixth major trophy in eight years as Arsenal boss. He can now be recognised as one of the finest managers in the history of English football.

Their triumph may not have been particularly attractive, but Graham demonstrated the art of winning football. With Ian Wright suspended, and John Jensen, David Hillier and Martin Keown all injured, George Graham had to rethink both his team and his tactics. As has been the case throughout the European campaign, his plan was carried out by a set of players who proved that commitment and spirit can be as important as individual skill. Parma may have been the more skillful team, man for man, but they were given little chance to display their ability because Arsenal closed down the space they need to play in.

Alan Smith, who was absolutely outstanding on his own up front, scored Arsenal's winning goal in the 19th minute. Lee Dixon took a throw-in to Smith who returned it to the right-back. Dixon's centre reached Minotti who tried to scissor-kick the ball clear but it spun to Smith who beat the diving Luca Bucci with a shot from 15 yards that entered the net via an upright.

Try as they might, Parma could not get back in the game and, when they did manage to break through the Arsenal midfield, they came up against the magnificent Tony Adams. Adams confirmed his reputation as one of the most effective and inspirational defenders in Europe. Arsenal's only real scare came when Tomas Brolin hit the post early in the first half.

The joy of the entire Arsenal squad, coaching staff, management and fans in the Parken Stadium was unconfined when referee Vaclav Krondl finally brought the match to an end after a remarkable 11 minutes and 31 seconds of stoppage time. Despite English failures at international level, Arsenal had shown that the traditional virtues of the English game could still beat Europe's elite.

Euro Cup-Winners' Cup Record

	P	W	D	L	F	A
ECWC Record 93-94	9	6	3	60	17	3
All-time ECWC Record	18	10	27	1	30	8

	Home	Away	Total
ECWC Attendances	119,837	136,825	256,662

Newcastle United (0) 2
Arsenal (0) 0

Saturday 7th May 1994, St. James' Park   Att.: 32,216

NEWCASTLE UNITED

1	Pavel	SRNICEK
2	Barry	VENISON
3	John	BERESFORD
15	Darren	PEACOCK
20	Alan	NEILSON
19	Steve	WATSON (†58)
7	Robert	LEE
5	Ruel	FOX
8	Peter	BEARDSLEY
9	Andy	COLE
11	Scott	SELLARS

ARSENAL

13	Alan	MILLER
2	Lee	DIXON (+81)
3	Nigel	WINTERBURN
4	Paul	DAVIS (†55)
12	Steve	BOULD
6	Tony	ADAMS
21	Steve	MORROW
8	Ian	WRIGHT
9	Alan	SMITH
22	Ian	SELLEY – Booked
11	Eddie	McGOLDRICK

Subs

12	Mark	ROBINSON (†58)
31	Michael	JEFFREY
30	Mike	HOOPER (gk)

5	Andy	LINIGHAN (+81)
23	Ray	PARLOUR (†55)
26	Jim	WILL (gk)

Match Facts

• Arsenal's second successive league defeat – the only time it happened all season.

• Andy Cole's strike was his 34th league goal of the season and his 41st in all competitions.

• It was only Arsenal's fourth away league defeat and their first since Saturday 4th December when they lost to Coventry City.

Score Sheet

A. COLE 46 min – 1-0

BEARDSLEY 66 min Pen – 1-1

Referee:
Mr. R. Dilkes (Mossley)

FA Carling Premiership

		P	W	D	L	F	A	Pts
2	Blackburn Rovers	42	25	9	8	63	36	84
3	Newcastle United	42	23	8	11	82	41	77
4	**Arsenal**	**42**	**18**	**17**	**7**	**53**	**28**	**71**
5	Leeds United	42	18	16	8	65	39	70
6	Wimbledon	42	18	11	13	56	53	65

Result of this Season's Fixture

Newcastle Utd
Arsenal

A Slight Hangover

Arsenal returned home from their wonderful night in Copenhagen to their last league match in the Premiership at Newcastle United. For the first time this season they suffered two successive league losses and the two goal defeat meant that they finished in fourth place – one place behind Newcastle.

Arsenal, with three changes from Wednesday's winning side, had only two serious attempts on goal in the 90 minutes. Ian Wright, put through by Steve Morrow, saw his angled shot well saved by Pavel Srnicek in the 19th minute and, in the 67th minute, substitute Ray Parlour brought another fine stop with a 15-yard shot.

Andy Cole got the goal he wanted against his old team just after the start of the second half. Peter Beardsley's impudent dribble through the entire Arsenal defence ended with a shot which goalkeeper Alan Miller could only knock out for Cole to score his 41st goal of the season.

Miller, deputising for the injured David Seaman, had denied Newcastle with a string of fine saves but was powerless to prevent Peter Beardsley adding a second goal from the penalty spot after Lee Dixon had brought down John Beresford.

Arsenal's Premiership season had therefore ended on a poor note with two consecutive defeats but after their display against Parma in the European Cup-Winners' Cup Final three days previously they could perhaps be forgiven an under-par performance in this game.

League Record

	P	W	D	L	F	A	Pts	Pos
93-94 Premiership Record	42	18	17	7	53	28	71	4th
All-time Premiership Record	84	33	28	23	93	66	127	
All-time League Record	3608	1570	898	1140	5937	4793		

	Home	Away	Total
League Attendances	641,833	492,786	1,134,619

Player by Player

Paul DAVIS

4

Date of Birth: 9th December 1961, Dulwich

Date signed for Arsenal	June 1979
Fee	–
Arsenal debut	v Tottenham Hotspur at White Hart Lane, April 1980. Won 2-1

Arsenal record

	Appearances	Goals
Football League	301/18	29
Premier League	27/1	
FA Cup	22/5	3
League Cup	44/5	4
Europe	15/1	
FA Charity Shield	2	

Honours	Football League Championship	1989, 1991
	FA Cup	1993
	Littlewoods Cup	1987
	Coca-Cola Cup	1993
	European Cup-Winners' Cup	1994

Previous Clubs and Appearance record

			Appearances			Goals		
Clubs	Signed	Fee	Lge	FLC	FAC	Lge	FLC	FAC
None								

Arsenal's current longest-serving player in the first team squad having made his debut back in 1980. He collected a winner's medal in the 1987 Littlewoods Cup Final win over Liverpool and was part of the two championship winning sides in 1989 and 1991. A nine match suspension and a succession of injuries meant he spent quite a lot of time on the sidelines, but he fought his way back to play an important role in Arsenal's winning double of the FA Cup and Coca-Cola Cup in 1993. He has won England U21 and 'B' honours but a full cap has always eluded him.

Estimated value: £800,000

PAUL MERSON

Date of Birth: 20th March 1968, Harlesden

10

Date signed for Arsenal	November 1985
Fee	–
Arsenal debut	v Manchester City at Highbury, November 1986. Won 3-0

Arsenal record

		Appearances	Goals
	Football League	139/28	50
	Premier League	56/10	13
	FA Cup	23/3	4
	League Cup	26/2	8
	Europe	12	3
	FA Charity Shield	3	
Honours	Football League Championship	1989, 1991	
	FA Cup	1993	
	Coca-Cola Cup	1993	
	European Cup-Winners' Cup	1994	

Previous Clubs and Appearance record

			Appearances			Goals		
Clubs	Signed	Fee	Lge	FLC	FAC	Lge	FLC	FAC
Brentford	1/87	Loan	6/1					

After making his debut in 1986, Paul took time establishing himself in the first team but, by the championship winning season of 1989/90, he had become a permanent fixture in the side. U21 caps for England followed and he was voted the 1989 Young Player of the Year by the PFA. A very versatile player who is equally at home in midfield, on the wing or as a central striker he has been a regular in full England international squads since 1992. Voted 'Man of the Match' in the 1993 Coca-Cola Cup Final win over Sheffield Wednesday, Paul also won a winner's medal in the FA Cup Final the same year. The 1993/94 season saw him in and out of the team but he did play a major part in Arsenal's European Cup-Winners' Cup success during the year.

Estimated value: £2,750,000

MARK FLATTS

Date of Birth: 14th October 1972, Islington

Date signed for Arsenal	December 1990
Fee	–
Arsenal debut	v Sheffield United at Bramall Lane, September 1992. Drew 1-1

Arsenal record

		Appearances	Goals
	Premier League	8/5	
	League Cup	0/1	
Honours	None		

Previous Clubs and Appearance record

			Appearances			Goals		
Clubs	Signed	Fee	Lge	FLC	FAC	Lge	FLC	FAC
None								

Mark broke into the first team in November during the 1992/93 season but injuries have restricted his appearances since. Joined Arsenal as a trainee from the FA School of Excellence in 1989 and won a South East Counties title medal and a Floodlit Cup winner's medal in 1991. Two stress fractures held up his development the next season. An England youth international.

Estimated value: £350,000

KEVIN CAMPBELL

7

Date of Birth: 4th February 1970, Lambeth

Date signed for Arsenal	February 1988
Fee	–
Arsenal debut	v Everton
	at Goodison Park, May 1988. Won 2-1

Arsenal record

		Appearances	Goals
	Football League	45/24	24
	Premier League	60/14	18
	FA Cup	12/5	2
	League Cup	9/7	2
	Europe	10/2	5
	FA Charity Shield	2	
Honours	Football League Championship	1991	
	FA Cup	1993	
	Coca-Cola Cup	1993	
	European Cup-Winners' Cup	1994	

Previous Clubs and Appearance record

			Appearances			Goals		
Club	Signed	Fee	Lge	FLC	FAC	Lge	FLC	FAC
Leyton Orient	1/89	Loan	16	9				
Leicester City	11/89	Loan	11	5				

Joined Arsenal as a trainee in 1986 and was a member of the FA Youth Cup winning side in 1988, scoring a hat-trick in the Final against Doncaster Rovers. After loan spells with Leyton Orient and Leicester City he established himself in the first team and won a League Championship medal in 1991. Since then he has also won FA Cup and Coca-Cola Cup winners medals in 1993 and played a prominent part in Arsenal's European Cup-Winners' Cup success in 1994 scoring four goals on the way to the Final. Capped at England U21 and 'B' level.

Estimated value: £2,600,000

ALAN SMITH

Date of Birth: 21st November 1962, Bromsgrove

Date signed for Arsenal	March 1987
Fee	£850,000
Arsenal debut	v Liverpool
	at Highbury, August 1987. Lost 1-2

Arsenal record

		Appearances	Goals
	Football League	177/12	78
	Premier League	47/8	6
	FA Cup	22/3	6
	League Cup	33/2	15
	Europe	11	6
	FA Charity Shield	2	
Honours	Football League Championship	1989, 1991	
	FA Cup	1993	
	Coca-Cola Cup	1993	
	European Cup-Winners' Cup	1994	

Previous Clubs and Appearance record

			Appearances			Goals		
Club	Signed	Fee	Lge	FLC	FAC	Lge	FLC	FAC
Leicester City	6/62	£22,000	190/10	8/1	8	76	4	4

Started his career with non-league Alvechurch before joining Leicester City and teaming up with Gary Lineker. Joined Arsenal in 1987 and has finished topscorer in four of his six seasons at Highbury, winning the Adidas 'Golden Shoe' award for the First Division's leading marksman. Won championship medals in 1989 and 1991 – scoring the first goal in the Gunners' dramatic 2-0 win at Liverpool in the last game of the 1988/89 season which won them the league. Further honours were gained in 1993 when he picked up FA Cup and Coca-Cola Cup winners' medals. 1993/94 saw him in and out of the first team but his season finished on a personal high when he scored the winning goal in the European Cup-Winners' Cup win over Parma in Copenhagen.

Estimated value: £750,000

IAN WRIGHT

Date of Birth: 3rd November 1963, Woolwich

Date signed for Arsenal	September 1991
Fee	£2,500,000
Arsenal debut	v Leicester City
	at Filbert Street, September 1991. Drew 1-1

Arsenal record

		Appearances	Goals
	Football League	30	24
	Premier League	69/1	38
	FA Cup	10	11
	League Cup	15	18
	Europe	6	4
	FA Charity Shield	1	
Honours	FA Cup		1993
	Coca-Cola Cup		1993
	ZDS Cup		1991

Previous Clubs and Appearance record

			Appearances			Goals		
Club	Signed	Fee	Lge	FLC	FAC	Lge	FLC	FAC
Crystal Palace	8/85	–	206/19	19	9/2	90	9	3

The club's record signing at £2.5million in September 1991 and he has been a huge success for the Gunners, finishing as the First Division's topscorer in his first season with 29 goals. 1992/93 saw Ian win the first major medals of his career with the Gunners' FA Cup and Coca-Cola Cup successes of that season. His phenomenal scoring record continued in the 1993/94 season, but he suffered huge personal disappointment when he was forced to sit out Arsenal's European Cup-Winners' Cup Final win over Parma because of suspension. His goals in six matches though, had been a huge contributory factor during the club's wonderful run. A valuable member of the England squad, although his prolific goalscoring club form has not been as proficient at international level. He did, however, score four of England's goals in their 7-1 win over San Marino which saw the end of the country's 1994 World Cup hopes.

Estimated value: £3,000,000

DAVID SEAMAN

Date of Birth: 19th September 1963, Rotherham

Date signed for Arsenal	May 1990
Fee	£1,300,000
Arsenal debut	v Wimbledon
	at Plough Lane, August 1990. Won 3-0

Arsenal record

		Appearances	*Goals*
	Football League	80	
	Premier League	78	
	FA Cup	20	
	League Cup	21	
	Europe	13	
	FA Charity Shield	2	
Honours	Football League Championship	1991	
	FA Cup	1993	
	Coca-Cola Cup	1993	
	European Cup-Winners' Cup	1994	

Previous Clubs and Appearance record

Club	Signed	Fee	*Appearances*			*Goals*		
			Lge	FLC	FAC	Lge	FLC	FAC
Leeds United	9/81	–						
Peterborough United	8/82	£4,000	91	10	3			
Birmingham City	10/84	£100,000	75	4	5			
QPR	8/86	£225,000	141	13	17			

Broke the British transfer record for a goalkeeper when he joined the club in 1990 for £1.3 million. In his first season he conceded just 18 goals and won a Championship medal. The 1992/93 season saw him add FA Cup and League Cup winners' medals to his collection. 1993/94 saw him establish himself as England's first choice goalkeeper and his season was made complete by a winners medal in the European Cup-Winners' Cup.

Estimated value: £2,500,000

ALAN MILLER

Date of Birth: 29th March 1970, Epping

Date signed for Arsenal	May 1988
Fee	–
Arsenal debut	v Leeds United
	at Elland Road, November 1992. Lost 0-3

Arsenal record

		Appearances	Goals
	Premier League	6/2	
Honours	European Cup-Winners' Cup	1994	

Previous Clubs and Appearance record

Club	Signed	Fee	Appearances			Goals		
			Lge	FLC	FAC	Lge	FLC	FAC
Plymouth Arg	11/88	Loan	13	2				
West Brom Alb	8/91	Loan	3					
Birmingham C	12/91	Loan	15					

Alan was the first goalkeeper from the FA School of Excellence to earn international recognition and the first to win U21 honours. A member of Arsenal's 1988 FA Youth Cup winning side. Spent loan spells with Plymouth Argyle, West Bromwich Albion and Birmingham City.

Estimated value: £500,000

LEE DIXON

Date of Birth: 17th March 1964, Manchester

Date signed for Arsenal	January 1988
Fee	£400,000
Arsenal debut	v Luton Town at Highbury, February 1988. Won 2-1

Arsenal record

		Appearances	Goals
	Football League	151/2	15
	Premier League	61/1	
	FA Cup	24	1
	League Cup	27	
	Europe	12	
	FA Charity Shield	3	
Honours	Football League Championship	1989, 1991	
	FA Cup	1993	
	European Cup-Winners' Cup	1994	

Previous Clubs and Appearance record

			Appearances			Goals		
Club:	Signed	Fee	Lge	FLC	FAC	Lge	FLC	FAC
Burnley	7/82	–	4	1				
Chester City	2/84	–	56/1	2	1	1		
Bury	7/85	£3,500	45	4	8	6		
Stoke City	7/86	£40,000	71	6	7	5		

Since arriving at Highbury in 1988, Lee has collected two championship medals, an FA Cup winners' medal and a European Cup-Winners' Cup medal. He missed Arsenal's Coca-Cola Cup win over Sheffield Wednesday in 1993 due to suspension. Despite two free transfers early in his career at Bury and Chester City, Lee showed that it is still possible for a rejected youngster to succeed at the highest level. Has won over 20 caps for England.

Estimated value: £1,500,000

NIGEL WINTERBURN

Date of Birth: 11th December 1963, Nuneaton

Date signed for Arsenal	May 1987
Fee	£400,000
Arsenal debut	v Southampton at Highbury, November 1987. Lost 0-1.

Arsenal record

		Appearances	Goals
	Football League	169/1	4
	Premier League	63	1
	FA Cup	28	
	League Cup	30	3
	Europe	13	
	FA Charity Shield	3	
Honours	Football League Championship	1989, 1991	
	FA Cup	1993	
	Coca-Cola Cup	1993	
	European Cup-Winners' Cup	1994	

Previous Clubs and Appearance record

			Appearances			Goals		
Club	Signed	Fee	Lge	FLC	FAC	Lge	FLC	FAC
Birmingham City	8/81	–						
Wimbledon	8/83	–	164/1	13	12	8		

Has proved to be one of George Graham's shrewdest signings since his arrival for £400,000 from Wimbledon in 1987. League championship medals from 1989 and 1991, FA Cup and Coca-Cola Cup winners medals in 1993 and a European Cup-Winners' Cup medal at the end of the 1993/94 season. One of the most consistent full backs in the Premiership and has two England caps.

Estimated value: £2,250,000

STEPHEN MORROW

Date of Birth: 2nd July 1970, Kilclenny, nr Belfast

Date signed for Arsenal	May 1988
Fee	–
Arsenal debut	v Norwich City at Carrow Road, April 1992. Won 3-1.

Arsenal record

		Appearances	Goals
	Football League	0/2	
	Premier League	20/7	
	FA Cup	2/2	
	League Cup	5/1	1
	Europe	1	
Honours	Coca-Cola Cup	1993	
	European Cup-Winners' Cup	1994	

Previous Clubs and Appearance record

			Appearances			Goals		
Club	Signed	Fee	Lge	FLC	FAC	Lge	FLC	FAC
Reading	1/91	Loan	10					
Watford	8/91	Loan	7/1					
Reading	10/91	Loan	3					
Barnet	3/92	Loan	1					

Remembered for his freak after-match injury in the Coca-Cola Cup Final in 1993, after he had scored Arsenal's winning goal. The injury ruled him out of the rest of the 1992/93 season. A member of the FA Youth Cup winning team in 1988, Stephen joined Arsenal as a trainee in 1987 after a year in Bangor's Irish League side. Capped 10 times for Northern Ireland.

Estimated value: £500,000

TONY ADAMS

Date of Birth: 10th October 1966, Romford

Date signed for Arsenal	April 1983
Fee	–
Arsenal debut	v Sunderland at Highbury, November 1983. Lost 1-2

Arsenal record

		Appearances	Goals
	Football League	248/1	20
	Premier League	68	
	FA Cup	29	5
	League Cup	44/1	2
	Europe	12	2
	FA Charity Shield	3	
Honours	Football League Championship	1989, 1991	
	FA Cup	1993	
	Littlewoods Cup	1987	
	Coca-Cola Cup	1993	
	European Cup-Winners' Cup	1994	

Previous Clubs and Appearance record

			Appearances			Goals		
Club	Signed	Fee	Lge	FLC	FAC	Lge	FLC	FAC
None								

Became one of Arsenal's youngest-ever captains when he was appointed in 1988. Voted PFA 'Young Player of the Year' in 1987 and won his first England cap the same year at the age of 20. He lost his international place after 1989 but fought his way back in 1993 and has now established himself in the England side again. Although he also has the ability to hit the headlines for occasional off-the-field activities, he is, nonetheless, an inspirational skipper and has earned himself a deserved reputation as one of the finest defenders in Europe. 31 England caps.

Estimated value: £3,000,000

ANDY LINIGHAN

5

Date of Birth: 18th June 1962, Hartlepool

Date signed for Arsenal	June 1990
Fee	£1,250,000
Arsenal debut	v Chelsea
	at Highbury, September 1990. Won 4-1

Arsenal record

		Appearances	Goals
	Football League	22/5	
	Premier League	39/4	2
	FA Cup	10/1	1
	League Cup	9/1	1
	Europe	3/1	1
	FA Charity Shield	1	
Honours	FA Cup	1993	
	Coca-Cola Cup	1993	
	European Cup-Winners' Cup	1994	

Previous Clubs and Appearance record

Club	Signed	Fee	Appearances			Goals		
			Lge	FLC	FAC	Lge	FLC	FAC
Hartlepool United	9/80	–	110	7/1	8	4	1	
Leeds United	5/84	£200,000	66	6	2	3	1	
Oldham Athletic	1/86	£65,000	87	8	3	6	2	
Norwich City	3/88	£350,000	86	6	10	8		

Became a Highbury hero when he scored the winning goal in the very last minute of Arsenal's FA Cup Final victory over Sheffield Wednesday in 1993. Before that he had struggled to gain a regular place in the Gunners' first team but he took his chance when Steve Bould was injured halfway through the 1992/93 season. His brother David plays for Ipswich Town.

Estimated value: £1,000,000

MARTIN KEOWN

Date of Birth: 24th July 1966, Oxford

Date signed for Arsenal	February 1984
Fee	–
Arsenal debut	v West Bromwich Albion at The Hawthorns, November 1985. Drew 0-0

Arsenal record

	Appearances	Goals
Football League	22	
Premier League	38/11	
FA Cup	7/1	
League Cup	3	
Europe	4/3	
FA Charity Shield	0/1	

| Honours | None |

Previous Clubs and Appearance record

Club	Signed	Fee	Appearances Lge	FLC	FAC	Goals Lge	FLC	FAC
Arsenal	2/84	–	22	5				
Brighton & HA	2/85	Loan	21/2	2	1	1		
Aston Villa	6/86	£200,000	109/3	12/1	6	3		
Everton	6/89	£750,000	79/4	7	10			

Came back to Highbury for a second spell in February 1993 after leaving Arsenal in 1986 to join Aston Villa. He joined Everton in 1989 for £750,000. One of the few successes in England's 1992 European Championship Finals side. Missed out on Arsenal's FA Cup and Coca-Cola successes in 1993 as he was cup-tied. Further disappointment followed at the end of the 1993/94 season when he was forced to miss the European Cup-Winners' Cup Final win over Parma because of injury.

Estimated value: £2,000,000

STEVE BOULD

Date of Birth: 16th November 1962, Stoke

Date signed for Arsenal	June 1989
Fee	£390,000
Arsenal debut	v Wimbledon
	at Plough Lane, August 1988. Won 5-1

Arsenal record

		Appearances	*Goals*
	Football League	107/5	3
	Premier League	47/2	2
	FA Cup	16	
	League Cup	17	
	Europe	5/2	
Honours	Football League Championship	1989, 1991	
	European Cup-Winners' Cup	1994	

Previous Clubs and Appearance record

			Appearances			*Goals*		
Club	Signed	Fee	Lge	FLC	FAC	Lge	FLC	FAC
Stoke City	11/80	–	179/4	13	10	6	1	
Torquay Utd	10/82	Loan	9	2				

After joining from Stoke City in 1988, Steve established himself alongside Tony Adams at the heart of the Arsenal defence and won Championship medals in 1989 and 1991. Injury forced him to miss the last three months of the 1992/93 season and he missed out on the club's FA Cup and Coca-Cola Cup success. The start of the 1993/94 season saw him struggling to get back into the first team but by November he had forced himself back into contention and was reunited with Tony Adams in defence. Having won a European Cup-Winners' Cup medal against Parma, he was called up to the England squad by Terry Venables, winning two caps against Greece and Norway at the end of May.

Estimated value: £1,000,000

DAVID HILLIER

Date of Birth: 19th December 1969, Blackheath

Date signed for Arsenal	February 1988
Fee	–
Arsenal debut	v Chester City at Moss Rose Ground, September 1990. Won 1-0

Arsenal record

		Appearances	Goals
	Football League	36/7	1
	Premier League	38/7	1
	FA Cup	11/6	
	League Cup	9/2	
	Europe	2/1	
	FA Charity Shield	1	
Honours	Football League Championship	1991	

Previous Clubs and Appearance record

			Appearances			Goals		
Club	Signed	Fee	Lge	FLC	FAC	Lge	FLC	FAC
None								

David suffered the heartbreak of missing the FA Cup and Coca-Cola wins in 1993 when he was injured two days after helping Arsenal beat Tottenham Hotspur in the FA Cup semi-final. He was also unfortunate to miss the European Cup-Winners' Cup Final win over Parma at the end of last season. Captained the 1988 FA Youth Cup winning side but has been unlucky with injuries since his first team debut in 1990. An effective midfield marker, David has been capped by the England U21 international side.

Estimated value: £650,000

JOHN JENSEN

Date of Birth: 3rd May 1965, Copenhagen

Date signed for Arsenal	August 1992
Fee	£1,100,000
Arsenal debut	v Norwich City at Highbury, August 1992. Lost 2-4

Arsenal record

	Appearances	Goals
Premier League	56/3	
FA Cup	4/1	
League Cup	8	
Europe	8	
FA Charity Shield	1	
Honours FA Cup		1993

Previous Clubs and Appearance record

Club	Signed	Fee	Appearances			Goals		
			Lge	FLC	FAC	Lge	FLC	FAC
Brondby								

After seeing John Jensen starring for Denmark in the 1992 European Championship Finals, when he scored the first goal in Denmark's 2-0 win over Germany, Arsenal manager George Graham was quick to sign the Danish midfielder from Brondby in August. He had to battle hard to adjust to the physical demands of the English game in his first season but he coped well enough to earn himself an FA Cup winner's medal in the Gunners' victory over Sheffield Wednesday. After distinguishing himself in Arsenal's European Cup-Winners' Cup campaign last season, John was forced to miss the Final in his home town of Copenhagen by a bad injury sustained whilst playing for Denmark. At the end of the 1993/94 season Highbury still expectantly awaited his first ever goal for the Gunners.

Estimated value: £1,300,000

RAY PARLOUR

Date of Birth: 7th March 1973, Romford

Date signed for Arsenal	July 1989
Fee	–
Arsenal debut	v Liverpool
	at Anfield, February 1992. Lost 0-2

Arsenal record

		Appearances	Goals
	Football League	2/4	1
	Premier League	40/8`	3
	FA Cup	14	2
	League Cup	5/1	
Honours	Coca-Cola Cup	1993	
	European Cup-Winners' Cup	1994	

Previous Clubs and Appearance record

			Appearances			Goals		
Club	Signed	Fee	Lge	FLC	FAC	Lge	FLC	FAC
None								

Made an immediate impression in his league debut in a live televised game at Liverpool early in 1992. The 1992/93 season saw him begin to establish himself in the first team and he won a Coca-Cola Cup winner's medal in the 2-1 victory over Sheffield Wednesday. He also played in the FA Cup Final against Wednesday but missed the replayed game five days later. An England U21 international with a bright future.

Estimated value: £850,000

IAN SELLEY

Date of Birth: 14th June 1974, Chertsey

Date signed for Arsenal	May 1992
Fee	–
Arsenal debut	v Blackburn Rovers at Highbury, September 1992.Lost 0-1

Arsenal record

		Appearances	Goals
	Premier League	26/2	
	FA Cup	3	
	League Cup	2/1	
	Europe	5/2	1
Honours	FA Cup	1993	
	Coca-Cola Cup	1993	
	European Cup-Winners' Cup	1994	

Previous Clubs and Appearance record

			Appearances			Goals		
Club	Signed	Fee	Lge	FLC	FAC	Lge	FLC	FAC
None								

Another youngster who has graduated through the Arsenal youth ranks and was just 18-years-old when he played in the FA Cup semi-final win over Tottenham in 1993. Was a non-playing substitute in the 1993 FA Cup and Coca-Cola Cup final winning sides. An England youth international, he also played for England in the U18 World Championships in Australia. Scored his first Arsenal goal in the Gunners' brilliant 7-0 win over Standard Liege in the European Cup-Winners' Cup in November and also picked up a winner's medal in the final against Parma.

Estimated value: £700,000

EDDIE McGOLDRICK

Date of Birth: 30th April 1965, Islington

Date signed for Arsenal	July 1993
Fee	£1,000,000
Arsenal debut	v Manchester United
	at Wembley, FA Charity Shield, August 1993. Drew 1-1

Arsenal record

		Appearances	Goals
	Premier League	23/3	
	FA Cup	1/1	
	League Cup	4	
	Europe	3/2	
	FA Charity Shield	0/1	
Honours	ZDS Cup	1991	
	European Cup-Winners' Cup	1994	

Previous Clubs and Appearance record

			Appearances			Goals		
Club	Signed	Fee	Lge	FLC	FAC	Lge	FLC	FAC
Northampton Town	8/86	£10,000	97/10	9	6/1	9	1	
Crystal Palace	1/89	£200,000	139/8	13/1	4	11		

Played in non-league football with Kettering Town and Nuneaton Borough before being signed by Northampton Town for £10,000 in 1986. After three years with the Cobblers he was signed by Crystal Palace for £200,000 and is equally at home in midfield or playing as sweeper. Capped by the Republic of Ireland and was a member of the European Cup-Winners' Cup winning squad at the end of the 1993/94 season.

Estimated value: £1,000,000

STEFAN SCHWARZ

Date of Birth: 18th April 1969, Sweden

Date signed for Arsenal	June 1994
Fee	£1,750,000
Arsenal debut	–

Arsenal record

	Appearances	Goals
Premier League		
FA Cup		
League Cup		

Previous Clubs and Appearance record

			Appearances			Goals		
Club	Signed	Fee	Lge	FLC	FAC	Lge	FLC	FAC
Malmo	1988							
Benfica	1991							

Made his debut for Malmo in the 1988/89 season and over the next three seasons made 29 league and eight European appearances for the Swedish side. Bayern Munich tried to sign him in 1990 and as his father was German they wanted him to take up German citizenship. Stefan refused as he wanted to play international football for Sweden. He joined Benfica in 1991 and played against Arsenal in the 1991/92 European Cup competition, which saw the Portuguese side knock out the Gunners. Signed for Arsenal in June 1994. Nearly 30 caps for Sweden and was a member of the 1994 World Cup squad, but was unfortunately sent off in the quarter-final match against Romania.

Estimated value: £1,750,000

Season's Records 1993-94

Attendances by Number – *FA Premier League*

Home			Away		
22/03/94	Manchester United	36,203	19/09/93	Manchester United	44,009
27/11/93	Newcastle United	36,091	02/10/93	Liverpool	42,750
06/12/93	Tottenham Hotspur	35,669	18/12/93	Leeds United	37,515
26/03/94	Liverpool	35,556	07/05/94	Newcastle United	32,216
26/02/94	Blackburn Rovers	35,030	23/04/94	Aston Villa	31,580
03/01/94	Queens Park Rangers	34,935	16/08/93	Tottenham Hotspur	28,355
16/04/94	Chelsea	34,314	20/11/93	Chelsea	26,839
30/04/94	West Ham United	33,701	21/08/93	Sheffield Wednesday	26,023
06/11/93	Aston Villa	31,773	15/01/94	Manchester City	25,642
02/04/94	Swindon Town	31,634	24/11/93	West Ham United	20,279
30/10/93	Norwich City	30,516	04/04/94	Sheffield United	20,019
16/10/93	Manchester City	29,567	19/02/94	Everton	19,891
28/08/93	Everton	29,063	05/03/94	Ipswich Town	18,656
24/08/93	Leeds United	29,042	13/02/94	Norwich City	17,667
11/09/93	Ipswich Town	28,563	27/12/93	Swindon Town	17,651
29/12/93	Sheffield United	27,035	10/03/94	Southampton	16,790
25/09/93	Southampton	26,902	01/01/94	Wimbledon	16,584
22/01/94	Oldham Athletic	26,524	01/09/93	Blackburn Rovers	14,051
14/08/93	Coventry City	26,397	04/12/93	Coventry City	12,722
12/12/93	Sheffield Wednesday	22,026	23/10/93	Oldham Athletic	12,105
19/04/94	Wimbledon	21,192	27/04/94	Queens Park Rangers	11,442

Attendances by Number – *European Cup-Winners' Cup*

Home			Away		
15/03/94	Torino	34,678	29/03/94	Paris St. Germain	46,000
12/04/94	Paris St. Germain	34,212	04/05/94	Parma	33,765
29/09/93	Odense Boldklub	25,689	02/03/94	Torino	32,480
20/10/93	Standard Liege	25,258	03/11/93	Standard Liege	15,000
			15/09/93	Odense Boldklub	9,580

Attendances by Number – *FA Cup*

Home			Away		
09/02/94	Bolton Wanderers	33,863	10/01/94	Millwall	20,093
			31/01/94	Bolton Wanderers	18,891

Attendances by Number – *Coca-Cola Cup*

	Home			Away	
30/11/93	Aston Villa	26,453	10/11/93	Norwich City	16,319
26/10/93	Norwich City	24,539	21/09/93	Huddersfield Town	14,275
05/10/93	Huddersfield Town	18,789			

Sendings Off

David	SEAMAN	24/11/93	v	West Ham United	(a)
Martin	KEOWN	09/02/93	v	Bolton Wanderers	(h)

Bookings

Tony	ADAMS	01/09/93	v	Blackburn Rovers	(a)
		26/10/93	v	Norwich City	(h)
		29/03/94	v	Paris St. Germain	(a)
		04/05/94	v	Parma	(a)
Steve	BOULD	30/10/93	v	Norwich City	(h)
		27/11/93	v	Newcastle United	(h)
		10/01/94	v	Millwall	(a)
Kevin	CAMPBELL	15/09/93	v	Odense Boldklub	(a)
		04/05/94	v	Parma	(a)
Paul	DAVIS	20/11/93	v	Chelsea	(a)
		23/04/94	v	Aston Villa	(a)
Lee	DIXON	23/10/93	v	Oldham Athletic	(a)
		04/12/93	v	Coventry City	(a)
David	HILLIER	27/12/93	v	Swindon Town	(a)
John	JENSEN	15/09/93	v	Odense Boldklub	(a)
		06/11/93	v	Aston Villa	(h)
Martin	KEOWN	16/08/93	v	Tottenham Hotspur	(a)
		19/09/93	v	Manchester United	(a)
		20/11/93	v	Chelsea	(a)
		29/09/93	v	Odense Boldklub	(h)
		16/04/94	v	Chelsea	(h)
Anders	LIMPAR	24/11/93	v	West Ham United	(a)
		18/12/93	v	Leeds United	(a)
		19/03/94	v	Southampton	(a)
Eddie	McGOLDRICK	15/09/93	v	Odense Boldklub	(a)
Paul	MERSON	22/03/94	v	Manchester United	(h)
		29/03/94	v	Paris St. Germain	(a)
Steve	MORROW	27/11/93	v	Newcastle United	(h)
Ray	PARLOUR	16/08/93	v	Tottenham Hotspur	(a)

Ian	SELLEY	04/12/93	v	Coventry City	(a)
		06/12/93	v	Tottenham Hotspur	(h)
		15/03/94	v	Torino	(h)
		04/05/94	v	Parma	(a)
		07/05/94	v	Newcastle United	(a)
Nigel	WINTERBURN	30/10/93	v	Norwich City	(h)
		04/12/93	v	Coventry City	(a)
		15/01/94	v	Manchester City	(a)
Ian	WRIGHT	16/08/93	v	Tottenham Hotspur	(a)
		24/08/93	v	Leeds United	(h)
		20/10/93	v	Standard Liege	(h)
		27/11/93	v	Newcastle United	(h)
		04/12/93	v	Coventry City	(a)
		27/12/93	v	Swindon Town	(a)
		03/01/94	v	Queens Park Rangers	(h)
		10/01/94	v	Millwall	(a)
		12/04/94	v	Paris St. Germain	(h)

Total Number of Bookings 46

9 Ian Wright

5 Martin Keown
   Ian Selley

4 Tony Adams

3 Nigel Winterburn
   Anders Limpar
   Steve Bould

2 John Jensen
   Kevin Campbell
   Lee Dixon
   Paul Davis
   Paul Merson

1 Ray Parlour
   Eddie McGoldrick
   Steve Morrow
   David Hillier

Total Dismissals   2

1 David Seaman
   Martin Keown

Summary of Appearances

Player		Apps	Subs	Goals	Y/Card	R/Card
David	Seaman	57	–	–	–	1
Ian	Wright	53	–	35	9	–
Nigel	Winterburn	51	–	–	3	–
Tony	Adams	49	–	4	4	–
Lee	Dixon	48	1	–	2	–
John	Jensen	41	1	–	2	–
Kevin	Campbell	40	13	19	2	–
Paul	Merson	39	10	9	2	–
Steve	Bould	34	3	1	3	–
Martin	Keown	32	15	–	5	1
Alan	Smith	32	8	7	–	–
Paul	Davis	32	3	–	2	–
Eddie	McGoldrick	31	7	1	1	–
Ray	Parlour	29	3	2	1	–
Andy	Linighan	26	3	–	–	–
Ian	Selley	23	5	1	5	–
David	Hillier	16	6	–	1	–
Anders	Limpar	12	6	–	3	–
Steve	Morrow	9	4	–	1	–
Alan	Miller	3	1	–	–	–
Mark	Flatts	2	1	–	–	–
Paul	Dickov	–	1	–	–	–
Own	Goal	–	–	3	–	–

All appearances cover FA Premiership, FA Cup, Coca-Cola Cup, European Cup-Winners' Cup and FA Charity Shield matches.

Goalscorers

		FAPL	FA Cup	CC Cup	ECW Cup	Ch Shield	Total
Ian	Wright	23	1	6	4	1	35
Kevin	Campbell	14	–	1	4	–	19
Paul	Merson	7	–	2	3	–	12
Alan	Smith	3	1	1	2	–	7
Tony	Adams	–	2	–	2	–	4
Ray	Parlour	2	–	–	–	–	2
Steve	Bould	1	–	–	–	–	1
Eddie	McGoldrick	–	–	–	1	–	1
Ian	Selley	–	–	–	1	–	1
Own	Goals	3	–	–	–	–	3

Goals For and Against by 5-minute Period

	For	Against		For	Against
0-5	5	3	45-50	3	2
5-10	1	2	50-55	8	2
10-15	4	0	55-60	6	3
15-20	6	2	60-65	7	2
20-25	2	2	65-70	4	4
25-30	6	1	70-75	3	1
30-35	3	3	75-80	5	2
35-40	8	3	80-85	3	1
40-45	5	1	85-90	6	4
			Extra Time	0	2

Transfers to Arsenal

Player	Date Bought	From	Fee
Stefan Schwarz	June 1994	Benfica	£1.75 million

Transfers from Arsenal

Player	Date Sold	To	Fee
Neil Heaney	March 1994	Southampton	£300,000
Anders Limpar	March 1994	Everton	£1.6 million

Loan Transfers

Player	Loan Club
Paul Dickov	Luton Town
	Brighton & Hove Albion
Mark Flatts	Cambridge United
Scott Marshall	Rotherham United
Jimmy Carter	Oxford United
Pål Lydersen	IK Start (Norway)

General Records

Football League

Record Win:	12-0	*v* Loughborough Town	12/03/1900
Record Defeat:	0-8	*v* Loughborough Town	12/12/1896
Highest Home Attendance:	73,295	*v* Sunderland Division 1	09/03/1935
Most Appearances:	517/30	David O'Leary	1975 -1992
Leading Scorer:	50	Cliff Bastin	1929 -1946
Most Goals in a Season:	42	Ted Drake	1934/35
Most League Wins in Season:	29	Division One	1970/71
Most League Defeats in Season:	23	Division One	1912/13 & 1924/25

Premier League

Record Win:	5-1	*v* Ipswich Town	05/03/1994
Record Defeat:	0-3	*v* Leeds United	21/11/1992
	0-3	*v* Coventry City	14/08/1993
Highest Home Attendance:	36,203	*v* Manchester United	22/03/1994
Most Appearances:	78	David Seaman	1992-1994
Leading Scorer:	38	Ian Wright	1992-1994
Most Goals in a Season:	23	Ian Wright	1993/94
Most League Wins in Season:	18	1993/94	
Most League Defeats in Season:	16	1992/93	

FA Cup

Record Win:	11-1	*v* Darwen -Round 1	09/01/1932
Record Defeat:	0-6	*v* Sunderland -Round 1	21/01/1893
	0-6	*v* Derby County -Round 1	28/01/1899
	0-6	*v* West Ham United -Round 3	05/01/1946
Most Appearances:	67	Pat Rice	1964 -1980
Leading Goalscorer:	26	Cliff Bastin	1929 -1946

League Cup

Record Win:	7-0	*v* Leeds Utd -Round 2	04/09/1979
Record Defeat:	2-6	*v* Manchester United – Round 4	28/11/1990
Most Appearances:	68/2	David O'Leary	1973 -1993
Leading Goalscorer:	14	Frank Stapleton	1972 -1981

Europe

Record Home Win:	7-1	*v* Dinamo Bacau European Fairs Cup, Round 4 18/03/70	
Record Home Win:	7-1	*v* Dinamo Bacau	
Record Away Win:	7-0	*v* Standard Liege European Cup-Winners' Cup, Round 2 03/11/93	
Record Home Defeat:	2-5	*v* Spartak Moscow UEFA Cup, Round 1 29/09/82	
Record Away Defeat:	1-3	*v* Standard Liege Inter-Cities Fairs Cup, Round 2 18/12/63 *and* *v* Anderlecht European Fairs Cup Final 22/04/70	
Record Aggregate Victory:	10-0	*v* Standard Liege (3-0 +7-0) European Cup-Winners' Cup, Round 2 1993-94	
Most Appearances:	26/1	Pat Rice 1964-80 *and* John Radford 1962-76	
Record Defeat:	2-5	*v* Spartak Moscow – Round1	29/09/1982
Most Appearances:	26/1	Pat Rice	1964 -1980
Leading Goalscorer:	11	John Radford	1962 -1976

JJ gunning for goal. Jonathan Pearce is waiting!

Arsenal

Arsenal Stadium, Avenell Road, Highbury, London N5 1BU

Nickname:	The Gunners
Colours:	Red and White shirts, White shorts, Red &White socks
Change:	Blue with Turquoise shirts,Blue shorts, Blue & Turquoise socks
Capacity:	39,497 **Pitch:** 110yds x 71yds

Officials

Chairman:	Peter Hill-Wood
Vice Chairman:	David Dein
Managing Director:	Ken Friar
Directors:	Sir Robert Bellinger, Roger Gibbs, Clive Carr, Richard Carr, Daniel Fisman.
Manager:	George Graham
First Team Coach:	Stewart Houston
Physiotherapist:	Gary Lewin
Assistant Secretary:	David Miles

Honours

Football League Champions:	1931, 1933, 1934, 1935, 1938, 1948, 1953, 1971, 1989, 1991
Runners-Up:	1926, 1932, 1973
FA Cup Winners:	1930, 1936, 1950, 1971, 1979, 1993
Runners-Up:	1927, 1932, 1952, 1972, 1978, 1980
League Cup Winners:	1987, 1993
Runners-Up:	1968, 1969, 1988

European Honours

European Fairs Cup Winners:	1970
European Cup-Winners' Cup:	Winners 1994
Runners-Up:	1980

Miscellaneous Records

FA Youth Cup Winners:	1966, 1971, 1988, 1994
Record Attendance:	73,295 *v* Sunderland Division 1 09/03/35

League History

1893	Elected to Division 2	1919 - 1992	Division 1
1904 - 1913	Division 1	1992 -	FA Premier League
1913 - 1919	Division 2		

Managers and Secretary-Managers

1894 - 1897	Sam Hollis	1947 - 1956	Tom Whittaker
1897 - 1898	Tom Mitchell	1956 - 1958	Jack Crayston
1898 - 1899	George Elcoat	1958 - 1962	George Swindin
1899 - 1904	Harry Bradshaw	1962 - 1966	Billy Wright
1904 - 1908	Phil Kelso	1966 - 1976	Bertie Mee
1908 - 1915	George Morrell	1976 - 1983	Terry Neill
1919 - 1925	Leslie Knighton	1984 - 1986	Don Howe
1925 - 1934	Herbert Chapman	1986 -	George Graham
1934 - 1947	George Allison		

Birth of The Gunners

Formed as Dial Square – a workshop in Woolwich Arsenal with a sundial over the
entrance – in October 1886 becoming Royal Arsenal later the same year. Turned
professional and became Woolwich Arsenal in 1891. Selected for an expanded
Football League Division Two in 1893, the first southern team to join.

Moved from the Manor Ground in Plumstead south-east London to Highbury in
1913, changing their name again at the same time. Elected from fifth in Division
Two to the expanded First Division for the 1919/20 season and have never been
relegated since. Premier League founder members in 1992.

Telephone Numbers

Main Switchboard	071 226 0304	Club Fax	071 226 0329
Match Information	071 359 0131	Dial-A-Ticket	071 226 4050
Box Office Enquiries	071 354 5404	Travel Club	071 359 0205
Commercial & Marketing	071 359 0808	Gunners Shop	071 226 9562
Arsenal World of Sport	071 272 1000	Clubcall Newsline	0891 202020
Mail Order/Credit Card Line	071 354 8397	Restaurant	071 704 8165

Arsenal FC

Directions:

From North:
M1 Junction 2 follow signs for City. After Holloway Road station take third left into Drayton Park. Then right into Aubert Street and 2nd left into Avenell Road.

From South:
Signs for Bank of England then Angel from London Bridge. Right at traffic lights towards Highbury roundabout. Follow Holloway Road then third right into Drayton Park. Thereafter as above.

From West:
A40(M) to A501 ring road. Left at Angel to Highbury roundabout then as above.

Rail:
Drayton Park/Finsbury Park

Tube:
(Piccadilly Line) Arsenal

Aston Villa

Villa Park, Trinity Rd, Birmingham, B6 6HE

Nickname: The Villains

Colours: Claret/Blue, White, Blue/Claret   **Change:** White, Black, White

All-seater Capacity: 40,530   **Pitch:** 115 yds x 75 yds

Directions:

M6 J6, follow signs for Birmingham NE. 3rd exit at roundabout then right into Ashton Hall Rd after ¹/₂ mile.

Rail: Witton

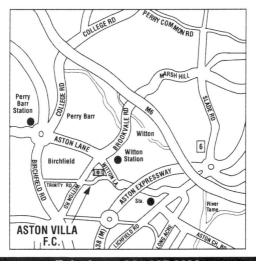

Telephone: 021-327 2299

172

Blackburn Rovers

Ewood Park, Blackburn, BB2 4JF

Nickname: Blue and Whites
Colours: Blue/White, White, Blue
All-seater Capacity: 30,591

Change: Black/Red, Black, Black/Red
Pitch: 115yds x 76yds

Directions:

From North, South & West: M6 J31 follow signs for Blackburn then Bolton Road.
Turn left after 1½ miles into Kidder Street.
From East: A677 or A679 following signs for Bolton Road, then as above.
Rail: Blackburn Central

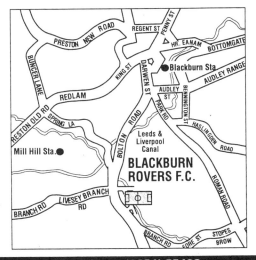

Telephone: (0254) 55432

Chelsea

Stamford Bridge, London SW6

Nickname: The Blues
Colours: Royal Blue, Royal Blue, White   **Change:** White/Red, Black, Black
All-seater Capacity: 41,050   **Pitch:** 110 yds x 72 yds

Directions:

From North & East: A1 or M1 to central London and Hyde Park corner. Follow signs for Guildford (A3) and then Knightsbridge (A4). After a mile turn left into Fulham Road. *From South:* A219 Putney Bridge then follow signs for West End joining A308 and then into Fulham Road. *From West:* M4 then A4 to central London. Follow A3220 to Westminster, after ¼ mile right at crossroads into Fulham Road.

Rail/Tube: Fulham Broadway (District line).

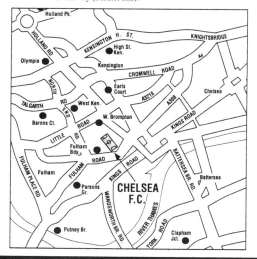

Telephone: 071-385 5545

Coventry City

Highfield Road Stadium, King Richard Street, Coventry, CV2 4FW

Nickname: Sky Blues
Colours: All Sky Blue   **Change:** Yellow, Blue, Yellow
All-seater Capacity: 24,021   **Pitch:** 110 yds x 75 yds

Directions:

From North & West: M6 J3, after 3½ miles turn left into Eagle Street and straight on to Swan Lane. *From South & East:* M1 to M45 then A45 to Ryton-on-Dunsmore where 3rd exit at roundabout is A423. After 1 mile turn right into B4110. Left at T-junction then right into Swan Lane.
Rail: Coventry

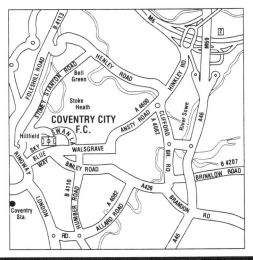

Telephone: (0203) 223535

Crystal Palace

Selhurst Park, London, SE25 6PU

Nickname: Eagles
Colours: Red/Blue, Red, Red
All-seater Capacity: 26,995

Change: Yellow, Light Blue, White
Pitch: 110 yds x 74 yds

Directions:

From North: M1 or A1 to A406 for Chiswick, then A205 to Wandsworth. A3 and then A214 for Streatham and then A23 to B273 for Whitehorse Lane.
From South: A23 and then B266. Turn right into High Street and then as above.
From East: A232 and then A215 to B266 for High Street and then as above.
From West: M4 to Chiswick and then as for the North.
Rail: Norwood Junction, Thornton Heath or Selhurst.

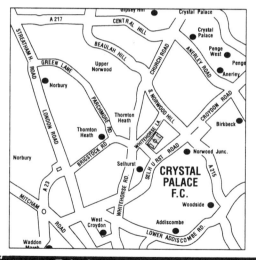

Telephone: 081-653 4462

Everton

Goodison Park, Liverpool, L4 4EL

Nickname: The Toffees
Colours: Royal Blue, White, Blue **Change:** Salmon/Dark Blue, Salmon, Salmon
All-seater Capacity: 40,160 **Pitch:** 112 yds x 78 yds

Directions:

From North: M6 J8 take A58 to A580 and follow into Walton Hall Avenue.
From South & East: M6 J21A to M62, turn right into Queen's Drive then, after 4 miles, left into Walton Hall Avenue.
From West: M53 through Wallasey Tunnel, follow signs for Preston on A580. Walton Hall Avenue is signposted.
Rail: Liverpool Lime Street

Telephone: 051-521 2020

Ipswich Town

Portman Road, Ipswich, Suffolk, IP1 2DA

Nickname: Blues or Town
Colours: Blue/White, White, Blue   **Change:** Red/Black, Black, Red/Black
All-seater Capacity: 22,823   **Pitch:** 112 yds x 70 yds

Directions:

Follow A45 and signs for Ipswich West. Through Post House traffic lights and turn right at second roundabout into West End Road. Ground is situated on the left.
Rail: Ipswich

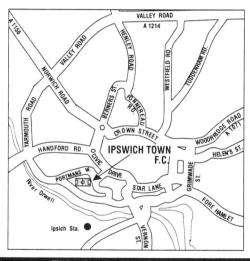

Telephone: (0473) 219211

Leeds United

Elland Road, Leeds, LS11 0ES

Nickname: United
Colours: All White
All-seater Capacity: 39,704

Change: All Yellow
Pitch: 117 yds x 76 yds

Directions:

From North & East: A58, A61, A63 or A64 into city centre and then onto M621.
Leave Motorway after 1½ miles onto A643 and Elland Road.
From West: take M62 to M621 then as above.
From South: M1 then M621 then as above
Rail: Leeds City

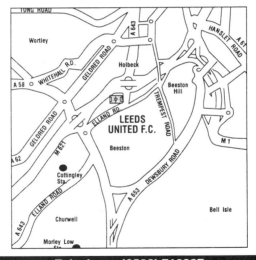

Telephone: (0532) 716037

Leicester City

City Stadium, Filbert Street, Leicester, LE2 7FL

Nickname: The Filberts or Foxes

Colours: Blue, White, Blue   **Change:** Red, Black, Black

All-seater Capacity: 27,722   **Pitch:** 112 yds x 75 yds

Directions:

From North: Leave M1 at J22 or take A46, A607 to town centre. Towards Rugby
via Almond Road, Sylestone Road and left into Walnut Street and Filbert Street.
From South: M1 or M69 and then A46 to Upperton Road and Filbert Street.
From East: A47 into town centre, right along Oxford Street to Aylestone Road and
then as North. *From West:* M69 and A50 to Aylestone Road and then as North.
Rail: Leicester

Telephone: (0533) 555000

Liverpool

Anfield Road, Liverpool L4 0TH

Nickname: Reds or Pool
Colours: All Red/White Trim
All-seater Capacity: 44,243

Change: Racing Green/White Trim
Pitch: 110 yds x 75 yds

Directions:

From North: M6 J8, follow A58 to Walton Hall Avenue and pass Stanley Park turning left into Anfield Road. *From South/East:* To end of M62 and right into Queens Drive (A5058). After 3 miles turn left into Utting Avenue and right after 1 mile into Anfield Road. *From West:* M53 through Wallasey Tunnel, follow signs for Preston then turn into Walton Hall Avenue and right into Anfield Road before Stanley Park. *Rail:* Liverpool Lime Street

Telephone: 051-263 2361

Manchester City

Maine Road, Moss Side, Manchester, M14 7WN

Nickname: Blues or City
Colours: Sky Blue, White, Sky Blue **Change:** Purple/Candystripe, Purple, Purple
All-seater Capacity: 45.053 **Pitch:** 117 yds x 77 yds

Directions:

From North & West: M61 to M63 J9. Follow signs into Manchester (A5103). Right after 3 miles into Claremont Road. Right after 400 yards into Maine Road.
From South: M6 J19 to A556 joining M56. Leave at J3 following A5103 as above.
From East: M62 J17 following signs for Manchester Airport (A56 and A57(M)). Then follow Birmingham signs to A5103. Left into Claremont Road after 1 mile then right into Maine Road. *Rail:* Manchester Piccadilly

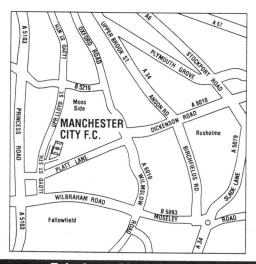

Manchester United

Old Trafford, Manchester, M16 0RA

Nickname: Red Devils
Colours: Red Shirts, White Shorts **Change:** All Black or Yellow/Green Halves
All-seater Capacity: 44,622 **Pitch:** 116 yds x 76 yds

Directions:

From North: M63 J4 follow signs for Manchester (A5081). Right after 2½ miles into Warwick Rd.
From South: M6 J19 follow A556 then A56 (Altrincham). From Altrincham follow signs for Manchester turning left into Warwick Rd after 6 miles.
From East: M62 J17 then A56 to Manchester. Follow signs South and then Chester. Turn right into Warwick Rd after 2 miles.
Rail: Manchester Victoria, Piccadilly, Old Trafford.

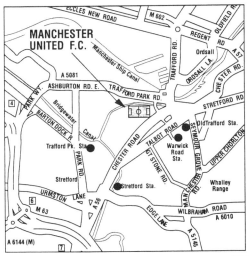

Telephone: 061-872 1661

Newcastle United

St James' Park, Newcastle-upon-Tyne, NE1 4ST

Nickname: Magpies

Colours: Black/White, Black, Black

All-seater Capacity: 36,401

Change: All Blue

Pitch: 115 yds x 75 yds.

Directions:

From South: Follow A1, A68 then A6127 to cross the Tyne. At roundabout, first exit into Moseley Street. Left into Neville Street, right at end for Clayton Street and then Newgate Street. Left for Leaze Park Road. *From West:* A69 towards city centre. Left into Clayton Street for Newgate Street, left again for Leaze Park Road. *From North:* A1 then follow signs for Hexham until Percy Street. Right into Leaze Park Road. *Rail:* Newcastle Central (¹/₂ mile).

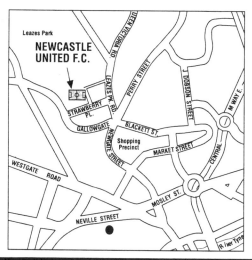

Telephone: 091-232 8361

Norwich City

Carrow Road, Norwich, NR1 1JE

Nickname: The Canaries

Colours: Yellow, Green, Yellow

All-seater Capacity: 25,000

Change: All White

Pitch: 114yds x 74 yds

Directions:

From North: A140 to ring road and follow signs for Yarmouth A47. Turn right at T junction after 3¹/₂ miles then left after ¹/₂ mile into Carrow Road.

From South & West: A11/A140 onto ring road. Follow signs for Yarmouth A47 etc as for North above.

From East: A47 into Norwich then left onto ring road.

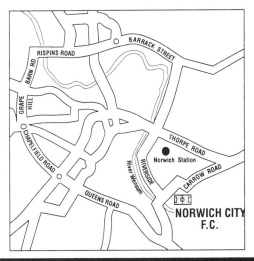

Telephone: (0603) 612131

185

Nottingham Forest

City Ground, Nottingham, NG2 5FJ

Nickname: The Reds or Forest
Colours: Red, White, Red
All-seater Capacity: 26,500

Change: Blue, Turquoise, Blue
Pitch: 115 yds x 78 yds

Directions:

From North: Leave the M1 J26 for the A610 and the A606. Left into Radcliffe Road for the ground. *From South:* Leave the M1 J24 to Trent Bridge, turning right into Radcliffe Road. *From East:* A52 to West Bridgford and right for the ground. *From West:* A52 to A606 and then as for the North.
Rail: Nottingham.

Telephone: (0602) 526000

Queens Park Rangers

South Africa Road, W12 7PA

Nickname: Rangers or R's
Colours: Blue/White, White, White   **Change:** Red/Black, Black, Black
All-seater Capacity: 19,300   **Pitch:** 112 yds x 72 yds

Directions:

From North: M1 to north circular A406 towards Neasden. Left onto A404 for Hammersmith, past White City Stadium then right into South Africa Road. *From South:* A3 across Putney Bridge and signs for Hammersmith. A219 to Shepherds Bush and join A4020 towards Acton. Turn right after ¼ mile into Loftus Road. *From East:* From A40(M) towards M41 roundabout. Take 3rd exit at roundabout to A4020 then as above. *From West:* M4 to Chiswick then A315 and A402 to Shepherd's Bush joining A4020 then as for South. *Rail:* Shepherds Bush *Tube:* White City (Central Line)

Telephone: 081-743 0262

187

Sheffield Wednesday

Hillsborough, Sheffield, S6 1SW

Nickname: The Owls

Colours: Blue/White, Blue, Blue   **Change:** All Black with Yellow/Grey trim

All-seater Capacity: 40,000   **Pitch:** 115 yds x 75 yds

Directions:

From North: M1 J34 then A6109 to Sheffield. At roundabout after 1¹/₂ miles take 3rd exit then turn left after 3 miles into Herries Road.

From South & East: M1 J31 or 33 to A57. At roundabout take Prince of Wales Road exit. A further 6 miles then turn left into Herries Road South.

From West: A57 to A6101 then turn left after 4 miles at T junction into Penistone Road.

Rail: Sheffield Midland

Southampton

The Dell, Milton Road, Southampton, SO9 4XX

Nickname: The Saints
Colours: Red/White, Black, Black   **Change:** Turquoise/Blue, Turquoise, Blue
All-seater Capacity: 15,288   **Pitch:** 110 yds x 72 yds

Directions:

From North: A33 into The Avenue then right into Northlands Road. Right at the
end into Archer's Road. *From East:* M27 then A334 and signs for Southampton
along A3024. Follow signs for the West into Commercial Road, right into Hill Lane
then first right into Milton Road.
From West: Take A35 then A3024 towards city centre. Left into Hill Lane and first
right into Milton Road.
Rail: Southampton Central

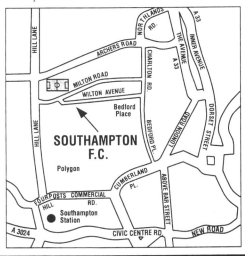

Telephone: (0703) 220505

189

Tottenham Hotspur

748 High Road, Tottenham, London, N17 0AP

Nickname: Spurs
Colours: White, Navy Blue, White
All-seater Capacity: 30,246

Change: All Yellow or all Sky Blue
Pitch: 110 yds x 73 yds

Directions:

A406 North Circular to Edmonton. At traffic lights follow signs for Tottenham along A1010 then Fore Street for ground.
Rail: White Hart Lane (adjacent)
Tube: Seven Sisters (Victoria Line) or Manor House (Piccadilly Line).

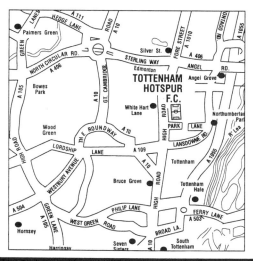

West Ham United

Boleyn Ground, Green Street, Upton Park, London E13

Nickname: The Hammers
Colours: Claret, White, White
All-seater Capacity: 24,500

Change: All Blue
Pitch: 112 yds x 72 yds

Directions:

From North & West: North Circular to East Ham then Barking Rd for 1½ miles until traffic lights. Turn right into Green Street.
From South: Blackwall Tunnel then A13 to Canning Town. Then A124 to East Ham, Green Street on left after 2 miles.
From East: A13 then A117 and A124. Green Street on right after ¼ miles.
Rail/Tube: Upton Park (¼ mile)

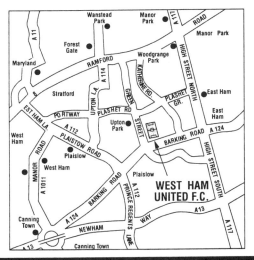

Wimbledon

Selhurst Park, London, SE25 6PU

Nickname: The Dons

Colours: All Blue with Yellow trim

All-seater Capacity: 26,995

Change: All Red

Pitch: 110 yds x 74 yds

Directions:

From North: M1/A1 to North Circular A406 and Chiswick. Follow South Circular A205 to Wandsworth then A3 and A214 towards Streatham and A23. Then left onto B273 for 1 mile and turn left at end into High Street and Whitehorse Lane. *From South:* On A23 follow signs for Crystal Palace along B266 going through Thornton Heath into Whitehorse Lane. *From East:* A232 Croydon Road to Shirley joining A215, Norwood Road. Turn left after 2½ miles into Whitehorse Lane. *From West:* M4 to Chiswick then as above.

Rail: Selhurst, Norwood Junction or Thornton Heath.

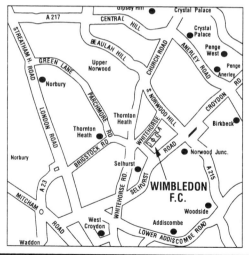

Telephone: 081-771 2233

All-time Records and Statistics

Arsenal Against Other Clubs – *Football League*

Club		Home					Away				
	P	W	D	L	F	A	W	D	L	F	A
Aston Villa	126	33	12	18	108	75	15	13	35	87	131
Barnsley	16	7	0	1	20	4	0	1	7	5	15
Birmingham City	110	35	16	4	109	37	13	13	29	66	108
Blackburn Rovers	72	21	10	5	80	32	12	12	12	56	69
Blackpool	72	26	8	2	85	34	12	13	11	57	50
Bolton Wanderers	92	26	13	7	104	45	10	13	23	60	86
Bradford PA	6	3	0	0	7	1	2	1	0	4	2
Bradford City	18	4	2	3	11	7	3	2	4	11	15
Brentford	10	1	3	1	6	6	1	0	4	2	8
Brighton & Hove Albion	8	3	1	0	8	1	2	0	2	6	3
Bristol City	28	7	4	3	23	13	9	2	3	23	10
Burnley	86	25	9	9	94	46	12	10	21	50	67
Burslem Port Vale	18	8	1	0	24	3	3	2	4	9	11
Burton United	22	8	1	2	31	6	3	0	8	12	25
Burton Wanderers	6	2	1	0	7	1	1	0	2	5	6
Bury	32	12	2	2	41	12	1	5	10	10	16
Cardiff City	30	7	5	3	26	14	4	6	5	19	24
Carlisle United	2	1	0	0	2	1	0	0	1	1	2
Charlton Athletic	36	10	4	4	43	28	10	5	3	40	21
Chelsea	110	25	14	16	88	71	18	19	18	72	68
Chesterfield	10	5	0	0	15	2	2	1	2	7	7
Coventry City	50	14	7	4	44	19	13	6	6	33	24
Crewe Alexandria	6	3	0	0	17	2	1	2	0	1	0
Crystal Palace	18	7	2	0	22	7	4	4	1	19	10
Darwen	10	4	0	1	15	4	2	1	2	11	10
Derby County	84	22	8	12	77	48	9	9	24	48	83
Doncaster Rovers	4	2	0	0	4	0	1	0	1	1	1
Everton	142	45	11	15	134	75	19	18	34	86	114
Fulham	28	13	1	0	38	13	5	4	5	24	28
Gainsborough Town	16	8	0	0	36	5	3	2	3	8	9
Glossop	14	6	1	0	16	1	6	0	1	13	4
Grimsby Town	42	16	4	1	76	18	4	6	11	26	31
Huddersfield Town	64	15	9	8	47	37	10	14	8	39	47
Hull City	4	1	1	0	2	1	1	0	1	2	2
Ipswich Town	42	10	5	6	33	25	9	3	9	24	28
Leeds City	4	2	0	0	3	0	0	2	0	2	2

Club	Home						Away				
	P	W	D	L	F	A	W	D	L	F	A
Leeds United	76	19	9	10	68	41	7	11	20	43	72
Leicester City	100	29	15	6	115	53	15	15	20	78	88
Leyton Orient	6	2	1	0	6	3	1	0	2	2	3
Lincoln City	26	10	3	0	39	11	3	4	6	18	31
Liverpool	136	31	22	15	107	63	18	11	39	74	132
Loughborough	10	5	0	0	26	1	2	1	2	7	13
Luton Town	38	16	1	2	46	19	6	7	6	21	28
Manchester City	138	41	15	13	132	68	23	19	27	93	103
Manchester United	146	44	11	18	151	84	12	20	41	70	143
Middlesbrough	90	29	11	5	111	43	13	13	19	55	68
Middlesbrough I	2	1	0	0	1	0	1	0	0	6	3
Millwall	4	1	1	0	2	0	2	0	0	4	2
New Brighton	6	3	0	0	11	1	1	0	2	3	4
Newcastle United	120	27	15	18	93	68	14	11	35	71	123
Northampton Town	2	0	1	0	1	1	0	1	0	1	1
Northwich Victoria	2	1	0	0	6	0	0	1	0	2	2
Norwich City	34	11	5	1	33	11	4	7	6	24	22
Nottingham Forest	82	23	12	6	76	38	16	7	18	52	57
Notts County	44	11	5	6	30	19	6	2	14	36	48
Oldham Athletic	16	3	4	1	10	7	0	5	3	3	10
Oxford United	6	2	1	0	4	1	0	2	1	0	3
Portsmouth	52	13	7	6	55	29	8	10	8	41	39
Preston North End	72	20	10	6	65	37	11	7	18	37	56
Queens Park Rangers	32	11	4	1	31	13	5	3	18	14	18
Rotherham	6	2	1	0	9	1	1	1	1	3	5
Sheffield United	88	28	7	9	106	49	8	12	24	60	97
Sheffield Wednesday	92	25	13	8	97	52	14	13	19	70	82
Southampton	44	12	8	2	36	18	8	4	10	30	31
Stockport County	12	6	0	0	20	4	1	3	2	3	6
Stoke City	74	27	5	5	74	21	9	13	15	38	47
Sunderland	108	27	12	15	103	60	10	18	26	65	110
Swansea City	4	1	0	1	2	3	1	0	1	2	3
Tottenham Hotspur	110	27	12	16	85	65	19	12	24	83	93
Walsall TS	14	4	3	0	19	4	1	0	6	9	20
Watford	12	2	1	3	9	10	1	0	5	6	14
West Bromwich Albion	104	30	13	9	112	63	19	12	21	65	76
West Ham United	76	17	12	9	66	47	13	13	12	57	57
Wimbledon	12	2	4	0	11	6	4	0	2	14	7
Wolverhampton W	90	24	13	8	108	65	16	11	18	67	81
Total	3524		412		3572		513		791		2954
		1024		326		1773		458		2272	

Arsenal Against Other Clubs - *FA Premiership*

Club		Home					Away				
	P	W	D	L	F	A	W	D	L	F	A
Aston Villa	4	0	0	2	1	3	1	0	1	2	2
Blackburn Rovers	4	1	0	1	1	1	0	1	1	1	2
Chelsea	4	2	0	0	3	1	1	0	1	2	1
Coventry City	4	1	0	1	3	3	1	0	1	2	1
Crystal Palace	2	1	0	0	3	0	1	0	0	2	1
Everton	4	2	0	0	4	0	0	2	0	1	1
Ipswich Town	4	1	1	0	4	0	2	0	0	7	2
Leeds United	4	1	1	0	2	1	0	0	2	1	5
Liverpool	4	1	0	1	1	1	1	1	0	2	0
Manchester City	4	1	1	0	1	0	1	0	1	1	0
Manchester United	4	0	1	1	2	3	0	1	1	0	1
Middlesbrough	2	0	1	0	1	1	0	0	1	0	1
Newcastle United	2	1	0	0	2	1	0	0	1	0	2
Norwich City	4	0	1	1	2	4	0	2	0	2	2
Nottingham Forest	2	0	1	0	1	1	1	0	0	1	0
Oldham Athletic	4	1	1	0	3	1	1	1	0	1	0
Queens Park Rangers	4	0	2	0	0	0	0	2	0	1	1
Sheffield United	4	1	1	0	4	1	0	2	0	2	2
Sheffield Wednesday	4	2	0	0	3	1	1	0	1	1	1
Southampton	4	2	0	0	5	3	1	0	1	4	2
Swindon Town	2	0	1	0	1	1	1	0	0	4	0
Tottenham Hotspur	4	0	1	1	2	4	1	0	1	1	1
West Ham United	2	0	0	1	0	2	0	1	0	0	0
Wimbledon	4	0	1	1	1	2	1	0	1	5	3
Total	84	18	14	10	50	35	15	14	13	43	31

Total Competitive Record

	P	W	D	L	F	A	W	D	L	F	A
Football League	3524	1024	412	326	3572	1773	513	458	791	2272	2954
Premiership	84	18	14	10	50	35	15	14	13	43	31
FA Cup	327	87	28	23	287	126	79	47	63	260	239
FA Cup Qualify	31	15	3	1	89	17	4	6	2	16	13
League Cup	140	51	13	11	141	51	25	22	18	98	76
Europe	64	23	4	4	73	22	10	11	12	43	30
Charity Shield	13	4	0	1	13	6	3	2	3	9	8
Totals	4183		474		4225		649		902		3351
		1222		376		2030		560		2741	

Arsenal's Full League Record

Season	Div	P	W	D	L	F	A	W	D	L	F	A	Pts	Pos
				Home					*Away*					
1893/94	2	28	9	1	4	33	19	3	3	8	19	36	28	9th
1894/95	2	30	11	3	1	54	20	3	3	9	21	28	34	8th
1895/96	2	30	11	1	3	43	11	3	3	9	16	31	29	7th
1896/97	2	30	10	1	4	42	20	3	3	9	26	50	30	10th
1897/98	2	30	10	4	1	41	14	6	1	8	28	35	37	5th
1898/99	2	34	14	2	1	55	10	4	3	10	17	31	41	7th
1899/00	2	34	13	1	3	47	12	3	3	11	14	31	36	8th
1900/01	2	34	13	3	1	30	11	2	3	12	9	24	36	7th
1901/02	2	34	13	2	2	35	9	5	5	8	15	17	42	4th
1902/03	2	34	14	2	1	46	9	6	6	5	20	21	48	3rd
1903/04	2	34	15	2	0	67	5	6	5	6	24	17	49	2nd
1904/05	1	34	9	5	3	19	12	3	4	10	17	28	33	10th
1905/06	1	38	12	4	3	43	21	3	3	13	19	43	37	12th
1906/07	1	38	15	1	3	38	15	5	3	11	28	44	44	7th
1907/08	1	38	9	8	2	32	18	3	4	12	19	45	36	14th=
1908/09	1	38	9	3	7	24	18	5	7	7	28	31	38	6th
1909/10	1	38	6	5	8	17	19	5	4	10	20	48	31	18th
1910/11	1	38	9	6	4	24	14	4	6	9	17	35	38	10th
1911/12	1	38	12	3	4	38	19	3	5	11	17	40	38	10th
1912/13	1	38	1	8	10	11	31	2	4	13	15	43	18	20th
1913/14	2	38	14	3	2	34	10	6	6	7	20	28	49	3rd
1914/15	2	38	15	1	3	52	13	4	4	11	17	28	43	5th
1919/20	1	42	11	5	5	32	21	4	7	10	24	37	42	10th
1920/21	1	42	9	7	5	31	25	6	7	8	28	38	44	9th
1921/22	1	42	10	6	5	27	19	5	1	15	20	37	37	17th
1922/23	1	42	13	4	4	38	16	3	6	12	23	46	42	11th
1923/24	1	42	8	5	8	25	24	4	4	13	15	39	33	19th
1924/25	1	42	12	3	6	33	17	2	2	17	13	41	33	20th
1925/26	1	42	16	2	3	57	19	6	6	9	30	44	52	2nd
1926/27	1	42	12	5	4	47	30	5	4	12	30	56	43	11th
1927/28	1	42	10	6	5	49	33	3	9	9	33	53	41	10th
1928/29	1	42	11	6	4	43	25	5	7	9	34	47	45	9th
1929/30	1	42	10	2	9	49	26	4	9	8	29	40	39	14th
1930/31	1	42	14	5	2	67	27	14	5	2	60	32	66	1st
1931/32	1	42	14	5	2	52	16	8	5	8	38	32	54	2nd
1932/33	1	42	14	3	4	70	27	11	5	5	48	34	58	1st
1933/34	1	42	15	4	2	55	19	10	5	6	30	28	59	1st
1934/35	1	42	15	4	2	74	17	8	8	5	41	29	58	1st
1935/36	1	42	9	9	3	44	22	6	6	9	34	26	45	6th

			Home					Away					
Season	Div	P	W	D	L	F	A	W	D	L	F	A	Pts	Pos
1936/37	1	42	10	10	1	43	20	8	6	7	37	29	52	3rd
1937/38	1	42	15	4	2	52	16	6	6	9	25	28	52	1st
1938/39	1	42	14	3	4	34	14	5	6	10	21	27	47	5th
1946/47	1	42	9	5	7	43	33	7	4	10	29	37	41	13th
1947/48	1	42	15	3	3	56	15	8	10	3	25	17	59	1st
1948/49	1	42	13	5	3	51	18	5	8	8	23	26	49	5th
1949/50	1	42	12	4	5	48	24	7	7	7	31	31	49	6th
1950/51	1	42	11	5	5	47	28	8	4	9	26	28	47	5th
1951/52	1	42	13	7	1	54	30	8	4	9	26	31	53	3rd
1952/53	1	42	15	3	3	60	30	6	9	6	37	34	54	1st
1953/54	1	42	8	8	5	42	37	7	5	9	33	36	43	12th
1954/55	1	42	12	3	6	44	25	5	6	10	25	38	43	9th
1955/56	1	42	13	4	4	38	22	5	6	10	22	39	46	5th
1956/57	1	42	12	5	4	45	21	9	3	9	40	48	50	5th
1957/58	1	42	10	4	7	48	39	6	3	12	25	46	39	12th
1958/59	1	42	14	3	4	53	29	7	5	9	35	39	50	3rd
1959/60	1	42	9	5	7	39	38	6	4	11	29	42	39	13th
1960/61	1	42	12	3	6	44	35	3	8	10	33	50	41	11th
1961/62	1	42	9	6	6	39	31	7	5	9	32	41	43	10th
1962/63	1	42	11	4	6	44	33	7	6	8	42	44	46	7th
1963/64	1	42	10	7	4	56	37	7	4	10	34	45	45	8th
1964/65	1	42	11	5	5	42	31	6	2	13	27	44	41	13th
1965/66	1	42	8	8	5	36	31	4	5	12	26	44	37	14th
1966/67	1	42	11	6	4	32	20	5	8	8	26	27	46	7th
1967/68	1	42	12	6	3	37	23	5	4	12	23	33	44	9th
1968/69	1	42	12	6	3	31	12	10	6	5	25	15	56	4th
1969/70	1	42	7	10	4	29	23	5	8	8	22	26	42	12th
1970/71	1	42	18	3	0	41	6	11	4	6	30	23	65	1st
1971/72	1	42	15	2	4	36	13	7	6	8	22	27	52	5th
1972/73	1	42	14	5	2	31	14	9	6	6	26	29	57	2nd
1973/74	1	42	9	7	5	23	16	5	7	9	26	35	42	10th
1974/75	1	42	10	6	5	31	16	3	5	13	16	33	37	16th
1975/76	1	42	11	4	6	33	19	2	6	13	14	34	36	17th
1976/77	1	42	11	6	4	37	20	5	5	11	27	39	43	8th
1977/78	1	42	14	5	2	38	12	7	5	9	22	25	52	5th
1978/79	1	42	11	8	2	37	18	6	6	9	24	30	48	7th
1979/80	1	42	8	9	4	24	12	10	7	4	28	24	52	5th
1980/81	1	42	13	8	0	36	17	6	7	8	25	28	53	3rd
1981/82	1	42	13	5	3	27	15	7	6	8	21	22	71	5th
1982/83	1	42	11	6	4	36	19	5	4	12	22	37	58	10th
1983/84	1	42	10	5	6	41	29	8	4	9	33	31	63	6th

		Home						Away						
Season	Div	P	W	D	L	F	A	W	D	L	F	A	Pts	Pos
1984/85	1	42	14	5	2	37	14	5	4	12	24	35	66	7th
1985/86	1	42	13	5	3	29	15	7	4	10	20	32	69	7th
1986/87	1	42	12	5	4	31	12	8	5	8	27	23	70	4th
1987/88	1	40	11	4	5	36	16	7	8	5	23	23	66	6th
1988/89	1	38	10	6	3	35	19	12	4	3	38	17	76	1st
1989/90	1	38	14	3	2	38	11	4	5	10	16	27	62	4th
1990/91	1	38	15	4	0	51	10	9	9	1	23	8	*83	1st
1991/92	1	42	12	7	2	51	22	7	8	6	30	24	72	4th
1992/93	FAPL	42	8	6	7	25	20	7	5	9	15	18	56	10th
1993/94	FAPL	42	10	8	3	25	15	8	9	4	28	13	71	4th

* 2 points deducted

Arsenal's League Cup Record

Season	P	W	D	L	F	A	Rnd	Season	P	W	D	L	F	A	Rnd
1966/67	4	1	2	1	8	5	3rd	1980/81	4	2	1	1	7	4	4th
1967/68	8	6	1	1	16	10	F	1981/82	5	2	1	2	3	4	4th
1968/69	7	5	1	1	17	7	F	1982/83	8	5	1	2	14	9	SF
1969/70	4	1	2	1	3	2	3rd	1983/84	4	2	1	1	5	4	4th
1970/71	5	2	2	1	5	2	4th	1984/85	3	1	1	1	7	4	3rd
1971/72	4	2	1	1	5	2	4th	1985/86	7	3	3	1	9	6	5th
1972/73	4	3	0	1	8	4	5th	1986/87	9	7	1	1	16	6	Win
1973/74	1	0	0	1	0	1	2nd	1987/88	8	7	0	1	15	4	F
1974/75	2	0	1	1	2	3	2nd	1988/89	5	2	2	1	7	4	3rd
1975/76	2	0	1	1	2	3	2nd	1989/90	4	3	0	1	10	4	4th
1976/77	6	3	2	1	9	6	5th	1990/91	4	3	0	1	10	7	4th
1977/78	7	4	2	1	12	5	SF	1991/92	3	1	1	1	3	2	3rd
1978/79	1	0	0	1	1	3	2nd	1992/93	9	6	3	0	15	6	Win
1979/80	7	3	3	1	18	7	5th	1993/94	5	2	2	1	10	3	4th

Arsenal's League Cup Record

Round	Opponents	Venue	Result	
1966/67				
2nd Round	Gillingham	H	Draw	0-0
Replay	Gillingham	A	Draw	1-1
2nd Replay	Gillingham	H	Win	5-0
3rd Round	West Ham United	H	Lose	1-3
1967/68				
2nd Round	Coventry City	A	Win	2-1
3rd Round	Reading	H	Win	1-0
4th Round	Blackburn Rovers	H	Win	2-1
5th Round	Burnley	A	Draw	3-3
Replay	Burnley	H	Win	2-1
S/F 1st Leg	Huddersfield Town	H	Win	3-2
S/F 2nd Leg	Huddersfield Town	A	Win	3-1
Final	Leeds United	N	Lose	0-1
1968/69				
2nd Round	Sunderland	H	Win	1-0
3rd Round	Scunthorpe United	A	Win	6-1
4th Round	Liverpool	H	Win	2-1
5th Round	Blackpool	H	Win	5-1
S/F 1st Leg	Tottenham Hotspur	H	Win	1-0
S/F 2nd Leg	Tottenham Hotspur	A	Draw	1-1
Final	Swindon Town	N	Lose	1-3
1969/70				
2nd Round	Southampton	A	Draw	1-1
Replay	Southampton	H	Win	2-0
3rd Round	Everton	H	Draw	0-0
Replay	Everton	A	Lose	0-1
1970/71				
2nd Round	Ipswich Town	A	Draw	0-0
Replay	Ipswich Town	H	Win	4-0
3rd Round	Luton Town	A	Win	1-0
4th Round	Crystal Palace	A	Draw	0-0
Replay	Crystal Palace	H	Lose	0-2
1971/72				
2nd Round	Barnsley	H	Win	1-0
3rd Round	Newcastle United	H	Win	4-0
4th Round	Sheffield United	H	Draw	0-0
Replay	Sheffield United	A	Lose	0-2

Round	Opponents	Venue	Result	
1972/73				
2nd Round	Everton	H	Win	1-0
3rd Round	Rotherham United	H	Win	5-0
4th Round	Sheffield United	A	Win	2-1
5th Round	Norwich City	H	Lose	0-3
1973/74				
2nd Round	Tranmere Rovers	H	Lose	0-1
1974/75				
2nd Round	Leicester City	H	Draw	1-1
Replay	Leicester City	A	Lose	1-2
1975/76				
2nd Round	Everton	A	Draw	2-2
Replay	Everton	H	Lose	0-1
1976/77				
2nd Round	Carlisle United	H	Win	3-2
3rd Round	Blackpool	A	Draw	1-1
Replay	Blackpool	H	Draw	0-0
2nd Replay	Blackpool	H	Win	2-0
4th Round	Chelsea	H	Win	2-1
5th Round	Queens Park Rangers	A	Lose	1-2
1977/78				
2nd Round	Manchester United	H	Win	3-2
3rd Round	Southampton	H	Win	2-0
4th Round	Hull City	H	Win	5-1
5th Round	Manchester City	A	Draw	0-0
Replay	Manchester City	H	Win	1-0
S/F 1st Leg	Liverpool	A	Lose	1-2
S/F 2nd Leg	Liverpool	H	Draw	0-0
1978/79				
2nd Round	Rotherham United	A	Lose	1-3
1979/80				
2nd Rd 1st Leg	Leeds United	A	Draw	1-1
2nd Rd 2nd Leg	Leeds United	H	Win	7-0
3rd Round	Southampton	H	Win	2-1
4th Round	Brighton & Hove Albion	A	Draw	0-0
Replay	Brighton & Hove Albion	H	Win	4-0
5th Round	Swindon Town	H	Draw	1-1
Replay	Swindon Town	A	Lose	3-4

Round	Opponents	Venue	Result	
1980/81				
2nd Rd 1st Leg	Swansea City	A	Draw	1-1
2nd Rd 2nd Leg	Swansea CIty	H	Win	3-1
3rd Round	Stockport County	A	Win	3-1
4th Round	Tottenham Hotspur	A	Lose	0-1
1981/82 Milk Cup				
2nd Rd 1st Leg	Sheffield United	A	Lose	0-1
2nd Rd 2nd Leg	Sheffield United	H	Win	2-0
3rd Round	Norwich City	H	Win	1-0
4th Round	Liverpool	H	Draw	0-0
Replay	Liverpool	A	Lose	0-3
1982/83 Milk Cup				
2nd Rd 1st Leg	Cardiff City	H	Win	2-1
2nd Rd 2nd Leg	Cardiff City	A	Win	3-1
3rd Round	Everton	A	Draw	1-1
Replay	Everton	H	Win	3-0
4th Round	Huddersfield Town	H	Win	1-0
5th Round	Sheffield Wednesday	H	Win	1-0
S/F 1st Leg	Manchester United	H	Lose	2-4
S/F 2nd Leg	Manchester United	A	Lose	1-2
1983/84 Milk Cup				
2nd Rd 1st Leg	Plymouth Argyle	A	Draw	1-1
2nd Rd 2nd Leg	Plymouth Argyle	H	Win	1-0
3rd Round	Tottenham Hotspur	A	Win	2-1
4th Round	Walsall	H	Lose	1-2
1984/85 Milk Cup				
2nd Rd 1st Leg	Bristol Rovers	H	Win	4-0
2nd Rd 2nd Leg	Bristol Rovers	A	Draw	1-1
3rd Round	Oxford United	A	Lose	2-3
1985/86 Milk Cup				
2nd Rd 1st Leg	Hereford United	A	Draw	0-0
2nd Rd 2nd Leg	Hereford United	H	Win	2-1
3rd Round	Manchester City	A	Win	2-1
4th Round	Southampton	H	Draw	0-0
Replay	Southampton	A	Win	3-1
5th Round	Aston Villa	A	Draw	1-1
Replay	Aston Villa	H	Lose	1-2

Round	Opponents	Venue	Result	
1986/87 Littlewoods Cup				
2nd Rd 1st Leg	Huddersfield Town	H	Win	2-0
2nd Rd 2nd Leg	Huddersfield Town	A	Draw	1-1
3rd Round	Manchester City	H	Win	3-1
4th Round	Charlton Athletic	H	Win	2-0
5th Round	Nottingham Forest	H	Win	2-0
S/F 1st Leg	Tottenham Hotspur	H	Lose	0-1
S/F 2nd Leg	Tottenham Hotspur	A	Win	2-1
Replay	Tottenham Hotspur	A	Win	2-1
Final	Liverpool	N	Win	2-1
1987/88 Littlewoods Cup				
2nd Rd 1st Leg	Doncaster Rovers	A	Win	3-0
2nd Rd 2nd Leg	Doncaster Rovers	H	Win	1-0
3rd Round	Bournemouth	H	Win	3-0
4th Round	Stoke City	H	Win	1-0
5th Round	Sheffield Wednesday	A	Win	1-0
S/F 1st Leg	Everton	A	Win	1-0
S/F 2nd Leg	Everton	H	Win	3-1
Final	Luton Town	N	Lose	2-3
1988/89 Littlewoods Cup				
2nd Rd 1st Leg	Hull City	A	Win	2-1
2nd Rd 2nd Leg	Hull City	H	Win	3-0
3rd Round	Liverpool	A	Draw	1-1
Replay	Liverpool	H	Draw	0-0
2nd Replay	Liverpool	N*	Lose	1-2
*At Aston Villa				
1989/90 Littlewoods Cup				
2nd Rd 1st leg	Plymouth Argyle	H	Win	2-0
2nd Rd 2nd Leg	Plymouth Argyle	A	Win	6-1
3rd Round	Liverpool	H	Win	1-0
4th Round	Oldham Athletic	A	Lose	1-3
1990/91 Rumbelows Cup				
2nd Rd 1st Leg	Chester City	A	Win	1-0
2nd Rd 2nd Leg	Chester City	H	Win	5-0
3rd Round	Manchester City	A	Win	2-1
4th Round	Manchester United	H	Lose	2-6
1991/92 Rumbelows Cup				
2nd Rd 1st Leg	Leicester City	A	Draw	1-1
2nd Rd 2nd Leg	Leicester City	H	Win	2-0
3rd Round	Coventry City	A	Lose	0-1

Round	Opponents	Venue	Result	
1992/93 Coca Cola Cup				
2nd Rd 1st Leg	Millwall	H	Draw	1-1
2nd Rd 2nd Leg	Millwall	A	Draw	1-1*
*Arsenal won 3-1 on pens.				
3rd Round	Derby County	A	Draw	1-1
Replay	Derby County	H	Win	2-1
4th Round	Scarborough	A	Win	1-0
5th Round	Nottingham Forest	H	Win	2-0
S/F 1st Leg	Crystal Palace	A	Win	3-1
S/F 2nd Leg	Crystal Palace	H	Win	2-0
Final	Sheffield Wednesday	N	Win	2-1
1993/94 Coca Cola Cup				
2nd Rd 1st Leg	Huddersfield Town	A	Win	5-0
2nd Rd 2nd Leg	Huddersfield Town	H	Draw	1-1
3rd Round	Norwich City	H	Draw	1-1
Replay	Norwich City	A	Win	3-0
4th Round	Aston Villa	H	Lose	0-1

League Cup full playing record up to end of 1993/94 season

	P	W	D	L	F	A
Total	140	76	35	29	236	126

Arsenal's FA Cup Record

Round	Opponents	Venue	Result	
1889/90				
1st QR	Lyndhurst	H	Win	11-0
2nd QR	Thorpe	A	Draw	2-2
(Thorpe withdrew from competition)				
3rd QR	Crusaders	H	Win	5-2
4th QR	Swifts	H	Lose	1-5
1890/91				
1st Round	Derby County	H	Lose	1-2
1891/92				
1st Round	Small Heath	A	Lose	1-5
1892/93				
1st QR	Highland Light Infantry	H	Win	3-0
2nd QR	City Ramblers	H	Win	10-1
3rd QR	Millwall	H	Win	3-2
4th QR	Clapton	H	Win	4-0
1st Round	Sunderland	A	Lose	0-6

Round	Opponents	Venue	Result	
1893/94				
1st QR	Ashford University	H	Win	12-0
2nd QR	Clapton	H	Win	6-2
3rd QR	Millwall	H	Win	2-0
4th QR	2nd Scots Guards	A	Win	2-1
1st Round	Sheffield Wednesday	H	Lose	1-2
1894/95				
1st Round	Bolton Wanderers	A	Lose	0-1
1895/96				
1st Round	Burnley	A	Lose	1-6
1896/97				
1st QR	Leyton	H	Win	5-2
2nd QR	Chatham	H	Win	4-0
3rd QR	Millwall	A	Lose	2-4
1897/98				
2nd QR	St Albans	H	Win	9-0
3rd QR	Sheppey United	H	Win	3-0
4th QR	New Brompton	H	Win	4-2
1st Round	Burnley	A	Lose	1-3
1898/99				
1st Round	Derby County	H	Lose	0-6
1899/00				
Qual. Round	New Brompton	H	Draw	1-1
Replay	New Brompton	A	Draw	0-0
2nd Replay	New Brompton	A	Draw	2-2
3rd Replay	New Brompton	A	Draw	1-1
4th Replay	New Brompton	A	Lose	0-1
1900/01				
Qual. Round	Darwen	A	Win	2-0
1st Round	Blackburn Rovers	H	Win	2-0
2nd Round	West Bromwich Alb.	H	Lose	0-1
1901/02				
Qual. Round	Luton Town	H	Draw	1-1
Replay	Luton Town	A	Win	2-0
1st Round	Newcastle United	H	Lose	0-2
1902/03				
Qual. Round	Brentford	A	Draw	1-1
Replay	Brentford	H	Win	5-0
1st Round	Sheffield United	H	Lose	1-3

Round	Opponents	Venue	Result	
1903/04				
Qual. Round	Bristol Rovers	A	Draw	1-1
Replay	Bristol Rovers	H	Draw	1-1
2nd Replay	Bristol Rovers	A	Win	1-0
1st Round	Fulham	H	Win	1-0
2nd Round	Manchester City	H	Lose	0-2
1904/05				
1st Round	Bristol City	H	Draw	0-0
Replay	Bristol City	A	Lose	0-1
1905/06				
1st Round	West Ham United	H	Draw	1-1
Replay	West Ham United	A	Win	3-2
2nd Round	Watford	H	Win	3-0
3rd Round	Sunderland	H	Win	5-0
4th Round	Manchester United	A	Win	3-2
Semi-Final	Newcastle United	N*	Lose	0-2
At Stoke				
1906/07				
1st Round	Grimsby Town	A	Draw	1-1
Replay	Grimsby Town	H	Win	3-0
2nd Round	Bristol City	H	Win	2-1
3rd Round	Bristol Rovers	H	Win	1-0
4th Round	Barnsley	A	Win	2-1
Semi-Final	Sheffield Wednesday	N*	Lose	1-3
At Birmingham				
1907/08				
1st Round	Hull City	H	Draw	0-0
Replay	Hull City	A	Lose	1-4
1908/09				
1st Round	Croydon Common	A	Draw	1-1
Replay	Croydon Common	H	Win	2-0
2nd Round	Millwall	H	Draw	1-1
Replay	Millwall	A	Lose	0-1
1909/10				
1st Round	Watford	H	Win	3-0
2nd Round	Everton	A	Lose	0-5

Round	Opponents	Venue	Result	
1910/11				
1st Round	Clapton Orient	A	Win	2-1
2nd Round	Swindon Town	A	Lose	0-1
1911/12				
1st Round	Bolton Wanderers	A	Lose	0-1
1912/13				
1st Round	Croydon Common	A	Draw	0-0
Replay	Croydon Common	H	Win	2-1
2nd Round	Liverpool	H	Lose	1-4
1913/14				
1st Round	Bradford Park Avenue	A	Lose	0-2
1914/15				
1st Round	Merthyr Town	H	Win	3-0
2nd Round	Chelsea	A	Lose	0-1
1919/20				
1st Round	Rochdale	H	Win	4-2
2nd Round	Bristol City	A	Lose	0-1
1920/21				
1st Round	Queens Park Rangers	A	Lose	0-2
1921/22				
1st Round	Queens Park Rangers	H	Draw	0-0
Replay	Queens Park Rangers	A	Win	2-1
2nd Round	Bradford City	A	Win	3-2
3rd Round	Leicester City	H	Win	3-0
4th Round	Preston North End	H	Draw	1-1
Replay	Preston North End	A	Lose	1-2
1922/23				
1st Round	Liverpool	A	Draw	0-0
Replay	Liverpool	H	Lose	1-4
1923/24				
1st Round	Luton Town	H	Win	4-1
2nd Round	Cardiff City	A	Lose	0-1
1924/25				
1st Round	West Ham United	A	Draw	0-0
Replay	West Ham United	H	Draw	2-2
2nd Replay	West Ham United	N	Lose	0-1
1925/26				
3rd Round	Wolverhampton W	A	Draw	1-1
Replay	Wolverhampton W	H	Win	1-0

Round	Opponents	Venue	Result	
4th Round	Blackburn Rovers	H	Win	3-1
5th Round	Aston Villa	A	Draw	1-1
Replay	Aston Villa	H	Win	2-0
6th Round	Swansea	A	Lose	1-2
1926/27				
3rd Round	Sheffield United	A	Win	3-2
4th Round	Port Vale	A	Draw	2-2
Replay	Port Vale	H	Win	1-0
5th Round	Liverpool	H	Win	2-0
6th Round	Wolverhampton W	H	Win	2-1
Semi-Final	Southampton	N*	Win	2-1
At Chelsea				
Final	Cardiff	N	Lose	0-1
1927/28				
3rd Round	West Bromwich Albion	H	Win	2-0
4th Round	Everton	H	Win	4-3
5th Round	Aston Villa	H	Win	4-1
6th Round	Stoke City	H	Win	4-1
Semi-Final	Blackburn Rovers	N	Lose	0-1
1928/29				
3rd Round	Stoke City	H	Win	2-1
4th Round	Mansfield Town	H	Win	2-0
5th Round	Swindon Town	A	Draw	0-0
Replay	Swindon Town	H	Win	1-0
6th Round	Aston Villa	A	Lose	0-1
1929/30				
3rd Round	Chelsea	H	Win	2-0
4th Round	Birmingham City	H	Draw	2-2
Replay	Birmingham City	A	Win	1-0
5th Round	Middlesbrough	A	Win	2-0
6th Round	West Ham United	A	Win	3-0
Semi-Final	Hull City	N*	Draw	2-2
At Leeds				
Replay	Hull City	N*	Win	1-0
At Aston Villa				
Final	Huddersfield Town	N	Win	2-0
1930/31				
3rd Round	Aston Villa	H	Draw	2-2
Replay	Aston Villa	A	Win	3-1
4th Round	Chelsea	A	Lose	1-2

Round	Opponents	Venue	Result	
1931/32				
3rd Round	Darwen	H	Win	11-1
4th Round	Plymouth	H	Win	4-2
5th Round	Portsmouth	A	Win	2-0
6th Round	Huddersfield Town	A	Win	1-0
Semi-Final	Manchester City	N*	Win	1-0
At Aston Villa				
Final	Newcastle United	N	Lose	1-2
1932/33				
3rd Round	Walsall	A	Lose	0-2
1933/34				
3rd Round	Luton Town	A	Win	1-0
4th Round	Crystal Palace	H	Win	7-0
5th Round	Derby County	H	Win	1-0
6th Round	Aston Villa	H	Lose	1-2
1934/35				
3rd Round	Brighton & Hove Albion	A	Win	2-0
4th Round	Leicester City	A	Win	1-0
5th Round	Reading	A	Win	1-0
6th Round	Sheffield Wednesday	A	Lose	1-2
1935/36				
3rd Round	Bristol Rovers	A	Win	5-1
4th Round	Liverpool	A	Win	2-0
5th Round	Newcastle United	A	Draw	3-3
Replay	Newcastle United	H	Win	3-0
6th Round	Barnsley	H	Win	4-1
Semi-Final	Grimsby Town	N*	Win	1-0
At Huddersfield				
Final	Sheffield United	N	Win	1-0
1936/37				
3rd Round	Chesterfield	A	Win	5-1
4th Round	Manchester United	H	Win	5-0
5th Round	Burnley	A	Win	7-1
6th Round	West Bromwich Albion	A	Lose	1-3
1937/38				
3rd Round	Bolton Wanderers	H	Win	3-1
4th Round	Wolverhampton W	A	Win	2-1
5th Round	Preston North End	H	Lose	0-1

Round	Opponents	Venue	Result	
1938/39				
3rd Round	Chelsea	A	Lose	1-2
1945/46				
3rd Round	West Ham United	A	Lose	0-6
3rd Round	West Ham United	H	Win	1-0
Played on two leg basis				
1946/47				
3rd Round	Chelsea	A	Draw	1-1
Replay	Chelsea	H	Draw	1-1
2nd Replay	Chelsea	N	Lose	0-2
1947/48				
3rd Round	Bradford City	H	Lose	0-1
1948/49				
3rd Round	Tottenham Hotspur	H	Win	3-0
4th Round	Derby County	A	Lose	0-1
1949/50				
3rd Round	Sheffield Wednesday	H	Win	1-0
4th Round	Swansea Town	H	Win	2-1
5th Round	Burnley	H	Win	2-0
6th Round	Leeds United	H	Win	1-0
Semi-Final	Chelsea	N	Draw	2-2
Replay	Chelsea	N*	Win	1-0
At Tottenham				
Final	Liverpool	N	Win	2-0
1950/51				
3rd Round	Carlisle United	H	Draw	0-0
Replay	Carlisle United	A	Win	4-1
4th Round	Northampton Town	H	Win	3-2
5th Round	Manchester United	A	Lose	0-1
1951/52				
3rd Round	Norwich City	A	Win	5-0
4th Round	Barnsley	H	Win	4-0
5th Round	Leyton Orient	A	Win	3-0
6th Round	Luton Town	A	Win	3-2
Semi-Final	Chelsea	N*	Draw	1-1
At Tottenham				
Replay	Chelsea	N*	Win	3-0
At Tottenham				
Final	Newcastle United	N	Lose	0-1

Round	Opponents	Venue	Result	
1952/53				
3rd Round	Doncaster Rovers	H	Win	4-0
4th Round	Bury	H	Win	6-2
5th Round	Burnley	A	Win	2-0
6th Round	Blackpool	H	Lose	1-2
1953/54				
3rd Round	Aston Villa	H	Win	5-1
4th Round	Norwich City	H	Lose	1-2
1954/55				
3rd Round	Cardiff City	H	Win	1-0
4th Round	Wolverhampton W	A	Lose	0-1
1955/56				
3rd Round	Bedford Town	H	Draw	2-2
Replay	Bedford Town	A	Win	2-1
4th Round	Aston Villa	H	Win	4-1
5th Round	Charlton Athletic	A	Win	2-0
6th Round	Birmingham City	H	Lose	1-3
1956/57				
3rd Round	Stoke City	H	Win	4-2
4th Round	Newport County	A	Win	2-0
5th Round	Preston North End	A	Draw	3-3
Replay	Preston North End	H	Win	2-1
6th Round	West Bromwich Albion	A	Draw	2-2
Replay	West Bromwich Albion	H	Lose	1-2
1957/58				
3rd Round	Northampton Town	A	Lose	1-3
1958/59				
3rd Round	Bury	A	Win	1-0
4th Round	Colchester United	A	Draw	2-2
Replay	Colchester United	H	Win	4-0
5th Round	Sheffield United	H	Draw	2-2
Replay	Sheffield United	A	Lose	0-3
1959/60				
3rd Round	Rotherham United	A	Draw	2-2
Replay	Rotherham United	H	Draw	1-1
2nd Replay	Rotherham United	N	Lose	0-2
At Sheffield Wednesday				
1960/61				
3rd Round	Sunderland	A	Lose	1-3

Round	Opponents	Venue	Result	
1961/62				
3rd Round	Bradford City	H	Win	3-0
4th Round	Manchester United	A	Lose	0-1
1962/63				
3rd Round	Oxford United	H	Win	5-1
4th Round	Sheffield Wednesday	H	Win	2-0
5th Round	Liverpool	H	Lose	1-2
1963/64				
3rd Round	Wolverhampton W	H	Win	2-1
4th Round	West Bromwich Albion	A	Draw	3-3
Replay	West Bromwich Albion	H	Win	2-0
5th Round	Liverpool	H	Lose	0-1
1964/65				
3rd Round	Darlington	A	Win	2-0
4th Round	Peterborough United	A	Lose	1-2
1965/66				
3rd Round	Blackburn Rovers	A	Lose	0-3
1966/67				
3rd Round	Bristol Rovers	A	Win	3-0
4th Round	Bolton Wanderers	A	Draw	0-0
Replay	Bolton Wanderers	H	Win	3-0
5th Round	Birmingham City	A	Lose	0-1
1967/68				
3rd Round	Shrewsbury Town	A	Draw	1-1
Replay	Shrewsbury Town	H	Win	2-0
4th Round	Swansea Town	A	Win	1-0
5th Round	Birmingham City	H	Draw	1-1
Replay	Birmingham City	A	Lose	1-2
1968/69				
3rd Round	Cardiff City	A	Draw	0-0
Replay	Cardiff City	H	Win	2-0
4th Round	Charlton Athletic	H	Win	2-0
5th Round	West Bromwich Albion	A	Lose	0-1
1969/70				
3rd Round	Blackpool	H	Draw	1-1
Replay	Blackpool	A	Lose	2-3
1970/71				
3rd Round	Yeovil Town	A	Win	3-0
4th Round	Portsmouth	A	Draw	1-1

Round	Opponents	Venue	Result	
Replay	Portsmouth	H	Win	3-2
5th Round	Manchester City	A	Win	2-1
6th Round	Leicester City	A	Draw	0-0
Replay	Leicester City	H	Win	1-0
Semi-Final	Stoke City	N*	Draw	2-2
*At Sheffield Wednesday				
Replay	Stoke City	N*	Win	2-0
*At Aston Villa				
Final	Liverpool	N	Win	2-1
1971/72				
3rd Round	Swindon Town	A	Win	2-0
4th Round	Reading	A	Win	2-0
5th Round	Derby County	A	Draw	2-2
Replay	Derby County	H	Draw	0-0
2nd Replay	Derby County	N	Win	1-0
*At Leicester City				
6th Round	Orient	A	Win	1-0
Semi-Final	Stoke City	N	Draw	1-1
*At Aston Villa				
Replay	Stoke City	N	Win	2-1
*At Everton				
Final	Leeds United	N	Lose	0-1
1972/73				
3rd Round	Leicester City	H	Draw	2-2
Replay	Leicester City	A	Win	2-1
4th Round	Bradford City	H	Win	2-0
5th Round	Carlisle United	A	Win	2-1
6th Round	Chelsea	A	Draw	2-2
Replay	Chelsea	H	Win	2-1
Semi-Final	Sunderland	N	Lose	1-2
*At Sheffield Wednesday				
1973/74				
3rd Round	Norwich City	A	Win	1-0
4th Round	Aston Villa	H	Draw	1-1
Replay	Aston Villa	A	Lose	0-2
1974/75				
3rd Round	York City	H	Draw	1-1
Replay	York City	A	Win	3-1
4th Round	Coventry City	A	Draw	1-1
Replay	Coventry City	H	Win	3-0
5th Round	Leicester City	H	Draw	0-0

Round	Opponents	Venue	Result	
Replay	Leicester City	A	Draw	1-1
2nd Replay	Leicester City	A	Win	1-0
6th Round	West Ham United	H	Lose	0-2
1975/76				
3rd Round	Wolverhampton W	A	Lose	0-3
1976/77				
3rd Round	Notts County	A	Win	1-0
4th Round	Coventry City	H	Win	3-1
5th Round	Middlesbrough	A	Lose	1-4
1977/78				
3rd Round	Sheffield United	A	Win	5-0
4th Round	Wolverhampton W	H	Win	2-1
5th Round	Walsall	H	Win	4-1
6th Round	Wrexham	A	Win	3-2
Semi-Final	Orient	N*	Win	3-0
*At Chelsea				
Final	Ipswich Town	N	Lose	0-1
1978/79				
3rd Round	Sheffield Wednesday	A	Draw	1-1
Replay	Sheffield Wednesday	H	Draw	1-1
2nd Replay	Sheffield Wednesday	N*	Draw	2-2
*At Leicester City				
3rd Replay	Sheffield Wednesday	N*	Draw	3-3
*At Leicester City				
4th Replay	Sheffield Wednesday	N*	Win	2-0
*At Leicester City				
4th Round	Notts County	H	Win	2-0
5th Round	Nottingham Forest	A	Win	1-0
6th Round	Southampton	A	Draw	1-1
Replay	Southampton	H	Win	2-0
Semi-Final	Wolverhampton Wand	N*	Win	2-0
*At Aston Villa				
Final	Manchester United	N	Win	3-2
1979/80				
3rd Round	Cardiff City	A	Draw	0-0
Replay	Cardiff City	H	Win	2-1
4th Round	Brighton & Hove Albion	H	Win	2-0
5th Round	Bolton Wanderers	A	Draw	1-1
Replay	Bolton Wanderers	H	Win	3-0
6th Round	Watford	A	Win	2-1

Round	Opponents	Venue	Result	
Semi-Final	Liverpool	N*	Draw	0-0
*At Sheffield Wed				
Replay	Liverpool	N*	Draw	1-1
*At Aston Villa				
2nd Replay	Liverpool	N*	Draw	1-1
*At Aston Villa				
3rd Replay	Liverpool	N*	Win	1-0
*At Coventry City				
Final	West Ham United	N	Lose	0-1
1980/81				
3rd Round	Everton	A	Lose	0-2
1981/82				
3rd Round	Tottenham Hotspur	A	Lose	0-1
1982/83				
3rd Round	Bolton Wanderers	H	Win	2-1
4th Round	Leeds United	H	Draw	1-1
Replay	Leeds United	A	Draw	0-0
2nd Replay	Leeds United	A	Win	2-1
5th Round	Middlesbrough	A	Draw	1-1
Replay	Middlesbrough	H	Win	3-2
6th Round	Aston Villa	H	Win	2-0
Semi-Final	Manchester United	N*	Lose	1-2
*At Aston Villa				
1983/84				
3rd Round	Middlesbrough	A	Lose	2-3
1984/85				
3rd Round	Hereford United	A	Draw	1-1
Replay	Hereford United	H	Win	7-2
4th Round	York City	A	Lose	0-1
1985/86				
3rd Round	Grimsby Town	A	Win	4-3
4th Round	Rotherham United	H	Win	5-1
5th Round	Luton Town	A	Draw	2-2
Replay	Luton Town	H	Draw	0-0
2nd Replay	Luton Town	A	Lose	0-3
1986/87				
3rd Round	Reading	A	Win	3-1
4th Round	Plymouth Argyle	H	Win	6-1
5th Round	Barnsley	H	Win	2-0
6th Round	Watford	H	Lose	1-3

Round	Opponents	Venue	Result	
1987/88				
3rd Round	Millwall	H	Win	2-0
4th Round	Brighton & Hove Albion	A	Win	2-1
5th Round	Manchester United	H	Win	2-1
6th Round	Nottingham Forest	H	Lose	1-2
1988/89				
3rd Round	West Ham United	A	Draw	2-2
Replay	West Ham United	H	Lose	0-1
1989/90				
3rd Round	Stoke City	A	Win	1-0
4th Round	Queens Park Rangers	H	Draw	0-0
Replay	Queens Park Rangers	A	Lose	0-2
1990/91				
3rd Round	Sunderland	H	Win	2-1
4th Round	Leeds United	H	Draw	0-0
Replay	Leeds United	A	Draw	1-1
2nd Replay	Leeds United	H	Draw	0-0
3rd Replay	Leeds United	A	Win	2-1
5th Round	Shrewsbury Town	A	Win	1-0
6th Round	Cambridge United	H	Win	2-1
Semi-Final	Tottenham Hotspur	N*	Lose	1-3
*At Wembley				
1991/92				
3rd Round	Wrexham	A	Lose	1-2
1992/93				
3rd Round	Yeovil Town	A	Win	3-1
4th Round	Leeds United	H	Draw	2-2
Replay	Leeds United	A	Win	3-2
5th Round	Nottingham Forest	H	Win	2-0
6th Round	Ipswich Town	A	Win	4-2
Semi-Final	Tottenham Hotspur	N*	Win	1-0
*At Wembley				
Final	Sheffield Wednesday	N	Draw	1-1
Replay	Sheffield Wednesday	N	Win	2-1

Summary of playing record in FA Cup, including qualifying games, up to end of 1993/94 season.

	P	W	D	L	F	A
Total	358	185	84	89	652	396

Arsenal in Europe – *European Cup*

Round	Leg	Opponents	Venue	Result	
1971/72					
1st	1st	Stromsgodset Drammen	A	Win	3-1
1st	2nd	Stromsgodset Drammen	H	Win	4-0
2nd	1st	Grasshoppers	A	Win	2-0
2nd	2nd	Grasshoppers	H	Win	3-0
3rd	1st	Ajax	A	Lose	1-2
3rd	2nd	Ajax	H	Lose	0-1
1991/92					
1st	1st	FK Austria	H	Win	6-1
1st	2nd	FK Austria	A	Lose	0-1
2nd	1st	Benfica	A	Draw	1-1
2nd	2nd	Benfica	H	Lose	1-3

Arsenal in Europe – *European Cup-Winners' Cup*

Round	Leg	Opponents	Venue	Result	
1979/80					
1st	1st	Fenerbahce	H	Win	2-0
1st	2nd	Fenerbahce	A	Draw	0-0
2nd	1st	Magdeburg	H	Win	2-1
2nd	2nd	Magdeburg	A	Draw	2-2
3rd	1st	IFK Gothenburg	H	Win	5-1
3rd	2nd	IFK Gothenburg	A	Draw	0-0
S/F	1st	Juventus	H	Draw	1-1
S/F	2nd	Juventus	A	Win	1-0
Final		Valencia	Brussels	Lose	0-0*

after extra time, lost 4-5 in penalty shoot-out

Round	Leg	Opponents	Venue	Result	
1993/94					
1st	1st	Odense Boldklub	A	Win	2-1
1st	2nd	Odense Boldklub	H	Draw	1-1
2nd	1st	Standard Liege	H	Win	3-0
2nd	2nd	Standard Liege	A	Win	7-0
3rd	1st	Torino	A	Draw	0-0
3rd	2nd	Torino	H	Win	1-0
S/F	1st	Paris St Germain	A	Draw	1-1
S/F	2nd	Paris St Germain	H	Win	1-0
Final		Parma	Copenhagen	Win	1-0

Arsenal in Europe – *Inter-Cities Fairs Cup*

Round	Leg	Opponents	Venue	Result	
1963/64					
1st	1st	Staevnet	A	Win	7-1
1st	2nd	Staevnet	H	Lose	2-3
1st	1st	R.F.C. Liege	H	Draw	1-1
1st	2nd	R.F.C. Liege	A	Lose	1-3

Arsenal in Europe – *European Fairs Cup*

Round	Leg	Opponents	Venue	Result	
1969/70					
1st	1st	Glentoran	H	Win	3-0
1st	2nd	Glentoran	A	Lose	0-1
2nd	1st	Sporting Lisbon	A	Draw	0-0
2nd	2nd	Sporting Lisbon	H	Win	3-0
3rd	1st	Rouen	A	Draw	0-0
3rd	2nd	Rouen	H	Win	1-0
4th	1st	Dinamo Bacau	A	Win	2-0
4th	2nd	Dinamo Bacau	H	Win	7-1
S/F	1st	Ajax	H	Win	3-0
S/F	2nd	Ajax	A	Lose	0-1
Final	1st	Anderlecht	A	Lose	1-3
Final	2nd	Anderlecht	H	Win	3-0
1970/71					
1st	1st	Lazio	A	Draw	2-2
1st	2nd	Lazio	H	Win	2-0
2nd	1st	Sturm Graz	A	Lose	0-1
2nd	2nd	Sturm Graz	H	Win	2-0
3rd	1st	Beveren-Waas	H	Win	4-0
3rd	2nd	Beveren-Waas	A	Win	0-0
4th	1st	IFC Cologne	H	Win	2-1
4th	2nd	IFC Cologne	A	Lose	0-1*

lost on away goals rule

Arsenal in Europe – *UEFA Cup*

Round	Leg	Opponents	Venue	Result	
1978/79					
1st	1st	Lokomotive Leipzig	H	Win	3-0
1st	2nd	Lokomotive Leipzig	A	Win	4-1
2nd	1st	Hajduk Split	A	Lose	1-2
2nd	2nd	Hajduk Split	H	Win	1-0*
3rd	1st	Red Star Belgrade	A	Lose	0-1
3rd	2nd	Red Star Belgrade	H	Draw	1-1
*won on away goals rule					
1981/82					
1st	1st	Panathinaikos	A	Win	2-0
1st	2nd	Panathinaikos	H	Win	1-0
2nd	1st	Winterslag	A	Lose	0-1
1st	2nd	Winterslag	H	Win	2-1*
*lost on away goals rule					
1982/83					
1st	1st	Spartak Moscow	A	Lose	2-3
1st	2nd	Spartak Moscow	H	Lose	2-5

Cup Final Teams – *FA Cup*

Date	Opponents	Result	
23rd April 1927	CARDIFF CITY	Lost	0-1

Team: Lewis, Parker, Kennedy, Baker, Butler, John, Hulme, Buchan, Brain, Blyth, Hoar.

| 23rd April 1932 | NEWCASTLE UNITED | Lost | 1-2 |

Team: Moss, Parker, Hapgood, Jones, Roberts, Male, Hulme, Jack, Lambert, Bastin, Jack. *Scorer:* John

| 25th April 1936 | SHEFFIELD UNITED | Won | 1-0 |

Team: Wilson, Male, Hapgood, Crayston, Roberts, Copping, Hulme, Bowden, Drake, James, Bastin. *Scorer:* Drake

| 28th April 1950 | LIVERPOOL | Won | 2-0 |

Team: Swindin, Scott, Barnes, Forbes, L. Compton, Mercer, Cox, Logie, Goring, Lewis, D. Compton. *Scorer:* Lewis 2

| 3rd May 1952 | NEWCASTLE UNITED | Lost | 0-1 |

Team: Swindin, Barnes, Smith, Forbes, Daniel, Mercer, Cox, Logie, Holton, Lishman, Roper.

Date	Opponents	Result

8th May 1971   LIVERPOOL   Won   2-1 aet
Team: Wilson, Rice, McNab, Storey (Kelly), McLintock, Simpson, Armstrong, Graham, Radford, Kennedy, George. *Scorers:* Kelly, George

6th May 1972   LEEDS UNITED   Lost   0-1
Team: Barnett, Rice, McNab, Storey, McLintock, Simpson, Armstrong, Ball, Radford (Kennedy), George, Graham.

6th May 1978   IPSWICH TOWN   Lost   0-1
Team: Jennings, Rice, Nelson, Price, O'Leary, Young, Brady (Rix), Sunderland, Macdonald, Stapleton, Hudson.

12th May 1979   MANCHESTER UNITED   Won   3-2
Team: Jennings, Rice, Nelson, Talbot, O'Leary, Young, Brady, Sunderland, Stapleton, Price (Walford), Rix. *Scorers:* Talbot, Stapleton, Sunderland

10th May 1980   WEST HAM UNITED   Lost   0-1
Team: Jennings, Rice, Devine (Nelson), Talbot, O'Leary, Young, Brady, Sunderland, Stapleton, Price, Rix.

15th May 1993   SHEFFIELD WEDNESDAY   Drew   1-1 aet
Team: Seaman, Dixon, Winterburn, Davis, Linighan, Adams, Jensen, Wright (O'Leary), Campbell, Merson, Parlour (Smith). *Scorer:* Wright

20th May 1993   SHEFFIELD WEDNESDAY   Won   2-1 aet
Team: Seaman, Dixon, Winterburn, Davis, Linighan, Adams, Jensen, Wright (O'Leary), Smith, Merson, Campbell. *Scorers:* Wright, Linighan

Cup Final Teams – *Football League Cup*

2nd March 1968   LEEDS UNITED   Lost   0-1
Team: Furnell, Storey, McNab, McLintock, Simpson, Ure, Radford, Jenkins (Neill), Graham, Sammels, Armstrong.

15th March 1969   SWINDON TOWN   Lost   1-3 aet
Team: Wilson. Storey, McNab, McLintock, Ure, Simpson (Graham), Radford, Sammels, Court, Gould, Armstrong. *Scorer:* Gould

Cup Final Teams – *Littlewoods Cup*

5th April 1987   LIVERPOOL   Won   2-1
Team: Lukic, Anderson, Sansom, Williams, O'Leary, Adams, Rocastle, Davis, Quinn (Groves), Nicholas, Hayes (Thomas). *Scorer:* Nicholas 2

24th April 1988   LUTON TOWN   Lost   2-3
Team: Lukic, Winterburn, Sansom, Thomas, Caesar, Adams, Rocastle, Davis, Smith, Groves (Hayes), Richardson. *Scorers:* Hayes, Smith

Cup Final Teams – *Coca Cola Cup*

18th April 1993   SHEFFIELD WEDNESDAY   Won   2-1
Team: Seaman, O'Leary, Winterburn, Morrow, Linighan, Adams, Davis, Wright, Campbell, Merson, Parlour. *Scorers:* Merson, Morrow

Cup Final Teams – *European Fairs Cup*

22nd April 1970   ANDERLECHT *in Brussels*   Lost   1-3
Team: Wilson, Storey, McNab, Kelly, McLintock, Simpson, Armstrong, Sammels, Radford, George (Kennedy), Graham. *Scorer:* Kennedy

28th April 1970   ANDERLECHT *at Highbury*   Won   3-0
Team: Wilson, Storey, McNab, Kelly, McLintock, Simpson, Armstrong, Sammels, Radford, George, Graham. *Scorers:* Kelly, Radford, Sammels

Cup Final Teams – *European Cup-Winners' Cup*

14th May 1980   VALENCIA *in Brussels*   Drew   0-0 aet
Lost 4-5 on penalties
Team: Jennings, Rice, Nelson, Talbot, O'Leary, Young, Brady, Sunderland, Stapleton, Price (Hollins), Rix.

4th May 1994   PARMA *in Copenhagen*   Won   1-0
Team: Seaman, Dixon, Winterburn, Davis, Bould, Adams, Campbell, Morrow, Smith, Merson (McGoldrick), Selley.

Arsenal – *Complete First Class Appearances*

Appearances are for all Premier League, Football League, FA Cup, Football League Cup & European matches from 1889. Charity Shield, other leagues (eg United League), wartime competitions, friendlies etc are excluded. FA Cup match totals include Qualifying Rounds. Figures are up to and including the end of the 1993/94 season.

Player	FAPL App	FAPL Goals	League App	League Goals	FACup App	FACup Goals	LgeCup App	LgeCup Goals	Europe App	Europe Goals	Totals App	Totals Goals
TA Adams (1983-)	68	–	248/1	20	29	5	42/1	2	12	2	399/2	29
C Addison (1966-67)			27/1	9	2	–	2	1			31/1	10
IJ Allinson (1983-87)			60/23	16	7/2	4	8/5	3			75/30	23
CJ Ambler (1891-96)			1	–	1	–					2	–
K Ampadu (1988-91)			12	–							12	–
E Anderson (1903-04)			2	–							2	–
J Anderson (1896-03)			144	10	9	1					153	11
TK Anderson (1959-65)			25	6					1	1	26	7
VA Anderson (1984-87)			120	9	12	3	18	3			150	15
W Anderson (1901-03)			28	10	2	1					30	11
G Armstrong (1961-77)			490/10	53	58/2	10	35	3	24/2	2	607/14	68
T Arnold (1905-06)			2	–							2	–
J Ashcroft (1900-08)			273	–	30	–					303	–
J Aston (1899-1900)			11	3	4	2					15	5
DR Bacuzzi (1958-64)			46	–	2	–					48	–
A Baker (1919-31)			310	23	41	3					351	26
JH Baker (1962-66)			144	93	10	4			2	3	156	100
T Baldwin (1962-66)			17	7			3	4			20	11
AJ Ball (1971-76)			177	45	28	7	12	–			217	52
W Bannister (1902-04)			18	–	4	–					22	–
H Barbour (1888-93)					5	4					5	4
JC Barley (1925-29)			8	1	2	–					10	1
W Barnes (1943-55)			267	11	25	1					292	12
GC Barnett (1969-76)			39	–	3	–	5	–	2	–	49	–

Player	FAPL		League		FACup		LgeCup		Europe		Totals	
	App	Goals	App	Goals	App	Goals	App	Goals	App	Goals	App	Goals
J Barnwell (1955-64)	–	–	138	23	10	–	–	–	3	1	151	24
PG Barron (1978-80)	–	–	8	–	–	–	–	–	–	–	8	–
ST Bassett (1906-10)	–	–	1	–	–	–	–	–	–	–	1	–
CS Bastin (1929-46)	–	–	350	150	42	26	–	–	–	–	392	176
JM Bates (188-91)	–	–	3	–	–	–	–	–	–	–	3	–
E Bateup (1905-11)	–	–	34	–	2	–	–	–	–	–	36	–
BM Batson (1969-74)	–	–	6/4	–	–	–	–	–	–	–	6/4	–
F Beardsley (1886-91)	–	–	–	–	2	–	–	–	–	–	2	–
E Bee (1890-93)	–	–	–	–	4	–	–	–	–	–	4	–
C Bell (1913-14)	–	–	1	2	–	–	–	–	–	–	1	2
J Bellamy (1903-07)	–	–	29	4	–	–	–	–	–	–	29	4
A Beney (1909-10)	–	–	16	6	1	–	–	–	–	–	17	6
RW Benson (1913-16)	–	–	52	7	2	–	–	–	–	–	54	7
JH Bigden (1904-08)	–	–	75	1	12	–	–	–	–	–	87	1
A Biggs (1955-58)	–	–	4	1	–	–	–	–	–	–	4	1
AG Biggs (1933-37)	–	–	3	–	–	–	–	–	–	–	3	–
RJ Birkett (1933-35)	–	–	19	7	2	1	–	–	–	–	21	8
T Black (1931-33)	–	–	–	–	1	1	–	–	–	–	1	1
J Blackwood (1900-01)	–	–	17	6	1	1	–	–	–	–	18	7
J Blair (1905-06)	–	–	13	3	–	–	–	–	–	–	13	3
JP Blockley (1972-75)	–	–	52	1	7	–	3	–	–	–	62	1
J Bloomfield (1954-60)	–	–	210	54	17	2	–	–	–	–	227	56
WN Blyth (1914-29)	–	–	314	45	29	6	–	–	–	–	343	51
MC Boot (1963-67)	–	–	3/1	2	–	–	1	–	–	–	4/1	2
C Booth (1892-94)	–	–	16	2	10	8	–	–	–	–	26	10

Player	FAPL App	Goals	League App	Goals	FACup App	Goals	LgeCup App	Goals	Europe App	Goals	Totals App	Goals
R Boreham (1921-25)	–	–	51	18	2	–	–	–	–	–	53	18
SA Bould (1988-)	47/2	2	107/5	3	16	–	17	–	5/2	–	192/9	5
FP Boulton (1936-38)	–	–	36	–	6	–	–	–	–	–	42	–
ER Bowden (1933-37)	–	–	123	42	13	5	–	–	–	–	136	47
DL Bowen (1950-59)	–	–	146	2	16	–	–	–	–	–	162	2
E Bowen (1926-28)	–	–	1	–	–	–	–	–	–	–	1	–
H Boyd (1894-97)	–	–	40	31	1	–	–	–	–	–	41	31
PA Boylan (1896-97)	–	–	11	–	–	–	–	–	–	–	11	–
J Boyle (1893-97)	–	–	61	7	5	2	–	–	–	–	66	9
F Bradshaw (1914-23)	–	–	132	14	10	–	–	–	–	–	142	14
W Bradshaw (1900-04)	–	–	4	2	–	–	–	–	–	–	4	2
WL Brady (1971-80)	–	–	227/8	43	31/4	2	23	10	13	4	294/12	59
J Brain (1923-31)	–	–	204	125	27	14	–	–	–	–	231	139
GH Bremner (1937-46)	–	–	15	4	–	–	–	–	–	–	15	4
T Briercliffe (1901-05)	–	–	122	33	11	1	–	–	–	–	133	34
S Briggs (1893)	–	–	2	–	–	–	–	–	–	–	2	–
SJ Brignall (1975-79)	–	–	0/1	–	–	–	–	–	–	–	0/1	–
J Brock (1896-98)	–	–	57	19	6	–	–	–	–	–	63	19
L Brown (1961-64)	–	–	101	2	5	–	–	–	3	–	109	2
T Bryan (1892-94)	–	–	9	1	–	–	–	–	–	–	9	1
CM Buchan (1925-28)	–	–	102	49	18	7	–	–	–	–	120	56
J Buchan (1904-05)	–	–	8	–	–	–	–	–	–	–	8	–
R Buchanan (1894-96)	–	–	42	16	2	–	–	–	–	–	44	16
W Buckenham (1909-10)	–	–	21	5	–	–	–	–	–	–	21	5
CS Buckley (1914-21)	–	–	56	3	3	–	–	–	–	–	59	3

Player	FAPL App	FAPL Goals	League App	League Goals	FACup App	FACup Goals	LgeCup App	LgeCup Goals	Europe App	Europe Goals	Totals App	Totals Goals
G Buist (1896-97)	–	–	6	–	–	–	–	–	–	–	6	–
R Buist (1891-94)	–	–	17	–	10	–	–	–	–	–	27	–
G Burdett (1910-12)	–	–	28	–	–	–	–	–	–	–	28	–
D Burgess (1919-22)	–	–	13	1	–	–	–	–	–	–	13	1
AJ Burns (1963-66)	–	–	31	–	2	–	–	–	–	–	33	–
G Burrell (1912-14)	–	–	23	3	1	–	–	–	–	–	24	3
L Burrows (1892-95)	–	–	10	–	–	–	–	–	–	–	10	–
W Busby (1903-05)	–	–	5	2	1	–	–	–	–	–	6	2
JD Butler (1914-30)	–	–	267	7	29	1	–	–	–	–	296	8
GC Caesar (1982-91)	–	–	27/17	–	0/1	–	3/2	–	–	–	30/20	–
A Caie (1897)	–	–	8	4	–	–	–	–	–	–	8	4
LA Calder (1911-13)	–	–	1	–	–	–	–	–	–	–	1	–
J Caldwell (1894-98)	–	–	93	2	4	–	–	–	–	–	97	2
JH Caldwell (1913-14)	–	–	3	–	–	–	–	–	–	–	3	–
A Calverley (1947)	–	–	11	–	–	–	–	–	–	–	11	–
FJ Calvert (1911-12)	–	–	2	1	–	–	–	–	–	–	2	1
KJ Campbell (1985-)	60/14	18	45/24	24	12/5	2	9/9	2	10/2	5	136/54	51
EM Carr (1935-40)	–	–	12	7	–	–	–	–	–	–	12	7
JW Carter (1991-)	11/5	2	5/1	–	2/1	–	–	–	–	–	19/7	2
S Cartwright (1931-46)	–	–	16	2	–	–	–	–	–	–	16	2
G Carver (1896-1900)	–	–	1	–	–	–	–	–	–	–	1	–
H Cassidy (1897)	–	–	1	–	–	–	–	–	–	–	1	–
TS Caton (1983-87)	–	–	81	2	4	–	10	1	–	–	95	3
J Chalmers (1910-12)	–	–	48	21	3	1	–	–	–	–	51	22

Player	FAPL App	FAPL Goals	League App	League Goals	FACup App	FACup Goals	LgeCup App	LgeCup Goals	Europe App	Europe Goals	Totals App	Totals Goals
B Chambers (1973-74)	–	–	1	–	–	–	0/1	–	–	–	1/1	–
LR Chapman (1982-83)	–	–	15/8	4	0/1	–	0/2	–	2	2	17/11	6
M Charles (1959-62)	–	–	60	26	4	2	–	–	–	–	64	28
S Charlton (1955-58)	–	–	99	–	11	3	–	–	–	–	110	3
JM Charteris (1888-90)	–	–	–	–	1	–	–	–	–	–	1	–
JC Chenell (1944-53)	–	–	16	–	–	–	–	–	–	–	16	–
N Chisholm (1907-10)	–	–	3	–	–	–	–	–	–	–	3	–
A Christmas (1890-91)	–	–	–	–	1	–	–	–	–	–	1	–
E Clamp (1961-62)	–	–	22	1	2	–	–	–	–	–	24	1
DR Clapton (1953-62)	–	–	207	25	18	2	–	–	–	–	225	27
DP Clapton (1957-61)	–	–	4	–	–	–	–	–	–	–	4	–
A Clark (1927-28)	–	–	1	–	–	–	–	–	–	–	1	–
JM Clark (1897-1900)	–	–	4	–	–	–	–	–	–	–	4	–
J Clark (1923-26)	–	–	6	–	–	–	–	–	–	–	6	–
FRG Clarke (1960-65)	–	–	26	–	2	–	–	–	–	–	28	–
T Coakley (1966-67)	–	–	9	1	–	–	4	1	–	–	13	2
D Cock (1925)	–	–	3	–	–	–	–	–	–	–	3	–
A Cole (1986-92)	–	–	0/1	–	–	–	–	–	–	–	0/1	–
E Coleman (1932-34)	–	–	45	26	1	–	–	–	–	–	46	26
JG Coleman (1902-08)	–	–	172	79	24	5	–	–	–	–	196	84
FG Coles (1900-04)	–	–	78	2	8	–	–	–	–	–	86	2
E Collett (1933-49)	–	–	20	–	1	–	–	–	–	–	21	–
A Common (1910-12)	–	–	77	23	3	–	–	–	–	–	80	23
DC Compton (1932-50)	–	–	54	15	5	1	–	–	–	–	59	16
LH Compton (1931-52)	–	–	253	5	17	1	–	–	–	–	270	6

Player	FAPL App	FAPL Goals	League App	League Goals	FACup App	FACup Goals	LgeCup App	LgeCup Goals	Europe App	Europe Goals	Totals App	Totals Goals
P Connolly (1888-93)	–	–	–	–	6	2	–	–	–	–	6	2
MJ Connor (1902)	–	–	14	2	2	1	–	–	–	–	16	3
J Cooper (1893-94)	–	–	6	–	2	2	–	–	–	–	8	2
W Coopland (1920-23)	–	–	1	–	–	–	–	–	–	–	1	–
HW Cope (1926-33)	–	–	65	–	11	–	–	–	–	–	76	–
W Copping (1934-39)	–	–	166	–	19	–	–	–	–	–	185	–
D Cork (1978-85)	–	–	5/2	1	1	–	–	–	–	–	6/2	1
EH Cottrell (1898-1901)	–	–	24	12	–	–	–	–	–	–	24	12
DJ Court (1959-70)	–	–	168/7	17	9/1	–	9/2	1	8	–	192/10	18
FF Cownley (1919-23)	–	–	15	–	–	–	–	–	–	–	15	–
FJA Cox (1949-53)	–	–	79	9	15	7	–	–	–	–	94	16
G Cox (1933-36)	–	–	7	1	1	–	–	–	–	–	8	1
G Crawford (1891-98)	–	–	122	4	16	4	–	–	–	–	138	8
HS Crawford (1911-13)	–	–	26	–	1	–	–	–	–	–	27	–
WJ Crayston (1934-43)	–	–	168	16	16	1	–	–	–	–	184	17
WW Creegan (1921-23)	–	–	5	–	1	–	–	–	–	–	6	–
AJ Cropley (1974-76)	–	–	29/1	5	2	–	2	1	–	–	33/1	6
AG Cross (1900-10)	–	–	132	4	17	–	–	–	–	–	149	–
A Crowe (1903-06)	–	–	6	4	–	–	–	–	–	–	6	4
J Crozier (1894)	–	–	1	–	–	–	–	–	–	–	1	–
RH Cumner (1938-46)	–	–	12	2	1	1	–	–	–	–	13	3
W Curle (1908-10)	–	–	3	–	–	–	–	–	–	–	3	–
GF Curtis (1936-47)	–	–	13	–	1	–	–	–	–	–	14	–
H Dailly (1898-99)	–	–	8	4	–	–	–	–	–	–	8	4

Player	FAPL		League		FACup		LgeCup		Europe		Totals	
	App	Goals	App	Goals	App	Goals	App	Goals	App	Goals	App	Goals
RW Daniel (1946-53)	–	–	87	5	12	–	–	–	–	–	99	5
A Davidson (1904-05)	–	–	1	–	–	–	–	–	–	–	1	–
RT Davidson (1935-37)	–	–	57	13	4	2	–	–	–	–	61	15
R Davidson (1964-69)	–	–	0/1	–	–	–	–	–	–	–	0/1	–
G Davie (1891-92)	–	–	–	–	4	3	–	–	–	–	4	3
P Davies (1968-72)	–	–	0/1	–	–	–	–	–	0/1	–	0/2	–
FW Davis (1893-99)	–	–	137	8	13	2	–	–	–	–	150	10
PV Davis (1978-)	27/1	–	301/18	29	22/5	3	44/5	4	15/1	–	409/30	36
A Devine (1913-14)	–	–	24	5	–	–	–	–	–	–	24	5
D Devine (1892-93)	–	–	2	–	2	–	–	–	–	–	4	–
JA Devine (1974-83)	–	–	86/3	–	6	–	8	–	8	–	108/3	–
J Devlin (1897-98)	–	–	1	–	–	–	–	–	–	–	1	–
J Dick (1898-1912)	–	–	262	12	22	1	–	–	–	–	284	13
P Dickov (1990-)	1/3	2	–	–	–	–	–	–	–	–	1/3	2
W Dickson (1953-56)	–	–	29	1	2	–	–	–	–	–	31	1
LM Dixon (1988-)	61/1	–	151/2	15	24	1	27	–	12	–	275/3	16
TH Docherty (1958-61)	–	–	83	–	7	–	–	–	–	–	90	–
W Dodgin (1952-61)	–	–	191	–	16	–	–	–	–	–	207	–
P Dougall (1933-37)	–	–	21	4	2	1	–	–	–	–	23	5
T Drain (1909-10)	–	–	2	–	–	–	–	–	–	–	2	–
EJ Drake (1934-45)	–	–	168	124	14	12	–	–	–	–	182	136
GB Drury (1938-46)	–	–	38	3	2	–	–	–	–	–	40	3
A Ducat (1905-12)	–	–	175	19	13	2	–	–	–	–	188	21
H Duff (1895-1900)	–	–	1	1	1	1	–	–	–	–	2	2
D Duncan (1912-13)	–	–	3	1	2	1	–	–	–	–	5	2

227

Player	FAPL		League		FACup		LgeCup		Europe		Totals	
	App	Goals	App	Goals	App	Goals	App	Goals	App	Goals	App	Goals
S Dunn (1919-25)	–	–	43	–	1	–	–	–	–	–	44	–
J Dunne (1933-36)	–	–	28	10	4	3	–	–	–	–	32	13
CR Dunsbee (1899-00)	–	–	8	–	3	–	–	–	–	–	11	–
F Dwight (1903-05)	–	–	1	–	–	–	–	–	–	–	1	–
F Dyer (1892-93)	–	–	–	–	5	–	–	–	–	–	5	–
SGJ Earle (1922-24)	–	–	4	3	–	–	–	–	–	–	4	3
GE Eastham (1960-66)	–	–	207	41	13	–	–	–	3	–	223	41
J Edgar (1901-02)	–	–	10	1	1	–	–	–	–	–	11	1
A Elliott (1892-94)	–	–	24	11	10	9	–	–	–	–	34	20
JR Elvey (1922-23)	–	–	–	–	–	–	–	–	–	–	–	–
DJ Evans (1951-63)	–	–	189	10	18	2	–	–	–	–	207	12
R Evans (1912-13)	–	–	1	1	1	–	–	–	–	–	2	1
MD Everitt (1956-61)	–	–	9	–	–	–	–	–	–	–	9	–
W Fairclough (1895-97)	–	–	26	–	1	–	–	–	–	–	27	–
GA Farmer (1896)	–	–	1	–	1	1	–	–	–	–	2	1
AM Farr (1937-40)	–	–	2	1	–	–	–	–	–	–	2	1
P Farrell (1897-98)	–	–	19	2	3	–	–	–	–	–	22	2
J Ferguson (1906-07)	–	–	–	–	–	–	–	–	–	–	–	–
G Ferry (1960-65)	–	–	11	–	–	–	–	–	–	–	11	–
J Fidler (1913-14)	–	–	25	–	–	–	–	–	–	–	25	–
AG Fields (1936-52)	–	–	19	–	–	–	–	–	–	–	19	–
G Fisher (1909)	–	–	2	–	–	–	–	–	–	–	2	–
TT Fitchie (1901-09)	–	–	56	27	7	3	–	–	–	–	63	30

Player	FAPL		League		FACup		LgeCup		Europe		Totals	
	App	Goals	App	Goals	App	Goals	App	Goals	App	Goals	App	Goals
J Flanaghan (1910-17)	–	–	114	28	7	–	–	–	–	–	121	28
MM Flatts (1990-)	8/5	–	–	–	–	–	–	–	–	–	9/5	–
A Fletcher (1914-15)	–	–	3	–	–	–	–	–	–	–	3	–
AR Forbes (1948-56)	–	–	217	20	22	–	–	–	–	–	239	20
GE Ford (1912-15)	–	–	9	–	1	–	–	–	–	–	10	–
R Foster (1889)	–	–	–	–	2	–	–	–	–	–	2	–
J Fotheringham (1949-59)	–	–	72	–	4	–	–	–	–	–	76	–
A Foxall (1901-02)	–	–	31	3	–	–	–	–	–	–	31	3
BC Freeman (1905-08)	–	–	44	21	5	3	–	–	–	–	49	24
J Furnell (1963-68)	–	–	141	–	13	–	12	–	1	–	167	–
J Fyfe (1898)	–	–	7	–	–	–	–	–	–	–	7	–
W Garbutt (1905-08)	–	–	52	8	13	6	–	–	–	–	65	14
J Garton (1899)	–	–	5	–	–	–	–	–	–	–	5	–
SP Gatting (1974-81)	–	–	50/8	5	9/1	1	3/1	–	3/1	–	65/11	6
R Gaudie (1899-1901)	–	–	47	24	3	–	–	–	–	–	50	24
D Gemmell (1892-94)	–	–	5	–	3	–	–	–	–	–	8	–
FC George (1966-75)	–	–	113/20	31	21/1	11	8	2	15/1	5	157/22	49
W Gilmer (1895-96)	–	–	3	–	–	–	–	–	–	–	3	–
DH Gloak (1889-91)	–	–	–	–	1	–	–	–	–	–	1	–
WH Gooing (1901-05)	–	–	94	45	12	3	–	–	–	–	106	48
R Gordon (1895-96)	–	–	20	6	–	–	–	–	–	–	20	6
H Goring (1948-60)	–	–	220	51	20	2	–	–	–	–	240	53
PA Gorman (1979-84)	–	–	5/1	–	–	–	–	–	–	–	5/1	–
RA Gould (1968-70)	–	–	57/8	16	7	3	6/3	3	2	1	72/11	24

Player	FAPL		League		FACup		LgeCup		Europe		Totals	
	App	Goals	App	Goals	App	Goals	App	Goals	App	Goals	App	Goals
RL Goulden (1953-61)	–	–	1	–	–	–	–	–	–	–	1	–
PJ Goy (1953-60)	–	–	2	–	–	–	–	–	–	–	2	–
A Graham (1911-24)	–	–	166	17	13	3	–	–	–	–	179	20
G Graham (1966-72)	–	–	219/8	59	27	2	27/2	9	23/2	7	296/12	77
J Graham (1899-1900)	–	–	1	–	–	–	–	–	–	–	1	–
T Graham (1891-92)	–	–	–	–	1	–	–	–	–	–	1	–
C Grant (1946)	–	–	2	–	–	–	–	–	–	–	2	–
GM Grant (1910-19)	–	–	54	4	3	–	–	–	–	–	57	4
JW Grant (1912)	–	–	4	3	–	–	–	–	–	–	4	3
A Gray (1904-12)	–	–	184	–	16	–	–	–	–	–	200	–
D Greenaway (1980-21)	–	–	161	13	9	–	–	–	–	–	170	13
NJ Grice (1906)	–	–	1	–	–	–	–	–	–	–	1	–
T Grieve (1900-01)	–	–	6	–	–	–	–	–	–	–	6	–
AT Griffiths (1961-62)	–	–	15	2	–	–	–	–	–	–	15	2
WM Griffiths (1936-38)	–	–	9	5	–	–	–	–	–	–	9	5
FW Groves (1912-21)	–	–	50	6	3	–	–	–	–	–	53	6
P Groves (1986-92)	0/1	–	91/64	21	11/6	1	18/8	6	0/4	–	120/83	28
VG Groves (1955-64)	–	–	185	31	16	6	–	–	2	–	203	37
A Gudmundsson (1946-47)	–	–	2	–	–	–	–	–	–	–	2	–
R Guthrie (1952-56)	–	–	2	–	–	–	–	–	–	–	2	–
S Haden (1922-27)	–	–	88	10	5	1	–	–	–	–	93	11
D Halliday (1929-30)	–	–	15	8	–	–	–	–	–	–	15	8
TS Hamilton (1898-00)	–	–	7	–	–	–	–	–	–	–	7	–
R Hankin (1981)	–	–	–	–	–	–	0/2	–	–	–	0/2	–

Player	FAPL App	FAPL Goals	League App	League Goals	FACup App	FACup Goals	LgeCup App	LgeCup Goals	Europe App	Europe Goals	Totals App	Totals Goals
E Hanks (1912-13)	–	–	4	1	–	–	–	–	–	–	4	1
D Hannah (1897-99)	–	–	46	17	4	–	–	–	–	–	50	17
R Hannigan (1899)	–	–	1	–	1	–	–	–	–	–	2	–
EA Hapgood (1927-45)	–	–	393	2	41	–	–	–	–	–	434	2
E Harding (1896)	–	–	–	–	1	–	–	–	–	–	1	–
HT Hardinge (1913-21)	–	–	54	14	1	–	–	–	–	–	55	14
CB Hare (1895-96)	–	–	19	7	1	–	–	–	–	–	20	7
W Harper (1925-31)	–	–	63	–	10	–	–	–	–	–	73	–
A Hartley (1899)	–	–	5	–	4	–	–	–	–	–	9	–
J Harvey (1977-80)	–	–	2/1	1	–	–	–	–	1	–	3/1	1
T Hatfield (1895-96)	–	–	2	–	–	–	–	–	–	–	2	–
J Haverty (1954-61)	–	–	114	25	8	1	–	–	–	–	122	26
JE Hawley (1981-83)	–	–	14/6	3	–	–	1	–	–	–	15/6	3
M Hayes (1981-90)	–	–	70/32	26	8/1	3	14/7	5	–	–	92/40	34
AE Haynes (1928-33)	–	–	29	–	1	–	–	–	–	–	30	–
A Haywood (1896-99)	–	–	84	31	7	5	–	–	–	–	91	36
NA Heaney (1987-94)	4/2	–	0/1	–	–	–	–	–	–	–	4/3	–
JF Heath (1893-99)	–	–	10	5	2	2	–	–	–	–	12	7
DM Heeley (1977-80)	–	–	9/6	–	–	–	–	–	4/1	–	13/7	–
J Henderson (1892-95)	–	–	38	18	9	12	–	–	–	–	47	30
JG Henderson (1958-62)	–	–	103	29	8	–	–	–	–	–	111	29
W Henderson (1921-23)	–	–	7	–	–	–	–	–	–	–	7	–
L Henley (1939-46)	–	–	–	–	1	–	–	–	–	–	1	–
F Heppinstall (1909-11)	–	–	23	–	–	–	–	–	–	–	23	–
DG Herd (1954-61)	–	–	166	97	14	10	–	–	–	–	180	107

Player	FAPL App	FAPL Goals	League App	League Goals	FACup App	FACup Goals	LgeCup App	LgeCup Goals	Europe App	Europe Goals	Totals App	Totals Goals
CF Hill (1979-86)	–	–	46	–	1	–	4	–	–	–	51	1
FR Hill (1932-36)	–	–	76	4	2	–	–	–	–	–	78	4
D Hillier (1985-)	38/7	1	36/7	1	11/6	–	9/2	–	2/1	–	96/23	2
S Hoar (1924-29)	–	–	100	16	17	2	–	–	–	–	117	18
GR Hoare (1907-12)	–	–	30	12	4	1	–	–	–	–	34	13
CL Hodges (1944-46)	–	–	2	–	–	–	–	–	–	–	2	2
JW Hollins (1979-83)	–	–	123/4	–	12	–	–	–	–	–	135/4	–
CC Holton (1947-58)	–	–	21	7	1	–	–	–	–	–	22	7
BG Hornsby (1970-76)	–	–	23/3	6	–	–	–	–	–	–	23/3	6
RT Horsington (1889-90)	–	–	–	–	2	–	–	–	–	–	2	–
P Howard (1976-77)	–	–	15/1	–	4	–	–	–	–	–	19/1	–
D Howat (1889-96)	–	–	56	2	16	1	–	–	–	–	72	3
D Howe (1964-67)	–	–	70	1	3	–	1	–	–	–	74	1
AA Hudson (1976-78)	–	–	36	–	7	–	3/1	–	–	–	46/1	–
J Hughes (1925)	–	–	1	–	–	–	–	–	–	–	1	–
JHA Hulme (1926-38)	–	–	333	107	39	17	–	–	–	–	372	124
AE Humpish (1930)	–	–	3	–	–	–	–	–	–	–	3	–
F Hunt (1897-1903)	–	–	72	30	9	5	–	–	–	–	81	35
GS Hunt (1937-38)	–	–	18	3	3	–	–	–	–	–	21	3
J Hunter (1904-05)	–	–	22	4	–	–	–	–	–	–	22	4
AV Hutchins (1916-23)	–	–	104	1	4	–	–	–	–	–	108	1
T Hynds (1906-07)	–	–	13	–	4	1	–	–	–	–	17	1
DBN Jack (1928-24)	–	–	181	113	25	10	–	–	–	–	206	123
J Jackson (1899-1905)	–	–	183	–	21	1	–	–	–	–	204	1

Player	FAPL		League		FACup		LgeCup		Europe		Totals	
	App	Goals	App	Goals	App	Goals	App	Goals	App	Goals	App	Goals
GH Jaques (1894)	–	–	2	2	–	–	–	–	–	–	2	2
AW James (1929-37)	–	–	231	26	28	1	–	–	–	–	259	27
WW Jeffrey (1892-94)	–	–	22	–	9	–	–	–	–	–	31	–
DJ Jenkins (1962-68)	–	–	16/1	3	2	1	6	5	–	–	24/1	9
CAL Jenkyns (1895-96)	–	–	27	6	–	–	–	–	–	–	27	6
PA Jennings (1977-85)	–	–	237	–	38	–	32	–	19	–	326	–
J Jensen (1992-)	56/3	–	–	–	4/1	–	8	–	8	–	76/4	3
G Jobey (1913-14)	–	–	28	3	–	–	–	–	–	–	28	3
RF John (192-37)	–	–	421	12	46	1	–	–	–	–	467	13
G Johnston (1967-69)	–	–	17/4	3	–	–	3/1	–	–	–	20/5	3
W Johnstone (1929-31)	–	–	9	4	–	–	–	–	–	–	9	4
B Jones (1938-49)	–	–	71	7	3	–	–	–	–	–	74	7
C Jones (1928-34)	–	–	176	8	17	–	–	–	–	–	193	8
FJ Jones (1923-24)	–	–	2	–	–	–	–	–	–	–	2	–
LJ Jones (1937-46)	–	–	46	3	4	–	–	–	–	–	50	3
S Jonsson (1989-91)	–	–	2/5	1	0/1	–	1	–	–	–	3/6	1
B Joy (1935-46)	–	–	86	–	6	–	–	–	–	–	92	–
JW Julian (1889-92)	–	–	–	–	4	–	–	–	–	–	4	–
LB Julians (1958-60)	–	–	18	7	6	3	–	–	–	–	24	10
ET Kane (1896-97)	–	–	1	–	–	–	–	–	–	–	1	–
P Kane (1960-63)	–	–	4	1	–	–	–	–	–	–	4	1
J Kay (1979-84)	–	–	13/1	–	–	–	–	–	–	–	13/1	–
EP Kelly (1966-76)	–	–	168/17	13	15/2	4	15	–	13/2	2	211/21	19
N Kelly (1947-50)	–	–	1	–	–	–	–	–	–	–	1	–

Player	FAPL App	FAPL Goals	League App	League Goals	FACup App	FACup Goals	LgeCup App	LgeCup Goals	Europe App	Europe Goals	Totals App	Totals Goals
AJ Kelsey (1949-62)	–	–	327	–	24	–	–	–	–	–	351	–
F Kemp (1905-06)	–	–	2	–	–	–	–	–	–	–	2	–
AR Kempton (1914-21)	–	–	–	–	–	–	–	–	–	–	1	–
AL Kennedy (1922-28)	–	–	122	–	7	–	–	–	–	–	129	–
R Kennedy (1968-74)	–	–	156/2	53	25/2	6	11	4	14/2	8	206/6	71
M Keown (181-86/93-)	38/11		22	–	7/1	–	3	–	4/3	–	74/15	–
GP Keyser (1930-31)	–	–	12	–	–	–	–	–	–	–	12	–
B Kidd (1974-76)	–	–	77	30	9	3	4	1	–	–	90	34
E King (1912-14)	–	–	11	–	2	–	–	–	–	–	13	–
HE King (1914-19)	–	–	37	26	2	3	–	–	–	–	39	29
E Kington (1895-98)	–	–	–	–	1	–	–	–	–	–	1	–
AJ Kirchen (1935-43)	–	–	92	38	7	6	–	–	–	–	99	44
FV Kirk (1892-94)	–	–	1	–	–	–	–	–	–	–	1	–
AJ Kosmina (1978-79)	–	–	0/1	–	–	–	–	–	1/2	–	1/3	–
P Kyle (1906-08)	–	–	52	21	8	2	–	–	–	–	60	23
J Laidlaw (1901)	–	–	3	2	–	–	–	–	–	–	3	2
J Lambert (1926-33)	–	–	143	98	16	11	–	–	–	–	159	109
ET Lawrence (1902-03)	–	–	20	3	3	–	–	–	–	–	23	3
W Lawrence (1909-10)	–	–	25	5	1	–	–	–	–	–	26	5
H Lawson (1924-27)	–	–	13	2	3	–	–	–	–	–	16	2
T Lawton (1953-56)	–	–	35	13	2	1	–	–	–	–	37	14
J Leather (1896-98)	–	–	8	–	2	–	–	–	–	–	10	–
HG Lee (1905-09)	–	–	41	15	–	–	–	–	–	–	41	15
JW Lee (1926-28)	–	–	7	–	–	–	–	–	–	–	7	–

Player	FAPL App	FAPL Goals	League App	League Goals	FACup App	FACup Goals	LgeCup App	LgeCup Goals	Europe App	Europe Goals	Totals App	Totals Goals
DL Le Roux (1957-58)			5								5	
CH Lewis (1907-21)			206	30	14	4					220	34
D Lewis (1924-31)			142		25						167	
R Lewis (1935-53)			154	103	21	13					175	116
E Liddell (1914-20)			2								2	
J Lievesley (1913-15)			73		2						75	
AE Limpar (1990-94)	21/12	2	55/8	15	7	2	9		3	1	95/20	20
A Linighan (1990-)	39/4	2	22/5		10/1	1	9/1	1	3/1		83/12	5
W Linward (1902-05)			47	10	3						50	10
DJ Lishman (1948-56)			226	125	17	10					243	135
F Lloyd (1899-1900)			18	3	3						21	1
H Logan (1910-11)			11								11	
P Logan (1899-1901)			28	7	1						29	7
JT Logie (1939-55)			296	68	30	8					326	76
AB Low (1906-08)			3								3	
TP Low (1900-01)			24	1	2	1					26	2
J Lukic (1983-90)			223		21		32				276	
P Lydersen (1991)	7/1		5/2				1				13/3	
AR Macaulay (1947-50)			103	1	4	1					107	2
J McAulcy (1897-98)			23	1	4	1					27	2
F McAvoy (1895-98)			44	8	3	2					47	10
J McAvoy (1898-99)			25		1						26	
J McBean (1889-92)					6						6	
J McClelland (1960-64)			46		3						49	

Player	FAPL App	FAPL Goals	League App	League Goals	FACup App	FACup Goals	LgeCup App	LgeCup Goals	Europe App	Europe Goals	Totals App	Totals Goals
A McConnell (1897-99)	–	–	37	1	1	–	–	–	–	–	38	1
A McCowie (1899-00)	–	–	28	7	5	–	–	–	–	–	33	7
W McCullough (1958-66)	–	–	253	4	11	–	–	–	4	–	268	4
B McDermott (1977-84)	–	–	38/23	12	0/1	–	3/1	–	3/3	1	44/28	13
D McDonald (1909-11)	–	–	26	–	1	–	–	–	–	–	27	–
H McDonald (1906-13)	–	–	94	–	9	–	–	–	–	–	103	–
M Macdonald (1976-79)	–	–	84	42	9	10	14	5	0/1	–	107/1	57
R McEachrane (1902-15)	–	–	313	–	33	–	–	–	–	–	346	–
A McFarlane (1896-97)	–	–	5	–	–	–	–	–	–	–	5	–
GA McGeoch (1897-99)	–	–	35	15	4	1	–	–	–	–	39	16
C McGibbon (1905-10)	–	–	4	3	–	–	–	–	–	–	4	3
JM McGill (1965-67)	–	–	6/4	–	–	–	2	–	–	–	8/4	–
E McGoldrick (1993-)	23/3	–	–	–	1/1	–	4	–	3/2	1	30/6	1
G McGowan (1992-)	0/2	–	–	–	–	–	–	–	–	–	0/2	–
I McKechnie (1958-64)	–	–	23	–	2	–	–	–	–	–	25	–
M McKellar (1909-10)	–	–	3	1	2	–	–	–	–	–	5	1
A McKenzie (1920-23)	–	–	15	2	1	–	–	–	–	–	16	2
JA Mackie (1921-28)	–	–	108	–	10	1	–	–	–	–	118	1
A McKinnon (1908-22)	–	–	211	4	6	–	–	–	–	–	217	4
J McLaughlan (1911-13)	–	–	16	3	–	–	–	–	–	–	16	3
JM McLeod (1961-64)	–	–	101	23	8	4	3	1	–	–	112	28
F McLintock (1964-73)	–	–	312/6	26	36	1	34	4	19	1	401/6	32
R McNab (1966-75)	–	–	277/1	4	39	–	26/1	2	20/1	–	362/3	6
W McNab (1893-94)	–	–	2	1	–	–	–	–	–	–	2	1
D McNichol (1899-03)	–	–	101	1	11	–	–	–	–	–	112	1

Player	FAPL App	FAPL Goals	League App	League Goals	FACup App	FACup Goals	LgeCup App	LgeCup Goals	Europe App	Europe Goals	Totals App	Totals Goals
J McPhee (1898-99)	–	–	7	–	1	–	–	–	–	–	8	–
I McPherson (1946-51)	–	–	152	19	11	2	–	–	–	–	163	21
J McQuilkie (1892-93)	–	–	–	–	2	–	–	–	–	–	2	–
DJ Madden (1983-84)	–	–	2	–	–	–	–	–	–	–	2	–
EJ McGill (1959-65)	–	–	116	–	11	–	–	–	4	–	131	–
A Main (1899-1903)	–	–	63	14	6	–	–	–	–	–	69	14
CG Male (1929-48)	–	–	285	–	29	–	–	–	–	–	314	–
TJ Mancini (1974-76)	–	–	52	1	8	2	–	–	–	–	60	3
RJ Marden (1950-55)	–	–	42	11	–	–	–	–	–	–	42	11
P Marinello (1970-73)	–	–	32/6	3	0/1	–	5	1	6/1	1	43/8	5
P Mariner (1984-86)	–	–	52/8	14	5/1	2	3/1	1	–	–	60/10	17
GW Marks (1936-46)	–	–	2	–	–	–	–	–	–	–	2	–
J Marshall (1934-35)	–	–	4	–	–	–	–	–	–	–	4	–
SR Marshall (1991-)	2	–	–	–	–	–	–	–	–	–	2	–
B Marwood (1988-90)	–	–	52	16	2	–	6	1	–	–	60	17
JM Matthews (1971-78)	–	–	38/7	2	4/2	1	6	2	–	–	48/9	5
J Maxwell (1908-09)	–	–	2	–	–	–	–	–	–	–	2	–
T Maxwell (1921)	–	–	1	–	–	–	–	–	–	–	1	–
WJ Maycock (1928-31)	–	–	1	–	–	–	–	–	–	–	1	–
RJ Meade (1978-85)	–	–	25/16	14	2/1	–	3/1	1	2/1	1	32/19	16
TG Meade (1893-97)	–	–	11	5	3	2	–	–	–	–	14	7
JW Meggs (1889-91)	–	–	–	–	5	4	–	–	–	–	5	4
J Mercer (1946-54)	–	–	247	2	26	–	–	–	–	–	273	2
PC Merson (1982-)	56/10	13	139/28	50	23/3	4	26/2	8	12	3	256/43	78
A Miller (1988-)	6/2	–	–	–	–	–	–	–	–	–	6/2	–

Player	FAPL App	Goals	League App	Goals	FACup App	Goals	LgeCup App	Goals	Europe App	Goals	Totals App	Goals
S Mills (1895-96)	–	–	24	3	1	–	–	–	–	–	25	3
JV Milne (1935-37)	–	–	49	19	3	–	–	–	–	–	52	19
W Milne (1921-27)	–	–	114	1	10	2	–	–	–	–	124	3
CA Milton (1945-55)	–	–	75	18	9	3	–	–	–	–	84	21
A Mitchell (1898-99)	–	–	10	2	–	–	–	–	–	–	10	2
JG Moir (1898-1900)	–	–	41	–	4	–	–	–	–	–	45	–
J Monteith (1897)	–	–	6	1	–	–	–	–	–	–	6	1
J Moody (1925-28)	–	–	6	–	–	–	–	–	–	–	6	–
J Mordue (1907-08)	–	–	26	1	2	–	–	–	–	–	28	1
AS Morgan (1938-48)	–	–	2	–	–	–	–	–	–	–	2	–
SJ Morrow (1987-)	20/7	–	0/2	–	2/2	–	5/1	1	1	–	28/12	1
P Mortimer (1894-96)	–	–	49	23	–	–	–	–	–	–	49	23
F Moss (1931-37)	–	–	143	1	16	–	–	–	–	–	159	1
J Murphy (1898-1900)	–	–	27	–	5	–	–	–	–	–	32	–
HR Murrell (1898-1900)	–	–	6	–	–	–	–	–	–	–	6	–
D Neave (1904-12)	–	–	154	30	14	2	–	–	–	–	168	32
A Neil (1924-26)	–	–	54	10	3	–	–	–	–	–	57	10
WJT Neill (1959-70)	–	–	240/1	8	12/1	1	15/1	–	5	–	272/3	10
G Ncilson (1964-68)	–	–	14	2	3	–	–	–	–	–	17	3
D Nelson (1936-46)	–	–	27	4	2	–	–	–	–	–	29	4
S Nelson (1966-81)	–	–	245/10	10	33/2	1	27	1	19/2	–	324/14	12
C Nicholas (1983-88)	–	–	145/6	34	11/2	10	20	10	–	–	176/8	54
P Nicholas (1981-83)	–	–	57/3	1	8	–	8	2	4	–	77/3	3
J Norman (1914-19)	–	–	4	–	–	–	–	–	–	–	4	–

Player	FAPL App	FAPL Goals	League App	League Goals	FACup App	FACup Goals	LgeCup App	LgeCup Goals	Europe App	Europe Goals	Totals App	Totals Goals
EJ North (1919-22)	–	–	23	6	–	–	–	–	–	–	23	6
GE Nutt (1955-60)	–	–	49	10	2	–	–	–	–	–	51	10
DJ Oakes (1945-55)	–	–	11	1	–	–	–	–	–	–	11	1
P O'Brien (1894-97)	–	–	63	27	4	2	–	–	–	–	67	29
HT Offer (1889-91)	–	–	–	–	4	–	–	–	–	–	4	–
K O'Flanagan (1945-49)	–	–	14	3	2	–	–	–	–	–	16	3
DA O'Leary (1973-93)	6/5	–	517/30	11	66/4	–	68/2	2	21	–	678/41	14
H Oliver (1909-10)	–	–	1	–	–	–	–	–	–	–	1	–
FS O'Neill (1958-61)	–	–	2	–	–	–	–	–	–	–	2	–
R Ord (1897-1900)	–	–	89	–	10	–	–	–	–	–	99	–
DE O'Shea (1978-84)	–	–	6	–	–	–	3	–	–	–	9	–
I Owens (1901-02)	–	–	9	2	2	–	–	–	–	–	11	2
RJ Pack (1962-66)	–	–	1	–	–	–	–	–	–	–	1	–
F Pagnam (1919-21)	–	–	50	26	3	–	–	–	–	–	53	27
TR Parker (1926-33)	–	–	258	17	34	–	–	–	–	–	292	17
R Parkin (1928-36)	–	–	25	11	1	–	–	–	–	–	26	11
R Parlour (1988-)	40/8	3	2/4	1	7	1	5/1	–	–	–	54/13	5
JA Paterson (1920-26)	–	–	70	1	7	–	–	–	–	–	77	2
W Paterson (1928-29)	–	–	15	–	–	–	–	–	–	–	15	–
CG Pates (1990-1993)	2/5	–	10/4	1	–	–	2	–	2	1	16/9	1
GC Pattison (1920-22)	–	–	9	–	1	–	–	–	–	–	10	–
GC Payne (1912-13)	–	–	3	–	–	–	–	–	–	–	3	–
CB Peachey (1891-92)	–	–	–	–	1	–	–	–	–	–	1	–

Player	FAPL App	FAPL Goals	League App	League Goals	FACup App	FACup Goals	LgeCup App	LgeCup Goals	Europe App	Europe Goals	Totals App	Totals Goals
HB Peel (1926-29)	–	–	47	5	5	1	–	–	–	–	52	6
V Petrovic (1983)	–	–	10/3	2	6	1	3	–	–	–	19/3	3
JWFJ Petts (1954-62)	–	–	32	–	–	–	–	–	–	–	32	–
W Place (1900-02)	–	–	42	6	3	1	–	–	–	–	45	7
EH Platt (1938-53)	–	–	53	–	4	–	–	–	–	–	57	–
J Powell (1892-96)	–	–	86	1	6	1	–	–	–	–	92	2
RF Powling (1971-81)	–	–	50/5	3	2	–	2	–	–	–	54/5	3
TP Pratt (1903-04)	–	–	8	2	2	–	–	–	–	–	10	2
CJF Preedy (1929-33)	–	–	37	–	2	–	–	–	–	–	39	–
DJ Price (1970-81)	–	–	116/10	16	26	1	11	–	11/1	2	164/11	19
D Pryde (1935-46)	–	–	4	–	–	–	–	–	–	–	4	–
SJ Pugh (1936-39)	–	–	1	–	–	–	–	–	–	–	1	–
JA Quayle (1907-11)	–	–	1	–	–	–	–	–	–	–	1	–
NJ Quinn (1983-90)	–	–	59/8	14	8/2	2	14/2	4	–	–	81/12	20
J Radford (1962-76)	–	–	375/4	111	42/2	15	34	12	24	11	475/6	149
JH Ramsey (1924-26)	–	–	69	11	6	–	–	–	–	–	75	11
CE Randall (1911-14)	–	–	43	12	1	–	–	–	–	–	44	12
A Rankin (1891-93)	–	–	–	–	3	–	–	–	–	–	3	–
F Ransom (1900-05)	–	–	1	–	–	–	–	–	–	–	1	–
SF Raybould (1908-09)	–	–	26	6	4	1	–	–	–	–	30	7
G Reece (1895)	–	–	1	–	–	–	–	–	–	–	1	–
PJ Rice (1964-80)	–	–	391/6	12	67	1	36	–	26/1	–	520/7	13
K Richardson (1987-90)	–	–	88/8	5	9	1	13/3	2	–	–	110/11	8

Player	FAPL App	FAPL Goals	League App	League Goals	FACup App	FACup Goals	LgeCup App	LgeCup Goals	Europe App	Europe Goals	Totals App	Totals Goals
JJ Rimmer (1974-77)	–	–	124	–	12	–	10	–	–	–	146	–
W Rippon (1910-11)	–	–	9	2	–	–	–	–	–	–	9	2
G Rix (1974-88)	–	–	338/13	41	42/2	7	45/2	2	21	1	446/17	51
H Roberts (1926-37)	–	–	297	4	36	1	–	–	–	–	333	5
JG Roberts (1969-72)	–	–	56/3	4	–	–	12	1	9/1	–	77/4	5
A Robertson (1891-92)	–	–	–	–	4	–	–	–	–	–	4	–
H Robertson (1889-90)	–	–	–	–	4	4	–	–	–	–	4	4
JG Robertson (1968-70)	–	–	45/1	7	4	1	4	–	5	–	58/1	8
JW Robertson (1948-53)	–	–	1	–	–	–	–	–	–	–	1	–
JH Robson (1921-26)	–	–	97	–	4	–	–	–	–	–	101	–
SI Robson (1980-87)	–	–	150/1	16	13	1	20	3	2	1	185/1	21
D Rocastle (1982-92)	–	–	204/13	24	18/2	4	32/1	6	4	–	258/16	34
J Rodger (1907-08)	–	–	1	–	–	–	–	–	–	–	1	–
Archie Roe (1922-23)	–	–	4	1	–	–	–	–	–	–	4	1
Arthur Roe (1925)	–	–	1	–	–	–	–	–	–	–	1	–
E Rogers (1935-36)	–	–	16	5	5	–	–	–	–	–	21	5
RL Rooke (1946-49)	–	–	88	68	5	1	–	–	–	–	93	69
LR Roose (1911-12)	–	–	13	–	–	–	–	–	–	–	13	–
DGB Roper (1947-57)	–	–	297	88	22	7	–	–	–	–	319	95
TW Ross (1972-77)	–	–	57/1	5	3	1	6	3	–	–	66/1	9
JW Rostron (1972-77)	–	–	12/5	2	2	1	1	–	–	–	14/5	3
TW Rudkin (1947)	–	–	5	2	–	–	–	–	–	–	5	2
AE Russell (1895-96)	–	–	–	–	1	–	–	–	–	–	1	–
J Russell (1896-97)	–	–	23	4	2	–	–	–	–	–	25	4
J Rutherford (1913-26)	–	–	222	25	10	2	–	–	–	–	232	27

<table>
<tr><th rowspan="2">Player</th><th colspan="2">FAPL</th><th colspan="2">League</th><th colspan="2">FACup</th><th colspan="2">LgeCup</th><th colspan="2">Europe</th><th colspan="2">Totals</th></tr>
<tr><th>App</th><th>Goals</th><th>App</th><th>Goals</th><th>App</th><th>Goals</th><th>App</th><th>Goals</th><th>App</th><th>Goals</th><th>App</th><th>Goals</th></tr>
<tr><td>JJ Rutherford (1924-27)</td><td>–</td><td>–</td><td>1</td><td>–</td><td>–</td><td>–</td><td>–</td><td>–</td><td>–</td><td>–</td><td>1</td><td>–</td></tr>
<tr><td>JC Sammels (1961-71)</td><td>–</td><td>–</td><td>212/3</td><td>39</td><td>20/1</td><td>3</td><td>19</td><td>3</td><td>15</td><td>7</td><td>266/4</td><td>52</td></tr>
<tr><td>M Sanders (1899-1900)</td><td>–</td><td>–</td><td>4</td><td>1</td><td>–</td><td>–</td><td>–</td><td>–</td><td>–</td><td>–</td><td>4</td><td>1</td></tr>
<tr><td>PR Sands (1902-19)</td><td>–</td><td>–</td><td>327</td><td>10</td><td>23</td><td>2</td><td>–</td><td>–</td><td>–</td><td>–</td><td>350</td><td>12</td></tr>
<tr><td>KG Sansom (1980-88)</td><td>–</td><td>–</td><td>314</td><td>6</td><td>26</td><td>–</td><td>48</td><td>–</td><td>6</td><td>–</td><td>394</td><td>6</td></tr>
<tr><td>C Satterthwaite (1904-10)</td><td>–</td><td>–</td><td>129</td><td>45</td><td>12</td><td>3</td><td>–</td><td>–</td><td>–</td><td>–</td><td>141</td><td>48</td></tr>
<tr><td>J Satterthwaite (1906-08)</td><td>–</td><td>–</td><td>5</td><td>1</td><td>–</td><td>–</td><td>–</td><td>–</td><td>–</td><td>–</td><td>5</td><td>1</td></tr>
<tr><td>L Scott (1937-51)</td><td>–</td><td>–</td><td>115</td><td>–</td><td>11</td><td>–</td><td>–</td><td>–</td><td>–</td><td>–</td><td>126</td><td>–</td></tr>
<tr><td>W Scott (1888-90)</td><td>–</td><td>–</td><td>–</td><td>–</td><td>3</td><td>4</td><td>–</td><td>–</td><td>–</td><td>–</td><td>3</td><td>4</td></tr>
<tr><td>DA Seaman (1990-)</td><td>78</td><td>–</td><td>80</td><td>–</td><td>20</td><td>–</td><td>21</td><td>–</td><td>13</td><td>–</td><td>212</td><td>–</td></tr>
<tr><td>WC Seddon (1924-32)</td><td>–</td><td>–</td><td>69</td><td>–</td><td>6</td><td>–</td><td>–</td><td>–</td><td>–</td><td>–</td><td>75</td><td>–</td></tr>
<tr><td>I Selley (1992-)</td><td>26/2</td><td>–</td><td>44</td><td>–</td><td>3</td><td>–</td><td>2/1</td><td>–</td><td>5/2</td><td>1</td><td>36/5</td><td>1</td></tr>
<tr><td>T Shanks (1903-04)</td><td>–</td><td>–</td><td>44</td><td>28</td><td>6</td><td>–</td><td>–</td><td>–</td><td>–</td><td>–</td><td>50</td><td>28</td></tr>
<tr><td>J Sharp (1905-08)</td><td>–</td><td>–</td><td>103</td><td>4</td><td>13</td><td>–</td><td>–</td><td>–</td><td>–</td><td>–</td><td>116</td><td>5</td></tr>
<tr><td>WH Sharp (1895-95)</td><td>–</td><td>–</td><td>13</td><td>4</td><td>1</td><td>–</td><td>–</td><td>–</td><td>–</td><td>–</td><td>14</td><td>4</td></tr>
<tr><td>A Shaw (1948-55)</td><td>–</td><td>–</td><td>57</td><td>–</td><td>4</td><td>–</td><td>–</td><td>–</td><td>–</td><td>–</td><td>61</td><td>–</td></tr>
<tr><td>B Shaw (1891-92)</td><td>–</td><td>–</td><td>–</td><td>–</td><td>1</td><td>–</td><td>–</td><td>–</td><td>–</td><td>–</td><td>1</td><td>–</td></tr>
<tr><td>H Shaw (1898-1900)</td><td>–</td><td>–</td><td>26</td><td>9</td><td>4</td><td>–</td><td>–</td><td>–</td><td>–</td><td>–</td><td>30</td><td>9</td></tr>
<tr><td>J Shaw (1926-30)</td><td>–</td><td>–</td><td>11</td><td>4</td><td>–</td><td>–</td><td>–</td><td>–</td><td>–</td><td>–</td><td>11</td><td>4</td></tr>
<tr><td>JE Shaw (1907-23)</td><td>–</td><td>–</td><td>309</td><td>–</td><td>17</td><td>–</td><td>–</td><td>–</td><td>–</td><td>–</td><td>326</td><td>–</td></tr>
<tr><td>WJ Shaw (1893-95)</td><td>–</td><td>–</td><td>19</td><td>11</td><td>5</td><td>1</td><td>–</td><td>–</td><td>–</td><td>–</td><td>24</td><td>12</td></tr>
<tr><td>M Shortt (1910)</td><td>–</td><td>–</td><td>4</td><td>–</td><td>–</td><td>–</td><td>–</td><td>–</td><td>–</td><td>–</td><td>4</td><td>–</td></tr>
<tr><td>T Shrewsbury (1896-00)</td><td>–</td><td>–</td><td>3</td><td>–</td><td>3</td><td>–</td><td>–</td><td>–</td><td>–</td><td>–</td><td>6</td><td>–</td></tr>
<tr><td>NW Sidey (1929-39)</td><td>–</td><td>–</td><td>40</td><td>–</td><td>3</td><td>–</td><td>–</td><td>–</td><td>–</td><td>–</td><td>43</td><td>–</td></tr>
</table>

Player	FAPL		League		FACup		LgeCup		Europe		Totals	
	App	Goals	App	Goals	App	Goals	App	Goals	App	Goals	App	Goals
PF Simpson (1960-78)	–	–	353/17	10	53	1	32/1	3	20/1	1	458/19	15
F Sinclair (1896-97)	–	–	26	–	2	–	–	–	–	–	28	–
AFG Skirton (1959-66)	–	–	144/1	53	8	–	–	–	1	1	153/1	54
D Slade (1913-14)	–	–	12	4	–	–	–	–	–	–	12	4
JW Sloan (1946-48)	–	–	33	1	3	–	–	–	–	–	36	1
A Smith (1946)	–	–	3	–	–	–	–	–	–	–	3	–
AM Smith (1987-)	47/8	6	177/12	78	22/3	6	33/2	15	11	6	290/25	111
J Smith (1920-21)	–	–	10	1	–	–	–	–	–	–	10	1
L Smith (1939-54)	–	–	162	–	18	–	–	–	–	–	180	–
R Smithson (1959-64)	–	–	2	–	–	–	–	–	–	–	2	–
JD Snedden (1958-65)	–	–	83	–	10	–	–	–	1	–	94	–
BE Sparrow (1977-84)	–	–	2	–	–	–	–	–	–	–	2	–
TA Spicer (1900-01)	–	–	4	–	–	–	–	–	–	–	4	–
WA Spittle (1912-19)	–	–	7	–	–	–	–	–	–	–	7	–
JA Standen (1952-60)	–	–	35	–	3	–	–	–	–	–	38	–
FA Stapleton (1972-81)	–	–	223/2	75	32	15	26/1	14	15	4	296/3	108
K Stead (1977-79)	–	–	1/1	–	–	–	–	–	–	–	1/1	–
A Steven (1897)	–	–	5	–	1	1	–	–	–	–	6	2
RC Stevens (1909-10)	–	–	7	1	–	–	–	–	–	–	7	1
R Stevenson (1894-95)	–	–	7	–	–	–	–	–	–	–	7	–
W Stewart (1889-93)	–	–	–	–	2	–	–	–	–	–	2	–
RR Stockill (1931-34)	–	–	7	4	–	–	–	–	–	–	7	4
S Stonley (1913-14)	–	–	38	14	1	–	–	–	–	–	39	14
H Storer (1894-95)	–	–	40	–	1	–	–	–	–	–	41	–
PE Storey (1961-77)	–	–	387/4	9	49/2	4	36/1	2	22	2	494/7	17

Player	FAPL		League		FACup		LgeCup		Europe		Totals	
	App	Goals	App	Goals	App	Goals	App	Goals	App	Goals	App	Goals
JA Storrs (1893-95)	–	–	12	–	4	–	–	–	–	–	16	–
GH Strong (1957-64)	–	–	125	69	8	5	–	–	4	3	137	77
J Stuart (1897)	–	–	2	1	–	–	–	–	–	–	2	1
CH Sullivan (1954-58)	–	–	28	–	4	–	–	–	–	–	32	–
A Sunderland (1977-84)	–	–	204/2	55	34	16	26	13	13/1	7	277/3	91
R Swallow (1952-58)	–	–	13	4	–	–	–	–	–	–	13	4
A Swan (1901)	–	–	7	2	–	–	–	–	–	–	7	2
GH Swindin (1936-54)	–	–	271	–	23	–	–	–	–	–	294	–
A Talbot (1896-97)	–	–	5	–	–	–	–	–	–	–	5	–
BE Talbot (1979-85)	–	–	245/9	40	29/1	7	26/1	1	15	1	315/11	49
DR Tapscott (1953-58)	–	–	119	26	13	6	–	–	–	–	132	32
B Tawse (1963-65)	–	–	5	–	–	–	–	–	–	–	5	–
R Templeton (1904-06)	–	–	33	1	8	–	–	–	–	–	41	1
J Tennant (1899-1901)	–	–	51	8	3	2	–	–	–	–	54	10
WS Theobald (1900-09)	–	–	24	–	–	–	–	–	–	–	24	–
ML Thomas (1982-91)	–	–	149/14	24	14/3	1	22/2	5	1/1	–	186/20	29
L Thompson (1928-33)	–	–	26	6	1	–	–	–	–	–	27	6
M Thomson (1908-14)	–	–	89	1	5	–	–	–	–	–	94	1
HC Thorpe (1903-04)	–	–	10	–	–	–	–	–	–	–	10	–
MD Tiddy (1955-58)	–	–	48	8	4	–	–	–	–	–	52	8
P Tilley (1952-53)	–	–	1	–	–	–	–	–	–	–	1	–
J Toner (1919-26)	–	–	89	6	11	–	–	–	–	–	100	6
FA Townrow (1921-26)	–	–	8	2	1	–	–	–	–	–	11	2
RW Tricker (1927-29)	–	–	12	5	–	–	–	–	–	–	12	5

Player	FAPL App	FAPL Goals	League App	League Goals	FACup App	FACup Goals	LgeCup App	LgeCup Goals	Europe App	Europe Goals	Totals App	Totals Goals
RF Trim (1933-37)	–	–	1	–	–	–	–	–	–	–	1	–
EW Tuckett (1932-37)	–	–	2	–	–	–	–	–	–	–	2	–
RH Turnbull (1921-24)	–	–	59	26	7	2	–	–	–	–	66	28
P Turner (1900-01)	–	–	33	5	3	–	–	–	–	–	36	5
A Tyrer (1965-67)	–	–	–	–	–	–	1/1	1	–	–	1/1	1
JF 'Ian' Ure (1963-69)	–	–	168	2	16	–	14	–	4	–	202	2
PL Vaessen (1977-82)	–	–	23/9	6	–	–	1/1	2	3/4	1	27/14	9
TH Vallance (1946-53)	–	–	15	2	–	–	–	–	–	–	15	2
JW Vaughan (1900-03)	–	–	–	–	1	–	–	–	–	–	1	–
CR Voysey (1919-26)	–	–	35	6	2	–	–	–	–	–	37	6
JS Ward (1944-56)	–	–	86	–	7	–	–	–	–	–	93	–
HA Walden (1920-21)	–	–	2	1	–	–	–	–	–	–	2	1
SJ Walford (1977-81)	–	–	64/13	3	5/5	–	5	1	3/2	–	77/20	4
H Waller (1937-47)	–	–	8	–	1	–	–	–	–	–	9	–
JT Walley (1964-67)	–	–	10/4	1	1	–	3	–	–	–	14/4	1
E Wallington (1923-24)	–	–	1	–	–	–	–	–	–	–	1	–
JB Walsh (1949-55)	–	–	17	–	–	–	–	–	–	–	17	–
CH Walsh (1930-33)	–	–	–	–	1	–	–	–	–	–	1	–
W Walsh (1935-39)	–	–	3	–	–	–	–	–	–	–	3	–
A Ward (1895)	–	–	7	–	–	–	–	–	–	–	7	–
G Ward (1952-63)	–	–	81	10	3	–	–	–	–	–	84	10
WH Warnes (1925-33)	–	–	–	–	1	–	–	–	–	–	1	–

Player	FAPL App	FAPL Goals	League App	League Goals	FACup App	FACup Goals	LgeCup App	LgeCup Goals	Europe App	Europe Goals	Totals App	Totals Goals
R Watson (1903-05)	–	–	9	1	1	–	–	–	–	–	10	1
MW Webster (1966-70)	–	–	3	–	–	–	2	–	1	–	6	–
R Westcott (1935-36)	–	–	2	1	–	–	–	–	–	–	2	1
HA White (1919-23)	–	–	101	40	8	5	–	–	–	–	109	45
W White (1897-99)	–	–	39	16	3	–	–	–	–	–	42	16
J Whitfield (1896-97)	–	–	2	–	–	–	–	–	–	–	2	–
TJ Whittaker (1919-25)	–	–	64	2	6	–	–	–	–	–	70	2
CA Whyte (1977-86)	–	–	86/4	8	5	–	14	–	3/1	–	108/4	8
J Wilkinson (1953-56)	–	–	1	–	–	–	–	–	–	–	1	–
CA Williams (1891-94)	–	–	19	–	4	–	–	–	–	–	23	–
E Williams (1889-90)	–	–	–	–	1	–	–	–	–	–	1	–
JJ Williams (1929-320)	–	–	22	5	4	–	–	–	–	–	26	5
SC Williams (1984-88)	–	–	93/2	4	11	–	15	1	–	–	119/2	5
W Williams (1893-95)	–	–	1	–	–	–	–	–	–	–	1	–
E Williamson (1919-23)	–	–	105	–	8	–	–	–	–	–	113	–
LE Wills (1949-62)	–	–	195	4	13	–	–	–	–	–	208	4
RJ Wimot (1977-89)	–	–	8	–	–	–	1	–	–	–	9	–
A Wilson (1933-41)	–	–	82	–	7	–	–	–	–	–	89	–
J Wilson (1896-97)	–	–	–	–	1	–	–	–	–	–	1	–
O Wilson (1912-13)	–	–	–	–	–	–	–	–	–	–	–	–
RP Wilson (1963-74)	–	–	234	–	32	–	18	–	24	–	308	–
T Winship (1910-15)	–	–	55	7	1	–	–	–	–	–	56	7
N Winterburn (1987-)	63	1	169/1	4	28	–	30	3	13	–	303/1	8
G Wolfe (1900-03)	–	–	5	–	–	–	–	–	–	–	5	–
G Wood (1980-83)	–	–	60	–	1	–	7	–	2	–	70	–

Player	FAPL App	FAPL Goals	League App	League Goals	FACup App	FACup Goals	LgeCup App	LgeCup Goals	Europe App	Europe Goals	Totals App	Totals Goals
Wood (1892)	–	–	–	–	1	–	–	–	–	–	1	–
A Woodcock (1982-86)	–	–	129/2	56	13/1	7	20/2	5	2	–	164/5	68
H Woods (1923-26)	–	–	70	21	5	1	–	–	–	–	75	22
J Woodward (1966-71)	–	–	2/1	–	–	–	1	–	–	–	3/1	–
A Worrall (1894)	–	–	4	1	–	–	–	–	–	–	4	1
IE Wright (1991-)	69/1	38	30	24	10	11	15	18	6	4	130/1	95
AR Young (1956-61)	–	–	4	–	–	–	–	–	–	–	4	–
A Young (1922-27)	–	–	68	9	3	–	–	–	–	–	71	9
WD Young (1977-81)	–	–	170	11	28	3	20	1	18	4	236	19

Players' International Appearances Whilst with Arsenal

The totals given are for appearances made whilst Arsenal players. Unofficial and wartime international appearances are not included. As at 31st May 1994.

England

ADAMS, T A	(31)	1987 v Spain, Turkey (2), Brazil, West Germany, Yugoslavia; 1988 v Holland (2), Hungary, Scotland, Colombia, Switzerland, Ireland, USSR; 1989 v Denmark, Sweden, Saudi Arabia; 1990 v Ireland; 1991 v Ireland; 1992 v Norway, Turkey; 1993 v San Marino, Turkey, Holland (2), Poland (2), Norway; 1994 v Denmark, Greece, Norway.
ANDERSON, V A	(16)	1984 v Turkey; 1985 v Northern Ireland, Ireland, Romania, Finland, Scotland, USA, Mexico; 1986 v USSR, Mexico, Sweden, Northern Ireland, Yugoslavia; 1987 v Spain, Northern Ireland, Turkey.
ASHCROFT, J	(3)	1906 v Northern Ireland, Wales, Scotland.
BAKER, A	(1)	1927 v Wales.
BAKER, J H	(3)	1965 v Northern Ireland, Spain; 1966 v Poland.
BALL, A J	(19)	1972 v West Germany (2), Scotland, Yugoslavia, Wales; 1973 v Wales (2), Scotland (2), Northern Ireland, Czechoslovakia, Poland; 1974 v Portugal (sub); 1975 v West Germany, Cyprus (2), Northern Ireland, Wales, Scotland.
BASTIN, C S	(21)	1931 v Wales; 1933 v Italy, Switzerland, Northern Ireland, Wales; 1934 v Scotland, Hungary, Czechoslovakia, Italy; 1935 v Northern Ireland, Scotland, Germany; 1936 v Wales (2), Scotland, Austria, Northern Ireland; 1938 v Scotland, Germany, Switzerland, France.
BLOCKLEY, J P	(1)	1972 v Yugoslavia.
BOULD, S	(2)	1994 v Greece, Denmark.
BOWDEN, E R	(6)	1934 v Wales, Italy; 1935 v Northern Ireland; 1936 v Wales, Austria, Hungary.
BUTLER, J D	(1)	1924 v Belgium.
CLAPTON, D R	(1)	1958 v Wales.
COLEMAN, J G	(1)	1907 v Northern Ireland.

COMPTON, L H	(2)	1950 v Wales, Yugoslavia.
COPPING, W	(13)	1934 v Italy, Northern Ireland; 1936 v Austria, Belgium; 1937 v Norway, Sweden, Finland. Northern Ireland, Wales, Czechoslovakia; 1938 v Scotland, Wales, Rest of Europe.
CRAYSTON, W J	(8)	1935 v Germany; 1936 v Wales, Scotland, Austria, Belgium; 1937 v Northern Ireland, Wales, Czechoslovakia.
DIXON, L M	21)	1990 v Czechoslovakia, Hungary, Poland, Ireland; 1991 v Cameroon, Ireland, Turkey (2), Argentina, Germany, Poland; 1992 v Czechoslovakia (sub), Norway, Turkey, Spain; 1993 v San Marino (2), Turkey, Holland, Norway, USA.
DRAKE, E J	(5)	1934 v Italy; 1935 v Northern Ireland; 1936 v Wales, Hungary; 1938 v France.
DUCAT, A	(3)	1910 v Northern Ireland, Wales, Scotland.
EASTHAM, G E	(19)	1963 v Brazil, Czechoslovakia, East Germany, Wales, Rest of World, Northern Ireland; 1964 v Scotland, Uruguay, Portugal, Ireland, USA, Brazil, Argentina; 1965 v Hungary, West Germany, Sweden. Spain; 1966 v Poland, Denmark.
HAPGOOD, E A	(30)	1933 v Italy, Switzerland, Northern Ireland, Wales; 1934 v Scotland, Hungary, Czechoslovakia, Wales, Italy; 1935 v Northern Ireland (2), Scotland, Holland, Germany; 1936 v Wales, Scotland, Austria, Belgium; 1937 v Finland; 1938 v Scotland, Germany, Switzerland, France, Wales, Rest of Europe, Norway, Northern Ireland; 1939 v Scotland, Italy, Yugoslavia.
HULME, J H A	(9)	1927 v Scotland, Belgium, France, Northern Ireland. Wales; 1928 v Scotland, Northern Ireland, Wales; 1933 v Scotland.
JACK, D B N	(5)	1930 v Scotland, Germany, Austria; 1932 v Wales, Austria.
JOY, B	(1)	1936 v Belgium.
KEOWN, M R	(2)	1993 v Holland, Germany (sub).
KIRCHEN, A J	(3)	1937 v Norway, Sweden, Finland.
McNAB, R	(4)	1968 v Romania (sub), Bulgaria; 1969 v Romania. Northern Ireland.
MALE, C G	(19)	1934 v Italy; 1935 v Northern Ireland (2), Scotland,

Holland, Germany; 1936 v Wales, Scotland,
Austria, Belgium. Northern Ireland, Hungary;
1937 v Scotland, Norway, Sweden, Finland;
1939 v Italy, Yugoslavia, Romania.

MARINER, P   (2)   1984 v East Germany; 1985 v Romania.

MARWOOD, B   (1)   1988 v Saudi Arabia (sub).

MERSON, P C   (14)   1991 v Germany (sub); 1992 v Czechoslovakia,
                            Hungary, Brazil (sub), Finland (sub), Denmark,
                            Sweden (sub), Norway (sub), Spain (sub);
                            1993 v Holland (2 including 1 as sub), Brazil (sub),
                            Germany; 1994 v Greece.

MILTON, C A   (1)   1951 v Austria.

MOSS, F   (4)   1934 v Scotland, Hungary, Czechoslovakia, Italy.

RADFORD, J   (2)   1969 v Romania; 1971 v Switzerland (sub).

RIMMER, J J   (1)   1976 v Italy.

RIX, G   (17)   1980 v Norway, Romania, Switzerland (sub);
                            1981 v Brazil, Wales, Scotland; 1982 v Holland
                            (sub), Finland (sub), France, Czechoslovakia,
                            Kuwait, West Germany, (2 incl. 1 sub), Spain,
                            Denmark; 1983 v Greece (sub); 1984 v Northern
                            Ireland.

ROBERTS, H   (1)   1931 v Scotland.

ROCASTLE, D   (14)   1988 v Denmark, Saudi Arabia; 1989 v Greece,
                            Albania (2), Poland (2 incl. 1 sub), Denmark, Sweden
                            (sub), Yugoslavia; 1990 v Denmark (sub);
                            1991 v Poland; 1992 v Czechoslovakia, Brazil (sub).

SANSOM, K G   (77)   1980 v Norway, Romania, Switzerland;
                            1981 v Spain, Romania, Brazil, Wales, Scotland,
                            Switzerland; 1982 v Northern Ireland, Wales,
                            Holland, Scotland, Finland, France,
                            Czechoslovakia, West Germany (2), Spain,
                            Denmark, Greece, Luxembourg; 1983 v Greece,
                            Holland (2), Northern Ireland, Scotland, Denmark,
                            Luxembourg; 1984 v France, Scotland, USSR,
                            Brazil, Uruguay, Chile, East, Germany, Finland,
                            Turkey; 1985 v Northern Ireland (2); Ireland,
                            Romania (2), Finland, Scotland, Italy, Mexico,
                            West Germany, USA, Turkey; 1986 v Egypt,
                            Israel, USSR, Spain, Mexico, Canada, Portugal,
                            Morocco, Poland, Paraguay, Argentina. Sweden,
                            Northern Ireland, Yugoslavia; 1987 v Spain,

		Northern Ireland, Turkey (2), West Germany, Yugoslavia; 1988 v Holland (2), Scotland, Colombia, Switzerland, Ireland, USSR.
SCOTT, L	(17)	1946 v Northern Ireland, Ireland, Wales, Holland; 1947 v Scotland, France, Switzerland, Portugal, Belgium, Wales, Northern Ireland, Sweden; 1948 v Scotland, Italy, Denmark, Northern Ireland, Wales.
SEAMAN, D A	(11)	1991 v Cameroon, Ireland, Turkey, Argentina; 1992 v Czechoslovakia, Hungary (sub); 1993 v Poland, Holland, San Marino; 1994 v Denmark, Norway.
SMITH, A M	(13)	1988 v Saudi Arabia (sub); 1989 v Greece, Albania (sub), Poland (sub); 1991 v Turkey (2); 1992 v USSR, Argentina, Germany, Poland (sub), Hungary (sub), Denmark, Sweden (sub).
SMITH, L	(6)	1950 v Wales; 1951 v Wales, Northern Ireland; 1952 v Wales, Belgium; 1953 v Scotland.
STOREY, P E	(19)	1971 v Greece, Northern Ireland, Scotland, Switzerland; 1972 v West Germany, Wales (2), Northern Ireland, Scotland, Yugoslavia; 1973 v Wales (2), Scotland (2), Northern Ireland, Czechoslovakia, Poland, USSR, Italy.
SUNDERLAND, A	(1)	1980 v Australia.
TALBOT, B E	(1)	1980 v Australia.
THOMAS, M L	(2)	1988 v Saudi Arabia; 1989 v Yugoslavia.
WILLIAMSON, E C	(2)	1923 v Sweden (2).
WINTERBURN, N	(2)	1989 v Italy (sub); 1993 v Germany (sub).
WOODCOCK, A S	(18)	1982 v West Germany (sub), Greece, Luxembourg; 1983 v Greece, Luxembourg; 1984 v France (sub), Northern Ireland, Wales, Scotland, Brazil, Uruguay (sub), East Germany, Finland, Turkey; 1985 v Northern Ireland, Romania (sub), Turkey (sub); 1986 v Israel (sub).
WRIGHT, I E	(13)	1992 v Hungary (sub), Norway, Turkey; 1993 v Turkey, Norway (sub), USA (sub), Brazil, Germany (sub), Poland, Holland (sub), San Marino; 1994 v Greece (sub), Norway (sub).

DOCHERTY, T H	(3)	1958 v Wales, Northern Ireland; 1959 v England.
FITCHIE, T T	(3)	1905 v Wales; 1906 v Wales, Northern Ireland.
FORBES, A R	(9)	1950 v England, Portugal, France, Wales, Northern Ireland, Austria; 1951 v Wales; 1952 v Denmark, Sweden.
GRAHAM, A	(1)	1921 v Northern Ireland.
GRAHAM, G	(8)	1971 v Portugal, Holland; 1972 v Northern Ireland, Yugoslavia, Czechoslovakia, Brazil, Denmark, (2).
HARPER, W	(2)	1926 v Northern Ireland, England.
HENDERSON, J G	(2)	1958 v Wales, Northern Ireland.
HERD, D G	(5)	1958 v Wales, Northern Ireland; 1959 v England; 1961 v Ireland, Czechoslovakia.
JAMES, A	(4)	1929 v Wales; 1930 v Northern Ireland, England; 1932 v Wales.
LOGIE, J T	(1)	1952 v Northern Ireland.
MACAULAY, A R	(6)	1947 v Northern Ireland, Wales; 1948 v England, Belgium, Switzerland, France.
McLINTOCK, F	(6)	1964 v Northern Ireland; 1967 v USSR; 1970 v Northern Ireland; 1971 v Wales, Northern Ireland, England.
NICHOLAS, C	(13)	1983 v Belgium; 1984 v France (sub), Yugoslavia, (sub), Iceland (sub); 1985 v Spain (sub), Wales (sub); 1986 v Israel, Romania (sub), England, Denmark, Uruguay (sub), Bulgaria; 1987 v England (sub).
SHARP, J	(3)	1907 v Wales, England; 1908 v England.
TEMPLETON, R B	(1)	1905 v Wales.
URE, J F	(3)	1963 v Northern Ireland, Norway; 1967 v Northern Ireland.
WILSON, R P	(2)	1971 v Portugal, Holland.
WOOD, G	(1)	1982 v Northern Ireland.

BARNES, W	(22)	1947 v England, Scotland; 1948 v Northern Ireland, Scotland, England; 1949 v Northern Ireland. England, Scotland, Belgium; 1950 v Northern Ireland, Scotland, England; 1951 v Northern Ireland, Portugal, England. Scotland, United Kingdom; 1952 v Northern Ireland; 1953 v England, Scotland; 1954 v Yugoslavia, Scotland.
BOWEN, D L	(19)	1954 v Yugoslavia, Scotland; 1957 v Northern Ireland, Czechoslovakia, East Germany (2), England, Scotland; 1958 v Israel (2), Northern Ireland, Hungary (2), Mexico, Sweden, Brazil, Scotland, England; 1959 v Northern Ireland.
CHARLES, M	(6)	1961 v Northern Ireland, Spain (2), Hungary, England, Scotland.
CUMNER, R H	(3)	1938 v England, Scotland; 1939 v Northern Ireland
DANIEL, R W	(12)	1950 v England, Northern Ireland. Portugal;1951 v England, Scotland, United Kingdom;1952 v Northern Ireland, Scotland, England 1953 v Northern Ireland, France, Yugoslavia.
JENKYNS. C A L	(1)	1896 v Scotland.
JOHN. R F	(15)	1923 v Scotland, Northern Ireland;1925 v Northern Ireland; 1926 v England;1927 v England (2); 1928 v Northern Ireland;1929 v Scotland, England; 1931 v England; 1932 v Northern Ireland; 1933 v France; 1935 v Northern Ireland. Scotland; 1936 v England.
JONES, B	(7)	1938 v England. Scotland; 1939 v Northern Ireland; 1946 v Scotland; 1947 v Northern Ireland, England; 1948 v Scotland.
JONES, C	(4)	1929 v Scotland, England; 1931 v England; 1933 v France.
JONES, L J	(4)	1937 v England; 1938 v Northern Ireland, England, Scotland.
KELSEY, A J	(41)	1954 v Northern Ireland, Austria, Yugoslavia, Scotland; 1955 v Northern Ireland, England, Scotland, Austria; 1956 v Northern Ireland, Scotland. England; 1957 v Northern Ireland. Czechoslovakia (2), East Germany, England, Scotland; 1958 v Israel (2), Northern Ireland,

253

		Hungary (2), Mexico, Sweden, Brazil, Scotland, England; 1959 v England, Scotland; 1960 v Northern Ireland, Scotland, England; 1961 v Northern Ireland, Spain (2), Hungary, England, Scotland; 1962, Northern Ireland, Brazil (2).
LEWIS, D	(3)	1927 v England; 1928 v Northern Ireland; 1929 v England.
NICHOLAS, P	(17)	1981 v Turkey, Scotland, England, USSR (2), Czechoslovakia, Iceland; 1982 v Spain, England, Scotland, Northern Ireland, France, Yugoslavia; 1983 v Bulgaria, Scotland, Northern Ireland, Norway.
ROBERTS, J G	(7)	1971 v Scotland, England, Northern Ireland, Finland (2); 1972 v England, Northern Ireland
TAPSCOTT, D R	(12)	1954 v Austria, Yugoslavia, Scotland, England; 1955 v Northern Ireland, England, Scotland, Austria; 1956 v Northern Ireland; 1957 v Northern Ireland, Czechoslovakia, East Germany.

Northern Ireland (Including Ireland before 1924)

DICKSON, W	(3)	1953 v England; 1954 v Wales, England.
JENNINGS, P A	(42)	1977 v Iceland, Holland, Belgium; 1978 v Ireland, Denmark; 1979 v Bulgaria (2), England (3), Scotland, Wales, Denmark, Ireland; 1980 v Israel; 1981 v Scotland (3), Portugal, Sweden, Israel; 1982 v England, Wales, Yugoslavia, Honduras, Spain, France; 1983 v Albania, Scotland (2), England, Wales, Austria, Turkey, West Germany; 1984 v Wales, Finland (2), Romania; 1985 v England, Spain, Turkey.
KENNEDY, A L	(2)	1923 v Wales; 1924 v England.
McCLELLAND, J	(5)	1960 v West Germany; 1961 v Wales, Italy, Greece, West Germany.
McCULLOUGH, W J	(9)	1961 v Italy; 1963 v Spain (2), Scotland, England; 1964 v Wales, Uruguay, England, Switzerland.
MACIE, J A	(1)	1923 v Wales.
MAGILL, E J	(21)	1961 v Scotland, Greece, England; 1962 v Poland (2), England, Scotland; 1963 v Wales, Spain (2), Scotland, England; 1964 v Wales, Uruguay, England, Switzerland (2), Scotland; 1965 v Holland, Albania, Scotland.

MORROW, S J	(12)	1990 v Uruguay (sub), Austria (sub); 1991 v Poland, Yugoslavia, Faroe Islands; 1992 v Scotland (sub), Germany (sub), Spain (sub); 1993 v Albania, Ireland; 1994 v Romania, Colombia.
NEILL, W J T	(44)	1961 v 1961 v Italy, Grece (2), West Germany, Scotland, England; 1962 v Wales, England, Poland; 1963 v Wales, Spain (2), England, Scotland: 1964 v Wales, Uruguay, England, Switzerland, Scotland; 1965 v Holland (2), Wales, Albania (2), Scotland, England; 1966 v Wales, West Germany, Mexico, Scotland; 1967 v Wales, Scotland, England; 1968 v Israel, Turkey (2); 1969 v England (2), vScotland (2), Wales (2), USSR (2).
NELSON, S	(48)	1970 v England (sub), Wales, Spain; 1971 v Cyprus, England, Scotland, Wales, USSR, (2); 1972 v Spain, Scotland, England, Wales; 1973 v Bugaria, Cyprus, Portugal; 1974 v Scotland, England, Sweden; 1975, Yugoslavia, Sweden, Norway; 1976 v Israel, England, Belgium (sub); 1977 v West Germany, Wales, Iceland (2), Holland, Belgium; 1978 v Wales (sub), Ireland, Denmark; 1979 v Bulgaria (2), England (3), Scotland, Wales, Denmark, Ireland, Denmark; 1980 v Israel; 1981 v Scotland (2), Portugal, Sweden.
RICE, P J	(49)	1968 v Israel; 1969 v USSR; 1971 v England, Scotland, Wales, USSR; 1972 v Spain, Scotland, England, Wales; 1973 v Bulgaria (2), Cyprus, England, Scotland, Wales, Portugal; 1974 v Scotland, England, Wales, Norway; 1975 v Yugoslavia (2), England, Wales, Scotland, Sweden, Norway; 1976 v Israel, Scotland, England, Wales, Holland, Belgium; 1977 v West Germany, England, Scotland, Iceland (2), Holland, Belgium; 1978 v Ireland. Denmark; 1979 v England (3), Scotland, Wales, Denmark.
SHANKS, T	(2)	1903 v Scotland; 1904 v Wales.
SLOAN, J W	(1)	1947 v Wales.
TONER, J	(6)	1922 v Wales; 1923 v Wales, England; 1924 v Wales, England; 1925 v Scotland.

BRADY, W L	(26)	1974 v USSR, Turkey; 1975 v Switzerland (2), USSR, Turkey; 1976 v Norway, Poland, England, Turkey, France; 1977 v France, Spain, Bulgaria (2); 1978 v Norway, Northern Ireland, England; 1979 v Denmark, Bulgaria (2), West Germany, Argentina, Wales; 1980 v England, Cyprus.
DEVINE, J A	(7)	1979 v Czechoslovakia, Northern Ireland; 1981 v Czechoslovakia, Holland; 1982 v Algeria, Spain; 1983 v Malta.
DUNNE, J	(3)	1936 v Switzerland, Hungary, Luxembourg.
HAVERTY, J	(15)	1956 v Holland, Denmark, West Germany; 1957 v Denmark, England (2); 1958 v Poland (2), Austria; 1959 v Sweden; 1960 v Chile, Wales, Norway; 1961 v Scotland (2).
McGOLDRICK, E J	(3)	1993 v Northern Ireland; 1994 v Russia, Holland, Czech Republic.
MANCINI, T J	(1)	1974 v USSR.
O'FLANAGAN, K P	(3)	1946 v England; 1947 v Spain, Portugal.
O'LEARY, D A	(68)	1976 v England, France; 1977 v France, Spain, Bulgaria (2); 1978 v Norway, Denmark, England; 1979 v Bulgaria (2), West Germany, Argentina, Wales, Northern Ireland; 1980 v England, Cyprus, Holland; 1981 v Czechoslovakia, Poland, Holland, France; 1982 v Holland, Iceland; 1983 v Spain; 1984 v Poland, Israel, China, USSR, Norway, Denmark; 1985 v Israel, England (sub), Norway, Spain, Switzerland (2), USSR, Denmark; 1986 v Wales; 1988 v Spain; 1989 v Malta (2), Hungary, West Germany, Northern Ireland (sub); 1990, v Wales (sub), USSR, Finland, Romania (sub), Turkey (2), Malta, Morocco, England; 1991 v England, Poland (2), Chile, Hungary, Turkey; 1992, Wales, Switzerland, USA, Italy, Portugal, Albania; 1993, Wales.
QUINN, N J	(13)	1986 v Iceland (sub), Czechoslovakia; 1987 v Bulgaria, (2 sub), Luxembourg (sub), Israel; 1988 v Romania (sub), Poland (sub), Norway (sub), England (sub), Tunisia (sub), Spain (sub), 1989 v Hungary (sub).
SCULLY, P J	(1)	1988 v Tunisia (sub).

SLOAN, J W   (2)   1946 v Portugal, Spain.

STAPLETON, F A   (24)   1976 v Turkey, France; 1977 v Spain, Bulgaria (2);
                            1978 v Norway, Denmark, Northern Ireland,
                            England (sub); 1979, Denmark, West Germany,
                            Argentina, Wales, Bulgaria. Northern Ireland;
                            1980 v England, Cyprus (2), Holland, Belgium,
                            France; 1981 v Belgium, Czechoslovakia, Poland.

Denmark

JENSEN, J   (15)   1992 v Latvia, Germany. Lithuania, Republic of
                            Ireland, Northern Ireland; 1993 v Spain(2), Latvia,
                            Republic of Ireland, Albania(2), Lithuania,
                            Northern Ireland; 1994 v England, Hungary.

Iceland

JONSSON, S   (5)   1990 v Czechoslovakia, Spain; 1991 v Denmark,
                            Spain, Cyprus.

Norway

LYDERSEN, P   (6)   1991 v Czechoslovakia, Italy; 1992 v Italy, Egypt,
                            Denmark. Sweden; 1993 v Portugal.

Sweden

LIMPAR, A E   (24)   1990 v Bulgaria; 1991 v Austria, Colombia,
                            Norway, Yugoslavia, Switzerland; 1992 v
                            Hungary, France, Denmark, England, Germany
                            (sub), Norway, Finland, Bulgaria; 1993 v Hungary,
                            Switzerland, France (sub), Bulgaria, Finland;
                            1994 v Colombia, USA (sub), Mexico.

Seaman!

Getting a grip: David Seaman, capped 11 times for England so far.

Miscellaneous

Managers

Thomas Mitchell   1897 – 1898

Arsenal's first professional manager joined the club from Blackburn Rovers and
remained at Plumstead for less than one season. During his period in charge the
club rose from tenth to fifth in the League and progressed through the qualifying
rounds of the FA Cup to the first round proper, where they were knocked out by
Burnley.

Despite the improved performances on the pitch, support continued to fall away
and the club's financial situation became very serious. Probably as a result of these
circumstances Mitchell resigned in March 1898.

George Elcoat   1898 – 1899

George Elcoat also only stayed for one season after succeeding Thomas Mitchell. A
native of Stockton-on-Tees, Elcoat signed several Scottish players and at one point
no less than eight of the first team were from over the border.

In the 1898/99 season Arsenal finished seventh in an expanded League. Although
exempt from the qualifying rounds of the FA Cup this season, the club lost 6-0 at
home to Derby County in the first round proper.

Financial problems still beset the club and several players had to be released to
prevent the club from sliding into bankruptcy. Unable to face the situation any
longer Elcoat left at the end of the season.

Harry Bradshaw   1899 – 1904

In the space of five years Harry Bradshaw transformed the fortunes of Arsenal
taking them from the point of bankruptcy to the building of a team which was to
win promotion to the First Division. Bradshaw had first made his name with
Burnley from 1891 to 1899 and, with little money available at Arsenal, he initially
recruited local talent. Adopting the Scottish-style short accurate passing game
Arsenal rose to fourth in the table by 1901/02. The improvement in results brought
an increase in support and the club were able to afford new players. Third position
in the League was achieved in 1902/03 and the following season promotion was at
last realised when they finished runners-up to Preston North End.

Having achieved this success Bradshaw stunned Arsenal by deciding to leave the
club and join Fulham taking his two sons, William and Joseph, with him. He was
equally successful at Fulham taking them from the Southern League into the
Football League and to a FA Cup semi-final before becoming the secretary of the
Southern League until his death in 1925.

Phil Kelso   1904 – 1908

A hard-rugged Scot associated with Hibernian for many years, Phil Kelso was
Arsenal's first manager in First Division football. His first priority was to
strengthen the attack with the signings of Satterthwaite, Fitchie and Templeton and
he also maintained a sound defence with the capture of Scottish full-backs Gary and
Sharp. In Kelso's second season with the club Arsenal reached the semi-final of the
FA Cup for the first time losing 2-0 to Newcastle United. The 1906/07 season was
the club's best so far – seventh in Division One and losing semi-finalists in the FA
Cup again.

Arsenal struggled the next season attendances dropped and the financial position
once again became unstable. Kelso was unable to cope with the situation and he
resigned before the end of the season, returning to Scotland to run a hotel.

Twelve months later he followed the path of Harry Bradshaw to Fulham, staying
as their manager until 1924 when he retired. He died in 1935 at the age of 64.

George Morrell   1908 – 1915

Kelso's replacement was another Scot, George Morrell, who had previous
experience with Glenure Athletic and Greenock Morton and who unfortunately
became the only Arsenal manager ever to suffer relegation.

Having turned around the financial fortunes of Greenock Morton, Morrell again
found himself at a club with similar problems. Despite being forced to part with
several key players in Morrell's first season, the club finished in a respectable sixth
position in the League. In an attempt to boost support Morrell brought in such well-
known players as Leigh Roose and Alf Common but, as the financial situation
worsened, they also had to be sold.

Relegation finally came in 1912/13 and with it the worst playing record in the
club's history. In search of better support Arsenal moved to North London and
Morrell became the club's first manager at Highbury. Despite two brave attempts to
regain their First Division status Arsenal's financial problems continued and
Morrell was forced to resign at the end of 1914-15 as the club officially closed
down because of war.

Leslie Knighton   1919 – 1925

The end of World War One saw Sir Henry Norris, the Arsenal chairman, use his
influence to secure First Division status for the Gunners and he then appointed
Leslie Knighton as manager.

With previous experience as assistant manager at Huddersfield and in charge at
Manchester City, where he built a young successful side, Knighton joined the club
in May 1919. On his arrival at Arsenal, Knighton's task was clearly defined by
Norris – to build a successful team without spending on big transfer fees and
preferably by developing his own players. Despite this restriction Knighton's
persuasive tongue managed to attract a good standard of player to Highbury during
his time in charge.

During his six seasons at Highbury the best League position achieved was ninth and relegation was narrowly avoided twice. In 1924/25 Knighton clashed with Norris over new signings and, with the club having been knocked out of the cup in the first round and in 20th place in the league, the chairman advertised for a new manager.

Knighton went on to manage Bournemouth, Birmingham – who he took to the 1931 FA Cup Final – Chelsea and Shrewsbury Town. He died after a major operation in 1959.

Herbert Chapman   1925 – 1934

The man who put Arsenal on top of the soccer world only came into football management by chance. A colleague at Tottenham Hotspur was offered the post of player-manager of Northampton Town and suggested to Chapman that he would be more suited to the job. His application was accepted and thus began the career of one of the game's greatest managers.

Born in 1878 at Kiveton Park near Sheffield, Chapman gained playing experience with several local clubs and Southern League Northampton Town before joining Tottenham in 1905. He took over as player-manager at Northampton in April 1907 and took the club to the Southern League title in his second season. Success continued at Leeds City – until they closed down because of financial irregularities – and Huddersfield Town. During his five years with the Leeds Road club they reached the FA Cup Final, were promoted to Division One and twice won the League Championship.

The challenge at Arsenal appealed to Chapman and he was appointed manager in 1925. He immediately persuaded chairman Norris to reverse his policy on transfer fees and set about strengthening the Arsenal side bringing in such players as Buchan, Harper, Parker, Hume and Lambert. He quickly lifted the club out of the relegation zone to second place in the League and reached the quarter-finals of the FA Cup. The introduction of Jack, James, Hapgood and Bastin brought the club its first major honour when they won the FA Cup in 1930. A year later the League Championship came to Highbury and in 1931/32 they just failed to win the League and Cup double – ending up runners-up in both. The end of the 1932/33 season saw the League Championship once again won.

Tragedy struck midway the following season though when Chapman died on the 6th of January 1934 after what he thought was no more than a heavy cold. His far-sighted ideas and methods had not only benefited Arsenal but professional football as a whole.

George Allison   1934 – 1947

The Arsenal directors faced a monumental task in replacing Herbert Chapman and eventually George Allison, himself a director of the club since 1926, was appointed on a permanent basis in June 1934.

In the meantime Arsenal had won their third League Championship in four seasons and Allison further strengthened the team with the signing of Ted Drake,

Jack Crayston and Wilf Copping. A further two Championships and the FA Cup were won before the outbreak of the Second World War. During wartime Allison practically ran Arsenal on his own for seven years.

Allison did not possess the same football knowledge as Chapman, leaving much of the management of the players to Joe Shaw and Tom Whittaker. Off the field he was equal to his predecessor in the field of public relations and overall he maintained the success of Herbert Chapman and kept Arsenal as the leading club in the country.

Allison finally retired in May 1947. He died of a heart attack at his Golders Green home at the age of 73 in 1957.

Tom Whittaker   1947 – 1956

Born in Aldershot in 1898 but brought up in the Newcastle area, Whittaker joined Arsenal as a player in 1919. A knee injury in 1925 terminated his playing career and he was appointed assistant-trainer in 1926, succeeding George Hardy as trainer in 1927. He gradually built up a reputation as the finest trainer in the game, not only to Arsenal in the 1920s and 1930s but also to the full England international touring team.

After the Second World War, Whittaker was appointed assistant to George Allison and together they rescued Arsenal from the threat of relegation. In June 1947 he succeeded Allison and in his first season Arsenal ran away with the Championship. Turning down the chance of rebuilding Turin following an air disaster, Allison guided Arsenal to an FA Cup Final victory over Liverpool in 1950. Two years later he again led the Gunners to Wembley where a ten-man team went down to Newcastle United.

Arsenal won their seventh League Championship in 1952/53 but, with an ageing team breaking up and poor results in the league, a transitional period followed. The lack of success caused Whittaker great concern and he was later found to be suffering from nervous exhaustion and ordered to take a complete rest. A short while later he died of a heart attack in October 1956.

Jack Crayston   1956 – 1958

Following the death of Tom Whittaker, Jack Crayston was appointed manager in November 1956. Born in Grange-over-Sands in 1910, he began his league career with Barrow in 1928. After two years he joined Bradford before Arsenal signed him in May 1934. In five seasons at Highbury before the war he made over 200 appearances and won every major honour in the game. A war injury ended his playing career and he returned to Highbury on the coaching staff becoming assistant-manager in 1947 and then manager in 1956.

His first season in charge saw Arsenal finish fifth in the league and reach the FA Cup Sixth Round. The following season was disappointing and Arsenal slipped to 12th place and lost in the FA Cup at Northampton Town. With Crayston become increasingly frustrated by the lack of money being made available, he resigned as manager in May 1958.

He moved back to Yorkshire becoming manager and then secretary of Doncaster Rovers until 1961 when he left football to run a newsagents and general stores business until his retirement.

George Swindin   1958 – 1962

Following a lot of success at Peterborough United, former goalkeeper George Swindin was appointed manager in the summer of 1958. Born near Doncaster, Swindin gained League experience with Bradford City before joining Arsenal in 1936 winning a Championship medal in 1937/38. After the war he became an automatic choice for Arsenal for a number of years, winning another Championship medal and winners' and runners-up medals in the FA Cup. He became player-manager of Peterborough United in 1954 guiding them to three Midland League Championships.

His first season saw a drastic overhaul of the playing staff and a satisfactory third place in the league after heading the table for part of the campaign. The next season was a big disappointment as Arsenal finished 13th and made an early exit from the FA Cup. Two more seasons of mediocrity followed, with the playing position showing no sign of improvement. Swindin was not helped by the huge success of Tottenham at this time and accepting responsibility for the club's poor league showing he resigned at the end of the 1961/62 season.

He later became manager at Norwich City and Cardiff City before finally retiring to Spain.

Billy Wright   1962 – 1966

Billy Wright became manager in May 1962 having previously declined the position of coach at Highbury a few months earlier. Wright was born at Ironbridge Shropshire in 1924 and joined the groundstaff at Wolverhampton Wanderers at the age of 14. He made his League debut straight after the war becoming one of the game's top stars and, for many years, captained Wolves and England winning three Championship medals and an FA Cup Winner's medal.

In his first season the signing of Joe Baker from Torino signalled his good intentions and the Gunners finished in seventh position in the League. But things did not improve and results, performances and attendances deteriorated culminating in a humiliating FA Cup defeat at Peterborough in 1964/65. The 1965/66 season was even more disappointing – 14th in the League knocked out of the FA Cup at the first hurdle and an all-time low attendance of just 4,554 for a home game against Leeds United.

In the summer of 1966 the directors, impatient for success and bowing to pressure from supporters, relieved Wright of his duties and he left football for a successful career in television sport.

Bertie Mee   1966 – 1976

Ex-physiotherapist and trainer Bertie Mee took over from Billy Wright on a
temporary basis in June 1966 and was officially appointed manager in March 1967.
Born at Bulwell Nottingham in 1918, Mee had his playing career with Derby
County and Mansfield Town cut short by injury. He qualified as a physiotherapist
and spent 12 years as a rehabilitation officer to disabled servicemen before joining
Arsenal in 1960.

On taking over from Wright, Mee brought in Colin Addison, George Graham and
Bob McNab and, at the end of the season, the club had finished a respectable
seventh in the League. Mee steered the club from strength to strength, reaching two
League Cup Finals in 1968 and 1969 but losing both. Success came a year later in
1970 when Anderlecht were beaten in the European Fairs Cup – the first trophy to
arrive at Highbury for 17 years.

The following season was the greatest in the club's history, as Mee and new
coach Don Howe guided Arsenal to the League and FA Cup double. Over the next
two seasons the club came close to further honours – FA Cup Finalists in 1971/72
and runners-up in the League and Cup semi-finalists in 1972/73. After that the
fortunes of the club began to decline and, after two difficult seasons, Mee
announced in March 1976 that he would be retiring at the end of the season.

He later joined Watford as general manager before becoming a director of the
Hornets on his retirement.

Terry Neill   1976 – 1983

Terry Neill was born in Belfast in 1942 and started his career with Bangor City
before joining Arsenal in 1959. He made 241 League appearances for the Gunners
before joining Hull City as player-manager in June 1970. He won a total of 50 caps
for Northern Ireland and after managerial experience with Hull and Northern
Ireland he succeeded Bill Nicholson at Tottenham Hotspur.

On joining Arsenal he immediately made his first signing Malcolm Macdonald,
but found difficulty in managing his old playing colleagues in the team. However,
Don Howe returned in 1977/78 and together they brought further honours to
Highbury. That season saw them lose to Ipswich Town in the FA Cup Final but
they returned the following year to beat Manchester United and Neill won his first
trophy in club management. The 1979/80 season saw the FA Cup Final reached
again but defeat followed against Second Division West Ham United. More
disappointment followed a few days later as Arsenal lost to Valencia in a penalty
shoot-out in the final of the European Cup-Winners' Cup.

Subsequent years promised much but no further honours came to Highbury and
Neill could never adequately replace the likes of Liam Brady and Frank Stapleton
on their departures. The semi-finals of the League Cup and the FA Cup were both
reached in 1982/83 but both ended in defeat and under mounting pressure from the
board and fans, Neill was sacked in December 1983.

Don Howe was appointed caretaker manager in December 1983 and confirmed as manager the following April. Born in October 1935, Howe had a distinguished playing career with West Bromwich Albion making nearly 350 appearances and winning 23 England caps. He joined Arsenal in April 1964 for £42,000 but suffered a broken leg in March 1966, becoming reserve team coach and then chief coach in succession to Dave Sexton in October 1967.

After the Fairs Cup and double triumph Howe left Arsenal to become manager at West Bromwich Albion and, after further spells as coach with Galatasaray and Leeds United. he returned to Highbury as chief coach in August 1977. He was also coach to the 1982 England World Cup team.

Taking over from Terry Neill in mid 1983/84, Howe guided Arsenal to sixth place in the League and they finished seventh twice in his other two seasons. Despite assembling one of the strongest squads in the country, Howe was unable to sustain a challenge for honours and there were also some disappointing results in both the cup competitions.

Hearing numerous rumours of a new manager coming to Highbury, Howe finally asked to be released from his contract in March 1986. He went on to help Wimbledon to their sensational FA Cup victory over Liverpool in 1988 and later managed Queens Park Rangers and Coventry City.

George Graham   1986 – present

Born at Bargeddie Lanark in 1944, George Graham was a Scottish Schoolboy international and started his career in English football with Aston Villa in 1961. He then moved to Chelsea in 1964 before being signed by Bertie Mee in September 1966. He was a member of the double winning side before leaving to join Manchester United and Portsmouth. He helped Crystal Palace to promotion to Division Two in 1976 before retiring from playing in 1980 and taking up coaching appointments with Palace and Queens Park Rangers.

His first managerial appointment was with Millwall in 1982, saving them from relegation to the Fourth Division that season. Under him the Lions won the Football League Trophy in 1983 and were promoted to the Second Division in 1985, when they also reached the FA Cup quarter-final.

He joined Arsenal in May 1986 and in his first season took the Gunners to fourth place in the League and a Littlewoods Cup win over Liverpool. The Gunners reached the Littlewoods Cup Final again the following year but this time were beaten by Luton Town. Graham continued to build and he led the club to the League Championship in 1988/89 joining the elite band of footballers who have won the game's top honour both as a player and as a manager.

A disappointing 1989/90 was followed by further League success in 1990/91 when Arsenal won the Championship again, losing just one league game all season. 1992/93 saw the unique double capture of the FA Cup and Coca-Cola Cup followed by the club's first European trophy for 24 years when Parma were beaten in the final of Cup-Winners' Cup in Copenhagen at the end of the 1993/94 season. Not only could George Graham be looked upon as possibly the greatest ever Arsenal manager, he could now also be looked upon as being one of the greatest football managers of all time.

The History of Arsenal Football Club

Arsenal Football Club was originally formed as Dial Square FC at a meeting held at the Prince of Wales public house in Plumstead in October 1886, when a group of football enthusiasts from the north all came south to work in the munitions factory in Woolwich Arsenal.

Their first match was at Millwall in December 1886 and they beat Eastern Wanderers 6-0. Two months later it was decided to change the club's name to Royal Arsenal and the first game under that banner took place in January 1887 against Erith.

The next season Arsenal rented the Sportsman Ground on Plumstead Marshes and entered the London Senior Cup for the first time, where they were beaten by Barnes. Increased support saw the club move to the Manor Ground and, in the 1889/90 season, they entered the FA Cup for the first time but were beaten 5-1 by Swifts in the last of the qualifying matches.

The 1890/91 season saw Royal Arsenal move to the Invicta Ground and the club also won their first trophy when they beat St Bartholomew's Hospital 6-0 in the final of the London Senior Cup. This increased success on the field prompted the club to adopt professionalism, a move which shocked the footballing authorities in the south. It led to Royal Arsenal being expelled by the London FA and being barred from southern cup competitions.

Arsenal continued to play friendly fixtures against the northern and midland professional teams for the next two seasons and, at the end of 1893, the decision was taken to form the club into a limited company. It gloried under the name of Woolwich Arsenal Football & Athletic Company Limited. An application was also made to join the Second Division of the Football League which was accepted.

Woolwich Arsenal made a reasonable start to their Football League career finishing ninth in the first season and, for the next decade, their results and placings continued to remain steady. In 1897/98 the club appointed Thomas Mitchell as its first professional manager, but he stayed only one season before being replaced by George Elcoat. Elcoat also only remained with the club for a year and Harry Bradshaw became the club's third manager in 1899/1900. He took Arsenal into the First Division within five years.

The financial situation of the club at this time was very perilous and their attendances were very poor, but Bradshaw managed to overcome all the off-the-field problems and take the club to runners-up position in season 1903/04. Somewhat surprisingly, Bradshaw then decided to leave and join Fulham; he was replaced by Phil Kelso. The club still continued to progress, finishing in comfortable mid-table league positions and reaching the FA Cup semi-final in 1906 and 1907, being beaten by Newcastle United and Sheffield Wednesday respectively.

Then, more financial problems beset the club and Phil Kelso left in 1908 to be succeeded by George Morrell. Morrell's first task was to sell a number of the star players to help Arsenal survive. The financial situation worsened and this in turn led to a decline in the club's playing fortunes with relegation – for the only time in its history – coming at the end of the 1912/13 season.

Henry Norris took over the club and he recognised the need for a move from Plumstead. After a long search, he found an easily accessible site at Highbury and Woolwich Arsenal started the 1913/14 season at their new ground. Promotion was just missed for the first two seasons and it was also decided during this period that the 'Woolwich' would be dropped from the title. The club became known as 'Arsenal FC'.

League football was suspended during World War One. When it started up again in 1919/20 Arsenal – thanks to some controversial behind-the-scenes lobbying – were placed back in the First Division. This despite the fact that they had finished in fifth place in the Second Division in the last pre-war season.

Leslie Knighton was appointed manager but six years of First Division football brought only moderate success and, after advertising the position, Henry Norris appointed Huddersfield Town's Herbert Chapman as Arsenal's new manager.

The appointment of Chapman in 1925 marked the start of the Arsenal success story. In his first season they finished runners-up in the league and a year later reached their first FA Cup Final, losing 1-0 to Cardiff City. In 1929/30 Arsenal, at last, won their first major trophy when they beat Huddersfield Town 2-0 in the FA Cup Final at Wembley. That triumph signalled the start of a decade of dominance by the Gunners, with the First Division title being won the following season and also in 1933, 1934, 1935 and 1938. The FA Cup was also won again in 1936.

This huge success was tinged with sadness in January 1934 however, when Herbert Chapman died following a short illness. Despite this crushing blow Arsenal continued to build on the foundations laid down by Chapman. George Allison was appointed manager and the success continued during the 1930s.

The Second World War again saw a suspension of the Football League programme and, when playing activities resumed in the 1946/47 season, Arsenal struggled. George Allison retired and Tom Whittaker was appointed as manager. In his first season Arsenal won the League Championship – for the sixth time – and, in 1950, won the FA Cup, when they beat Liverpool 2-0 at Wembley.

The League Championship was again won in 1953, but this win marked the start of a barren period in the club's history. That title success was to be Arsenal's last major honour for 17 years. Tom Whittaker died in 1956 and the next ten years saw four different managers appointed as the club attempted to regain their former glories. Ex-players Jack Crayston and George Swindin both managed adequately but without producing consistently successful teams, whilst ex-Wolves and England captain, Billy Wright, suffered from a lack of managerial experience.

The appointment of Bertie Mee in 1966 proved to be the turning point in the club's fortunes. Backed up by excellent coaching from Dave Sexton and Don Howe, he soon restored Arsenal's challenge for honours. Football League Cup Finals were reached in 1968 and 1969, both lost to Leeds United and Swindon Town respectively, before 1969/70 saw Arsenal's 17-year wait for a trophy end with a 4-3 aggregate win over Anderlecht in the European Fairs Cup Final. Twelve months later came the greatest achievement in the club's history – the winning of the League and FA Cup double.

Under pressure to try and maintain this sort of high standard, Mee retired at the end of the 1975/76 season and ex-player Terry Neill was appointed in his place. The return of Don Howe as coach saw the club begin to mount further challenges for honours and three successive FA Cup Finals were reached in 1978, 1979 and 1980, although only Manchester United, in 1979, were beaten. 1980 also saw Arsenal lose to Valencia on penalty kicks in the final of the European Cup-Winners' Cup.

The early eighties saw two cup semi-finals reached, but the inability of Neill to find adequate replacements for players like Liam Brady and Frank Stapleton finally led to his dismissal in 1983. Don Howe was appointed manager but his two seasons in charge were only satisfactory, not outstanding. When he heard rumours that the Arsenal directors were interested in appointing Terry Venables as manager, he resigned in March 1986.

The rumours turned out to be unfounded and Millwall manager, George Graham, took up the reins at the start of the 1986/87 season. His first season brought fresh honours back to Highbury as Liverpool were defeated in the final of the Littlewoods Cup. The Gunners returned to Wembley a year later in the same competition but lost 3-2 to Luton Town in a dramatic match.

The 1988/89 season saw Arsenal needing to win by at least two goals against Liverpool, at Anfield, to win the League Championship in the final match of an extended season. Before the game few people outside the club gave Arsenal much chance of causing such an upset but they won 2-0 scoring their second goal in the game's dying moments. Following an inconsistent 1989/90, the First Division trophy was again won in 1990/91 with the Gunners only suffering one league defeat. Disappointment followed in the 1991/92 season with failure in the European Cup and no domestic trophies.

1992/93 saw the club back to winning ways and a unique cup double was achieved with the capture of the FA Cup and Coca-Cola Cup – both against Sheffield Wednesday. 1993/94 again saw an inconsistent league season, with a final placing of fourth, but further success came in the shape of the European Cup-Winners' Cup, when Italian side Parma – the cup holders and favourites – were beaten 1-0 in the final in Copenhagen.

Reserves

Neville Ovenden Football Combination 1993/94

17/08/93	v Norwich City	(h)	0-5
25/08/93	v Swindon Town	(h)	2-1
01/09/93	v Wimbledon	(a)	2-2
07/09/93	v Oxford United	(h)	3-0
13/09/93	v Portsmouth	(h)	2-0
21/09/93	v West Ham United	(h)	1-3
07/10/93	v Queens Park Rangers	(h)	1-2
12/10/93	v Watford	(a)	4-3
23/10/93	v Southampton	(h)	4-1
27/10/93	v Tottenham Hotspur	(a)	2-2
03/11/93	v Swindon Town	(a)	1-2
09/11/93	v Tottenham Hotspur	(h)	1-2
17/11/93	v Luton Town	(a)	1-1
20/11/93	v Southampton	(a)	1-2
30/11/93	v Queens Park Rangers	(a)	1-1
08/12/93	v Watford	(h)	4-3
11/12/93	v Portsmouth	(a)	3-1
14/12/93	v Luton Town	(h)	2-3
12/01/94	v Millwall	(h)	1-2
18/01/94	v Chelsea	(h)	0-2
26/01/94	v Ipswich Town	(a)	0-4
29/01/94	v Wimbledon	(h)	4-0
01/02/94	v Millwall	(a)	6-3
07/02/94	v Bristol Rovers	(a)	0-3
10/02/94	v Bristol City	(a)	0-0
15/02/94	v Ipswich Town	(h)	2-3
23/02/94	v Brighton & Hove Albion	(a)	1-0
01/03/94	v Bristol Rovers	(h)	2-3
09/03/94	v Norwich City	(a)	1-0
14/03/94	v Chelsea	(a)	1-2
31/03/94	v Oxford United	(a)	0-1
06/04/94	v Charlton Athletic	(a)	0-2
19/04/94	v Crystal Palace	(a)	1-5
23/04/94	v Brighton & Hove Albion	(h)	2-2
26/04/94	v Bristol City	(h)	5-3
03/05/94	v Crystal Palace	(h)	2-4
06/05/94	v Charlton Athletic	(h)	3-1
11/05/94	v West Ham United	(a)	1-2

Player	Apps	Sub	Goals	Player	Apps	Sub	Goals
Alan Miller	11	–	–	Anders Limpar	3	–	1
Ryan Kirby	21	3	–	Kevin Campbell	4	–	3
Pål Lydersen	19	–	–	Kenny Webster	20	2	1
David Hillier	12	–	2	Noel Imber	1	–	–
Matthew Rose	3	3	–	Alex Welsh	2	–	–
Scott Marshall	19	–	2	Tony Adams	1	–	–
Mark Flatts	17	3	4	Andy Linighan	13	–	–
Ian Selley	15	–	2	Paul Davis	7	–	1
Alan Smith	9	–	5	Eddie McGoldrick	3	1	–
Paul Dickov	18	1	16	Nigel Winterburn	2	–	–
Neil Heaney	21	4	5	Martin Keown	4	–	–
Paul Shaw	24	5	12	Stephen Hughes	5	1	–
Stuart Campbell	10	4	–	Paul Merson	4	–	–
Neil Fewing	4	–	–	Chris McDonald	1	–	–
Roy O'Brien	26	1	–	Gavin McGowan	2	1	–
Adrian Clarke	15	6	3	Michael Black	–	2	–
Jim Will	22	–	–	Matthew Rawlins	–	1	–
Tony Connolly	2	3	1	Greg Tello	1	–	–
Soner Zumrutel	11	2	2	Jamie Howell	1	1	–
Steve Bould	4	1	–	Robbie Drake	1	–	–
Jimmy Carter	23	1	1	Orlando Hollinsworth	–	1	–
Paul Read	9	11	3	Evan Allen	–	1	–
Lee Dixon	1	–	–	L. Harper	2	–	–
Ray Parlour	9	1	2	M. Parrish	1	–	–
Stephen Morrow	13	–	1	C. McLeod	1	–	–
Perry Marshall	1	–	–				

The Neville Ovenden Football Combination – Final League Table

Pos.	Team	P	W	D	L	F	A	Pts
1	Chelsea	38	24	8	6	79	41	80
2	Ipswich Town	38	19	8	11	71	52	65
3	Tottenham H	38	19	6	13	69	47	63
4	Crystal Palace	38	17	11	10	63	40	62
5	Norwich City	38	18	7	13	68	54	61
6	Wimbledon	38	16	13	9	53	48	61
7	QPR	38	17	8	13	58	49	59
8	West Ham Utd	38	16	10	12	59	45	58
9	Swindon Town	38	18	4	16	54	53	58
10	Bristol Rovers	38	15	12	11	50	52	57
11	Southampton	38	15	10	13	62	66	55

12	Millwall	38	12	11	15	57	67	47
13	Charlton Ath	38	13	7	18	61	62	46
14	Luton Town	38	12	9	17	64	70	45
15	**Arsenal**	**38**	**13**	**6**	**19**	**67**	**76**	**45**
16	Oxford United	38	11	10	17	53	66	43
17	Portsmouth	38	10	11	17	43	60	41
18	Brighton & H A	38	9	10	19	38	58	37
19	Watford	38	9	8	21	49	75	35
20	Bristol City	38	8	9	21	47	84	33

Youth Team

South East Counties League 1993/94

14/8/93	Chelsea	(a)	3-1
21/8/93	Gillingham	(h)	3-1
28/8/93	Charlton Athletic	(a)	5-2
04/09/93	Leyton Orient	(a)	0-0
06/09/93	Ipswich Town (SJFC1)	(h)	2-1
11/09/93	Watford	(a)	6-3
18/09/93	Bristol City (SECLC1)	(h)	1-1
25/09/93	Bristol City (SECLC1R)	(a)	2-3
09/10/93	Cambridge United	(a)	1-1
16/10/93	Norwich City	(h)	2-0
23/10/93	Ipswich Town	(a)	3-2
30/10/93	Ipswich Town	(h)	1-2
06/11/93	Southend United	(h)	7-1
13/11/93	Millwall	(a)	3-0
20/11/93	Portsmouth	(h)	1-1
23/11/93	Luton Town (SJFC2)	(h)	2-1
27/11/93	Fulham	(a)	0-3
29/11/93	Colchester United (FAYC2)	(a)	3-2
04/12/93	West Ham United	(a)	3-1
11/12/93	West Ham United	(h)	3-3
01/01/94	Chelsea	(h)	0-2
12/01/94	Brentford (FAYC3)	(h)	1-1
15/01/94	Charlton Athletic	(h)	3-1
17/01/94	Brentford (FAYC3R)	(h)	3-1
22/01/94	Leyton Orient	(h)	1-1
24/01/94	Brighton & HA (SJFC3)	(a)	0-1
29/01/94	Watford	(h)	0-2
31/01/94	Burnley (FAYC4)	(a)	1-0
05/02/94	Queens Park Rangers	(h)	1-2
12/02/94	Fulham	(h)	2-2

19/02/94	Cambridge United	(h)	1-2
21/02/94	Stoke City (FAYCQF)	(h)	3-1
12/03/94	Southend United	(a)	5-1
19/03/94	Millwall	(h)	2-2
26/03/94	Portsmouth	(a)	3-0
02/04/94	Queens Park Rangers	(a)	3-1
09/04/94	Tottenham Hotspur	(h)	0-2
11/04/94	Bradford City (FAYCSF)	(a)	1-0
20/04/94	Bradford City (FAYCSF)	(h)	1-0
30/04/94	Tottenham Hotspur	(a)	0-2
02/05/94	Norwich City	(a)	2-1
03/05/94	Gillingham	(a)	2-0
06/05/94	Millwall (FAYCFinal1)	(a)	2-3
12/05/94	Millwall (FAYCFinal2)	(h)	3-0

Youth Team Appearances & Goalscorers 1993/94

Player	SECL Apps	SECL Goals	FAYC Apps	FAYC Goals	SECL Cup Apps	SECL Cup Goals	SJF Cup Apps	SJF Cup Goals
M. Black	22/2	5	7	1	2	–	2	–
T. Clarke	19/6	11	6/1	2	1	1	2	–
C. Coffey	1	–	–	–	–	–	–	–
R. Crawley	4	–	–	–	–	–	–	–
K. Dennis	11/4	2	1	1	0/1	–	1	–
R. Drake	20	6	1/1	–	1/1	–	–	–
D. Gladman	1	–	–	–	–	–	–	–
T. Griggs	24/3	–	7	–	2	–	2	–
G. Hall	19	–	8/1	–	–	–	2	–
O. Hollinsworth	4/3	–	2	–	–	–	1	–
J. Howell	23/1	2	6/1	1	2	–	2/1	–
S. Hughes	21/3	5	9	3	2	1	3	–
N. Imber	28	–	9	–	2	–	3	–
C. McDonald	22/1	4	7	–	2	–	2	1
G. McGowan	20/2	2	7	2	2	–	3	–
D. Owen	1	–	–	–	–	–	–	–
R. Parsons	1	–	–	–	–	–	–	–
I. Rankine	4/10	–	2/1	1	–	–	1	1
M. Rawlins	22/4	22	9	5	2	–	1	1
M. Rose	21/1	1	9	2	2	–	3	1
R. Taylor	24/1	2	9	–	2	–	3	–
G. Tello	7/1	–	–	–	0/1	–	–	–
J. Woolsey	4	–	–	–	–	–	–	–
J. Wynter	7/2	2	0/1	–	–	–	0/1	–
own goals	–	2	–	–	–	–	–	–

SECL	–	South East Counties League
FAYC	–	FA Youth Cup
SECL Cup	–	South East Counies League Cup
SJF Cup	–	Southern Junior Floodlit Cup

Arsenal in the FA Youth Cup – Winning Squads

Date	Opponents	Venue	Result

1965/66

29th April 1966   Sunderland   (a)   1-2
Team: E. Adams, Rice, Youlden, Gillibrand, Woodward, Rhodes, Leven, Cumming, Milne, Simmons, Bristow. *Scorer:* Simmons

9th May 1966   Sunderland   (h)   4-1
Team: E. Adams, Rice, Youlden, Boot, Woodward, Gillibrand, Leven, Cumming, Milne, Simmons, Nelson. *Scorers:* Milne, Boot, Simmons, Leven
       Matches are played over two legs. Arsenal won 5-3 on Aggregate.

1970/71

28th April 1971   Cardiff City   (h)   0-0
Team: Horn, Donaldson, Shovelar, Price, Batson, de Garis Hornsby, Newton, P. Davies, Burton, Kennerley.

5th May 1971   Cardiff City   (a)   2-0
Team: Horn, Donaldson, Shovelar, Price, Batson, de Garis, Hornsby, Newton, P. Davies, Burton, Kennerley. *Scorers:* Kennerley, Burton.
       Matches are played over two legs. Arsenal won 2-0 on Aggregate.

1987/88

29th April 1988   Doncaster Rovers   (a)   5-0
Team: Miller, Francis, Carstairs, Hillier, Hannigan, Morrow, Heaney, Cagigao, Campbell (Lee), Ball, McKeown. *Scorers:* Campbell(3), Ball(pen), Lee.

3rd May 1988   Doncaster Rovers   (h)   1-1
Team: Miller, Francis, Carstairs, Hillier, Hannigan, Morrow, Heaney, Cagigao, Campbell (Lee), Ball, McKeown. *Scorer:* McKeown.
       Matches are played over two legs. Arsenal won 6-1 on Aggregate.

1993/94

6th May 1994   Millwall   (a)   2-3
Team: Imber, Griggs, Taylor, Howell, Hall, McDonald, Black, Rose, Rawlins, McGowan, Hughes. *Scorers:* Rawlings, McGowan.

12th May 1994   Millwall   (h)   3-0
Team: Imber, Griggs, Taylor, Clarke, Hall, McDonald, Black, Rose (Howell), Rawlins (Drake), McGowan, Hughes. *Scorers:* Clarke, Rawlins, Hughes.
       Matches are played over two legs. Arsenal won 5-3 on Aggregate.

Arsenal's 1994/5 Season in Prospect

	1992/93 result		1993/94 result		1994/95 fixture date	
	Home	Away	Home	Away	Home	Away
Aston Villa	0-1	0-1	1-2	2-1	26/12	17/04
Blackburn Rovers	0-1	0-1	1-0	1-1	30/08	07/03
Chelsea	2-1	0-1	1-0	2-0	15/10	13/05
Coventry City	3-0	2-0	0-3	0-1	22/10	21/01
Crystal Palace	3-0	2-1	–	–	01/10	25/02
Everton	2-0	0-0	2-0	1-1	14/01	29/10
Ipswich Town	0-0	2-1	4-0	5-1	15/04	27/12
Leeds United	0-0	0-3	2-1	1-2	17/12	23/08
Leicester City	–	–	–	–	11/02	02/11
Liverpool	0-1	2-0	1-0	0-0	11/03	27/08
Manchester City	1-0	1-0	0-0	0-0	20/08	10/12
Manchester United	0-1	0-0	2-2	0-1	26/11	18/02
Newcastle United	–	–	2-1	0-2	17/09	18/03
Norwich City	2-4	1-1	0-0	1-1	01/04	10/09
Nottingham Forest	1-1	1-0	–	–	21/02	03/12
Queens Park Rangers	0-0	0-0	0-0	1-1	31/12	08/04
Sheffield Wednesday	2-1	0-1	1-0	1-0	05/11	04/02
Southampton	4-3	0-2	1-0	4-0	24/01	19/11
Tottenham Hotspur	1-3	0-1	1-1	1-0	29/04	02/01
West Ham United	–	–	0-2	0-0	04/03	24/09
Wimbledon	0-1	2-3	1-1	3-0	06/05	08/10

1994/95 Squad Numbers

1	David	Seaman	10	Paul	Merson	19	Jimmy	Carter
2	Lee	Dixon	11	Eddie	McGoldrick	20	Pål	Lydersen
3	Nigel	Winterburn	12	Steve	Bould	21	Steve	Morrow
4	Paul	Davis	13	Alan	Miller	22	Ian	Selley
5	Andy	Linighan	14	Martin	Keown	23	Ray	Parlour
6	Tony	Adams	15	Stefan	Schwarz	24	Mark	Flatts
7	Kevin	Campbell	16		–	25		–
8	Ian	Wright	17	John	Jensen	26	Jim	Will
9	Alan	Smith	18	David	Hillier	27	Paul	Dickov

FA Carling Premiership Final Table 1993-94

		HOME					AWAY					
	P	W	D	L	F	A	W	D	L	F	A	Pts
Manchester United	42	14	6	1	39	13	13	5	3	41	25	92
Blackburn Rovers	42	14	5	2	31	11	11	4	6	32	25	84
Newcastle United	42	14	4	3	51	14	9	4	8	31	27	77
ARSENAL	42	10	8	3	25	15	8	9	4	28	13	71
Leeds United	42	13	6	2	37	18	5	10	6	28	21	70
Wimbledon	42	12	5	4	35	21	6	6	9	21	32	65
Sheffield Wednesday	42	10	7	4	48	24	6	9	6	28	30	64
Liverpool	42	12	4	5	33	23	5	5	11	26	32	60
Queens Park Rangers	42	8	7	6	32	29	8	5	8	30	32	60
Aston Villa	42	8	5	8	23	18	7	7	7	23	32	57
Coventry City	42	9	7	5	23	17	5	7	9	20	28	56
Norwich City	42	4	9	8	26	29	8	8	5	39	32	53
West Ham United	42	6	7	8	26	31	7	6	8	21	27	52
Chelsea	42	11	5	5	31	20	2	7	12	18	33	51
Tottenham Hotspur	42	4	8	9	29	33	7	4	10	25	26	45
Manchester City	42	6	10	5	24	22	3	8	10	14	27	45
Everton	42	8	4	9	26	30	4	4	13	16	33	44
Southampton	42	9	2	10	30	31	3	5	13	19	35	43
Ipswich Town	42	5	8	8	21	32	4	8	9	14	26	43
Sheffield United	42	6	10	5	24	23	2	8	11	18	37	42
Oldham Athletic	42	5	8	8	24	33	4	5	12	18	35	40
Swindon Town	42	4	7	10	25	45	1	8	12	22	55	30

A jubilant Ian Wright celebrates Arsenal's 1-0 win over Parma in the European Cup-Winners' Cup final despite spending the whole of the match on the bench.

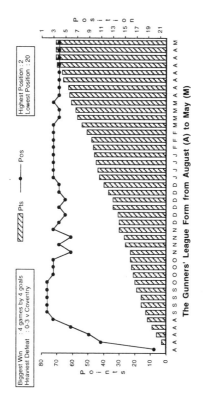

The Gunners' League Form from August (A) to May (M)

Highest Position : 2
Lowest Position : 20

Pts

Pos

Biggest Win : 4 games by 4 goals
Heaviest Defeat : 0-3 v Coventry

Who's Scored the Goals

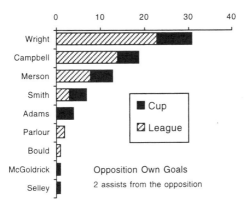

Average Goals per Match

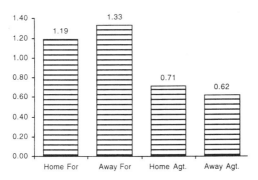

Who was Booked

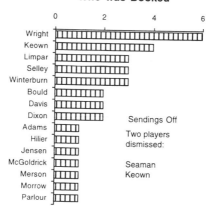

Sendings Off

Two players
dismissed:

Seaman
Keown

Bookings Breakdown

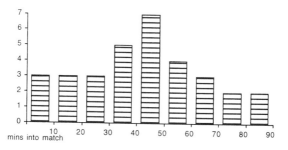

mins into match

The Season On-Screen

Keep the memories alive with these videos of your favourite teams in the 1993-94 season!

Race for the Premiership 1994   **£10.99**

The full season round-up – and the chase for the championship – on video for you to keep. A Polygram video.

Liverpool Season 93-94   **£11.99**

Telstar Video's coverage of Liverpool's year, the last for the Kop.

Arsenal – Season Review 93-94   **£11.99**

A great season in Europe for the Gunners, recorded on video for your enjoyment by VVL/Polygram.

Newcastle United 93-94   **£10.99**

Warner Video's complete look at the club's first Premier season.

Manchester United 93-94   **£10.99**

The double season captured on tape. The best-seller.

Ordering Details

Ordering your video couldn't be easier. Write the video(s) of your choice and your name and address details on a sheet of paper. Send this together with a postal order or cheque made out to *Words on Sport Ltd* or send your credit card details – number, expiry date, name of holder – to:

Words on Sport, Freepost 282,
PO Box 382, St Albans, AL2 3BR.

Telephone your order 24 hours a day on (0923) 894355.
Please allow 28 days for delivery. No P&P to pay.

Collector's Item

A Centenary Celebration from the Archives

History of the Amateur Cup   £11.99

This video history delves deep into the archives to celebrate the centenary of the Amateur Cup. Today many of the famous names who took part in the Amateur Cup compete in either the FA Trophy or Vase competitions. Premier club and 1988 FA Cup winners Wimbledon won the Amateur Cup in 1963 and were runners-up twice. They are the only club to have won both cups. Other star teams to enjoy are Wycombe Wanderers, Barnet, Wealdstone, Enfield and Bishops Stortford. The Amateur Cup exploits of these, and many other, famous teams feature on a new permanent record created by Trans Video Productions in conjunction with The Football Association.

Young Hopefuls

Advice from the Football Association

The Schoolboy Dream   £10.99

Want to become a professional footballer? Produced in conjunction with the Football Association and introduced by Bobby Robson, this video takes you through all the stages of becoming a professional footballer. Parents will find the information and helpful guidance invaluable. A whimsical cartoon character, Barney the Frog, fancies his chances of becoming a future football star. See how he fares along with all the other young hopefuls at the Nottingham Forest school of excellence. A Trans Video production.

See ordering instructions on page 281.

Other Great Pocket Annuals from

Mail-Order:

In case of difficulty obtaining the pocket annual of your choice, send a cheque or P/O made out to Words on Sport or give your credit card details (number/expiry/address of card holder) on 0923 894355 (24 hours) and we'll send you your book by return.

Send for your own detailed catalogue with information about all the great new titles from Words on Sport.

Send you name and address to:
Words on Sport, PO Box 382, St Albans, Herts, AL2 3JD

Trade Sales:
Derek Searle Associates,
14 High Street, Slough, Berks, SL1 1EE

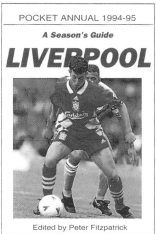

POCKET ANNUAL 1994-95

A Season's Guide

LIVERPOOL

Edited by Peter Fitzpatrick

Liverpool Pocket Annual 1994-95

Edited by Peter Fitzpatrick, 288 pages, £3.99
ISBN: 1-898351-10-4

Also available as a 10 Copy Counter Pack, £39.90, ISBN: 1-898351-17-1

Re-live the season – match-by-match, fact-by-fact and goal-by-goal as Peter Fitzpatrick provides a report on every Liverpool game as it happened! Look up all the line-ups, appearance details and goal-scoring records of all the current stars and debate for yourself their current transfer value. The Liverpool Pocket Annual provides complete records in all competitions and against every club! This year's annual includes a special look at the history – and future – of the legendary Kop. Don't leave home without it – it'll even give you directions to all the Premiership grounds. All the facts at your fingertips in a handy pocket size, with photos of your favourite footballers.

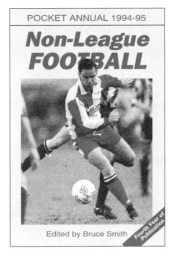

POCKET ANNUAL 1994-95

Non-League FOOTBALL

Edited by Bruce Smith

Fourth Year of Publication

Non-League Football Pocket Annual 1994-95

Edited by Bruce Smith, 288 pages, £3.99
ISBN: 1-898351-07-4

Also available as a 10 Copy Counter Pack, £39.90, ISBN: 1-898351-14-7

Now in its fourth year, Bruce Smith's famous *Non-League Football Annual* is the perfect pocket travelling companion for all followers of the Non-League game. Cram-packed with information and histories on all the major Pyramid clubs, it includes full details and reviews of all the major cup competitions including the FA Cup, FA Trophy and FA Vase. Unique five-year records allow you to see for yourself how the top club sides have fared. There are even appearance records for all the Vauxhall Conference sides. Great for groundhoppers and arm-chair enthusiasts.

Bruce Smith

FA Carling Premiership Pocket Annual 1994-95

Edited by Bruce Smith, 288 pages, £3.99
ISBN: 1-898351-06-6

Also available as a 10 Copy Counter Pack, £39.90, ISBN: 1-898351-13-9

Having sold out in its first year, the second edition of the *FA Carling Premiership Pocket Annual* has been revamped to make it even clearer, more informative and better value than ever before. It contains a complete Premiership club directory with season reviews, club and player records in the Premiership and former Football League, and is packed with unique statistics and records every fan will want to know. Make sure you have the complete record of this and every Premiership season. Illustrated with detailed guides to all the Premiership League grounds and photographs of all the season's action – and all for just £3.99!

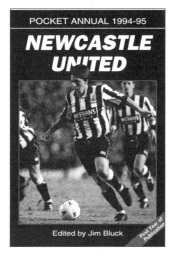

Newcastle United Pocket Annual 1994-95

Edited by Jim Bluck, 256 pages, £3.99
ISBN: 1-898351-11-2

Also available as a 10 Copy Counter Pack, £39.90, ISBN: 1-898351-18-X

H'away the lads! The Magpies made an incredible impact on the Premiership so don't fail to re-savour every moment with this match-by-match, fact-by-fact, blow-by-blow account of the season as Andy Cole scores the quickest ever 30-goals in Newcastle United's history! With records of all the current Newcastle stars debate their transfer values as estimated by our panel of editors, walk down memory lane as you scan through United's complete record in all competitions and against every other club. Take it with you to matches – it'll slip into your pocket and even give you directions to all the Premiership grounds.

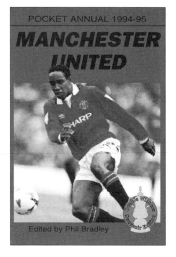

POCKET ANNUAL 1994-95

MANCHESTER UNITED

SHARP

Edited by Phil Bradley

Manchester United Pocket Annual 1994-95

Edited by Phil Bradley, 288 pages, £3.99
ISBN: 1-898351-08-2

Also available as a 10 Copy Counter Pack, £39.90, ISBN: 1-898351-15-9

The debate was all about *The Treble*. What went right and what went wrong as United set the Premiership alight with their brilliant brand of football? Every match, every goal and all the facts on every player as it's happened since United's formation in 1878 as Newton Heath. Is Ryan Giggs really worth £12 million? Debate for yourself our valuation of him and the other United players. Also included is United's record in all competitions and against every club. Don't leave home without it – it'll even give you directions to all the Premiership grounds.